W9-BLX-370

The Riverside Literature Series

THE

LADY OF THE LAKE

BY

SIR WALTER SCOTT, BART.

EDITED WITH NOTES BY

WILLIAM J. ROLFE, A. M., LITT. D.

FORMERLY HEAD MASTER OF THE HIGH SCHOOL, CAMBRIDGE, MASS

REVISED AND ENLARGED EDITION

HOUGHTON MIFFLIN COMPANY

The Riverside Press Cambridge

The Riverside Press
CAMBRIDGE · MASSACHUSETTS
PRINTED IN THE U.S.A.

PREFACE.

WHEN I first saw the beautiful illustrated Holiday Edition of *The Lady of the Lake*, I asked to be allowed to use some of the cuts in a cheaper annotated edition for school and household use; and the present volume is the result.

The *text* of the poem has given me unexpected trouble. When I edited some of Gray's poems several years ago, I found that they had not been correctly printed for more than half a century; but in the case of Scott I supposed that the text of Black's so-called "Author's Edition" could be depended upon as accurate. Almost at the start, however, I detected sundry obvious misprints in one of the many forms in which this edition is issued, and an examination of others showed that they were as bad in their way. The "Shilling" issue was no worse than the costly illustrated one of 1853, which had its own assortment of slips of the type. No two editions that I could obtain agreed exactly in their readings. I tried in vain to find a copy of the *editio princeps* (1810) in Cambridge and Boston, but succeeded in getting one through a London bookseller. This I compared, line by line, with the Edinburgh edition of 1821 (from the Harvard Library), with Lockhart's first edition, the "Globe" edition, and about a dozen others, English and American. I found many misprints and corruptions in all except the edition of 1821, and a few even in that. For instance, in i. 217 Scott wrote "Found in each clift a narrow bower," and it is so printed in the first edition; but in *every* other that I have seen "cliff" appears in place of *clift*, to the manifest injury of the passage. In ii. 685, every edition that I have seen since that of 1821 has "I meant not all my *heart* might say," which is worse than nonsense, the correct reading being "my *heat*." In vi. 396, the Scottish "boune" (though it occurs twice in other parts of the poem) has been changed to "bound" in all editions since 1821; and, eight lines below, the old word "barded" has become "barbed." Scores of similar corruptions are recorded in my Notes. [See also "Addendum," p. 269 below.]

I have restored the reading of the first edition, except in cases where I have no doubt that the latter reading is the poet's own correction or alteration. There are obvious misprints in the first edition which Scott himself overlooked (see on ii. 115, 217, vi. 527, etc.), and it is sometimes difficult to decide whether a later reading — a change of a plural to a singular, or like trivial variation — is a misprint or the author's correction of an earlier misprint. I have done the best I could, with the means at my command, to settle these questions, and am at least certain that the text as I give it is nearer right than in any edition since 1821. All *variæ lectiones* are recorded in the Notes.

I have retained all Scott's *Notes* (a few of them have been somewhat abridged) and all those added by Lockhart.[1] My own I have made as concise as possible. There are, of course, many of them which many of my readers will not need, but I think there are none that may not be of service, or at least of interest, to some of them; and I hope that no one will turn to them for help without finding it.

Prefatory Note to the Revised Edition.

In this edition an "Historical Introduction" (pp. vii–xvi) and a "Pronouncing Glossary" of Scottish words (p. 274) have been incorporated.

I may add that down to the present time (1908) all or most of the misprints and corruptions noted by me have been retained in both school and "standard" editions (including one "edited" by Mr. Andrew Lang a few years ago), except in the few that have adopted my text, with or without giving me credit.

[1] One of Scott's (on vi. 47) has suffered badly in Lockhart's edition. In a quotation from Lord Berners's *Froissart* (which I omit) *a whole page* seems to have dropped out, and the last sentence, as it now stands, is made up of parts of the one preceding and the one following the lost matter. It reads thus (I mark the gap): "There all the companyons made them [. . .] breke no poynt of that ye have ordayned and commaunded." This is palpable nonsense, but it has been repeated without correction in every reprint of Lockhart's edition for the last fifty years.

HISTORICAL INTRODUCTION.

The Lady of the Lake, the third of Scott's "metrical romances" (*The Lay of the Last Minstrel* and *Marmion* having preceded it in 1805 and 1808), was, like its predecessors, founded upon history, though, as the author explained in his preface of 1830 (see page 175 below), it varies somewhat from the facts of history, as the earlier poems did, and as historical novels (Scott's and others) always do. While it was intended to be true in the main to the manners and customs of the ancient Highlanders of Scotland, it was "an idealized picture" of their character and life.

Until the middle of the eighteenth century these people of northern Scotland were little known to their English neighbors, only about five hundred miles away. Macaulay, in his *History of England* (chap. xiii.) says of that period: "In the south of our island scarcely anything was known about the Celtic part of Scotland; and what was known excited no feeling but contempt and loathing. The crags and the glens, the woods and the waters, were indeed the same that now swarm every autumn with admiring gazers and sketchers; . . . yet none of these sights had power to attract a single poet or painter from more opulent and more tranquil regions. . . . About the year 1730, Captain Burt, one of the first Englishmen who caught a glimpse of the spots which now allure tourists from every part of the civilized world, wrote an account of his wanderings. He was evidently a man of a quick, an observant, and a cultivated mind, and would doubtless, had he lived in our age, have looked with mingled awe and delight on the mountains of Invernesshire. But, writing with the feeling which was universal in his own age, he pronounced those mountains monstrous excrescences. Their deformity, he said, was such that the most sterile plains seemed lovely by comparison. Fine weather, he complained, only made bad worse; for, the clearer the sky, the more disagreeably did these misshapen masses of gloomy brown and dirty purple affect the eye. . . . Goldsmith was one of the very few Saxons who [in 1753] ventured to explore the Highlands. He was disgusted by the hideous wilderness, and declared that he greatly preferred the charming country round Leyden" — a flat but fertile and highly cultivated region.

Macaulay explains this feeling of Goldsmith by the difficulty and danger of travel in a region where there were no roads worthy of the name, no bridges over the rivulets, and where inns had not succeeded to the dens of robbers; but Goldsmith held the same view of mountain scenery where travel was safer and more comfortable. He shared the feeling of the people of his time at which Macaulay had already hinted, — the ancient, the mediæval, and the modern view of mountains till almost the dawn of the nineteenth century, — that there was nothing beautiful or attractive in them. They were viewed with dread or with dislike, and never introduced into a poetic landscape to add a charm to it. Compare Goldsmith's description of Switzerland in *The Traveller* with Byron's and others of more recent days. Goldsmith saw nothing in Alpine scenery but the struggle of man with nature: —

> "No product here the barren hills afford
> But man and steel, the soldier and his sword;
> No vernal blooms the torpid rocks array,
> But winter lingering chills the lap of May;

> No zephyr fondly sues the mountain's breast,
> But meteors glare, and stormy glooms invest."

Doubtless, however, Goldsmith's dislike of the Highlands, —"an unfruitful country," with "hills all brown with heath, and valleys scarce able to feed a rabbit — every part of it presenting the same dismal landscape" (as he writes to a friend in Edinburgh), — was intensified by the fact that the natives seemed to him, as to the Saxons generally then, mere savages.

But, as Macaulay remarks, "it is strange that, considered as savages, they should not have been objects of interest and curiosity," like the Laplanders and Hottentots, Mohawks and Malays. "The only barbarian about whom there was no wish to have any information was the Highlander." The English knew almost nothing about him, and cared less. In a book of three hundred pages, describing a *Journey through Scotland* in 1723, "two contemptuous passages were thought sufficient for the Highlands and the Highlanders."

Macaulay adds: "While the old Gaelic institutions were in full vigor, no account of them was given by any observer qualified to judge of them fairly. Had such an observer studied the character of the Highlanders, . . . he would have found that the people had no love for their country or for their king; that they had no attachment to any commonwealth larger than the clan, or to any magistrate superior to the chief. He would have found that life was governed by a code of morality and honor widely different from that which is established in peaceful and prosperous societies. He would have learned that a stab in the back, or a shot from behind a fragment of rock, were approved modes of taking satisfaction for insults. . . . He would have found that robbery was held to be a calling, not merely innocent but honorable. He would have seen, wherever he turned, that dislike of steady industry, and that disposition to throw on the weaker sex the heaviest part of manual labor, which are characteristic of savages. . . . Nor did the women repine at their hard lot. In their view, it was quite fit that a man . . . should take his ease except when he was fighting, hunting, or marauding. To mention his name in connection with commerce or with any mechanical art was an insult. Agriculture was indeed less despised. Yet a high-born warrior was much more becomingly employed in plundering the land of others than in tilling his own. The religion of the greater part of the Highlands was a rude mixture of Popery and Paganism. . . . Baptized men poured libations of ale to one demon, and set out drink-offerings of milk for another. Seers wrapped themselves up in bulls' hides, and awaited, in that vesture, the inspiration which was to reveal the future. Even among those minstrels and genealogists whose hereditary vocation was to preserve the memory of past events, an inquirer would have found very few who could read. In truth, he might easily have journeyed from sea to sea without discovering a page of Gaelic printed or written. The price which he would have had to pay for his knowledge of the country would have been heavy. . . . In many dwellings, the furniture, the food, the clothing, nay, the very hair and skin of his hosts, would have put his philosophy to the proof. His lodging would sometimes have been in a hut of which every nook would have swarmed with vermin. At supper, grain fit only for horses would have been set before him, accompanied by a cake of blood drawn from living cows. . . . His couch would have been the bare earth, dry or wet as the weather might be; and from that he would have risen half poisoned with stench and half blinded with the reek of turf" — used for fuel.

"This is not an attractive picture. And yet an enlightened and dispassionate observer would have found in the character and manners of this rude people something which might well excite admiration and a good hope. Their courage would be what great exploits achieved in all the four quarters of the globe have since proved it to be. Their intense attachment to their own tribe and their own patriarch, though politically a great evil, partook of the nature of virtue. . . . There must be some elevation of soul in a man who loves the society of which he is a member and the leader whom he follows with a love stronger than the love of life. The Highlander had no scruple about shedding the blood of an enemy; but he had high notions of the duty of observing faith to allies and hospitality to guests. His predatory habits were most pernicious to the commonwealth; yet those erred greatly who imagined that he bore any resemblance to villains who, in rich and well-governed communities, live by stealing. When he drove before him the herds of Lowland farmers up the pass which led to his native glen, he no more considered himself as a thief than the Raleighs and the Drakes considered themselves as thieves when they divided the cargoes of Spanish galleons. He was a warrior seizing the lawful prize of war, of war never intermitted during the thirty-five generations which had passed away since the Teutonic invaders had driven the children of the soil to the mountains. . . . His inordinate pride of birth and his contempt for labor and trade were indeed great weaknesses, and had done far more than the inclemency of the air and the sterility of the soil to keep his country poor and rude. Yet even here there was some compensation. . . . As there was no other part of the island where men, sordidly clothed, lodged, and fed, indulged themselves to such a degree in the idle, sauntering habits of an aristocracy, so there was no other part where such men had in such a degree the better qualities of an aristocracy, grace and dignity of manner, self-respect, and that noble sensibility which makes dishonor more terrible than death." They had as little book-learning as English plowboys; but the arts of poetry and rhetoric may thrive where books are wholly or almost wholly unknown. "At the Highland banquets, minstrels who did not know their letters sometimes poured forth rhapsodies in which a discerning critic might have found passages which might have reminded him of the tenderness of Otway or the vigor of Dryden."

But the Saxons who dwelt far from the Gaelic provinces knew little about the Highlander, and those who were near those provinces could not judge him impartially. "The enmity between the Highland borderer and the Lowland borderer was the growth of ages, and was kept fresh by constant injuries. Thus the Highlander was an object of hatred to his Saxon neighbors, and from these neighbors those Saxons who dwelt far away learned the very little they cared to know about his habits. When the English condescended to think of him at all, they considered him as a filthy savage, a slave, a cut-throat, and a thief."

This state of things lasted until the year 1745, and was soon followed by the conflict in which the Highlands were completely subjugated by England. A political and social revolution followed through the whole Celtic region. The power of the chiefs was destroyed, the old predatory habits were broken up; and soon — though not quite so speedily as Macaulay implies — "a strange reflux of public feeling began, and pity succeeded to aversion." He dwells at great length on the change, but a sentence or two will suffice to indicate the tenor of it: "As long as there were Gaelic marauders, they had been regarded by the Saxon population as hateful vermin who ought to be exterminated without mercy; as soon as the extermination had been accomplished, . . . the freebooter was exalted into a hero of mance. . . . The Gaelic monuments, the Gaelic usages, the Gaelic superstitions, the Gaelic verses, disdainfully neglected during many ages, began to attract the attention of the learned. . . . Where the Highlands were concerned, men of sense gave ready credence to stories without evidence; and men of taste gave rapturous applause to compositions without merit. Epic poems, which any skilful and dispassionate critic would at a glance have perceived to be almost entirely modern, . . . were pronounced to be fifteen hundred years old, and were gravely classed with the Iliad."

This refers to Macpherson's alleged translations of Ossian, and the entire passage alludes to his poems and those of others who wrote about the same time (1747 to 1763, when the Ossian poems appeared) — half a century or so before Scott's metrical romances were published. The "correctness" of the latter, so far as substantial truth to the old Highland life and character is concerned, Macaulay recognizes in his essay on Moore's *Life of Byron*, where he says: "We are sure that the Greeks of Shakespeare [in *Troilus and Cressida*] bear a far greater resemblance than the Greeks of Racine to the real Greeks who besieged Troy; the Greeks of Shakespeare are human beings, and the Greeks of Racine mere names." So Scott, he says, is a more correct poet than some, like Pope and Addison, "who are commonly extolled as the models of correctness. . . . No man can possibly think that the Romans of Addison [in *Cato*] resemble the real Romans so closely as the moss-troopers of Scott resemble the real moss-troopers."

In the chapter of his *History* from which I have quoted above, Macaulay apparently includes Scott among the "writers of a very different order" from Macpherson and others (but, like those, not mentioned by name) who have given us "skilful pictures of the old Highland life," in which "whatever was repulsive was softened down, whatever was graceful and noble was brought prominently forward." "Some of these works," he adds, "were executed with such admirable art that, like the historical plays of Shakespeare, they superseded history. The visions of the poet were realities to his readers; the places which he described became holy ground, and were visited by thousands of pilgrims."

This was eminently true of the region in which the story of *The Lady of the Lake* is laid. The poem was published in June, 1810, and crowds of tourists rushed to Loch Katrine before the summer was over. A Miss Spence, who was at Callander in August, records that "the number of persons attracted to the far-famed spot in consequence of Mr. Walter Scott's beautiful poem exceeds calculation."

And yet, as Professor Minto shows, in his scholarly edition of the poem (Oxford, 1891), the common opinion that in this poem and his subsequent novels Scott "originally created the romantic interest in Scotland is not quite accurate. He did not so much create this interest as popularize it. It had grown up slowly among literary people in the course of the century, and Scott gave it a sudden and wide expansion." There had been an enthusiastic description of the Trosachs in Sir John Sinclair's *Statistical Account of Scotland*, published in 1794. The Hon. Mrs. Murray travelled there in 1796, and her account of her tour was printed in 1799. Wordsworth and his sister Dorothy visited the Trosachs in 1803. A road had been opened along the north shore of Loch Katrine twenty years before Scott made the district famous by his poem.

In the Introduction of 1830, referred to above, and in the notes appended to the poem (mostly given in full in the present edition), Scott has taken special pains to indicate where he has followed sober history and where he has varied from it, and also to justify many incidents in the plot by quoting authorities to prove that these are true to Highland manners, customs, beliefs, and superstitions. I fancy that the average reader — and sometimes the teacher and the student — is inclined to "skip" the longer notes at least; but they deserve careful attention for the light they throw on Highland history and life, and also on the poet's treatment of his subject and materials. See particularly the notes on canto i. 460, 585, 622; ii. 7, 109, 131, 142, 200, 229, 306, 309, 363, 408, 422, 615, 634, 801, 809; iii. 18, 19, 71, 149, 168, 169, 191, 300, 369, 452, 600, 622, 672; iv. 63, 98, 132, 298, 301, 306, 345, 747, 762; v. 124, 126, 165, 270, 315, 380, 383, 406, 551, 562, 564, 614, 630; vi. 47, 127, 348, 369, 740, 789. The information given by Scott in these notes, if formally grouped and arranged, would furnish matter for a much longer introduction to the poem than the present one; and that teachers sometimes overlook it is evident from the fact that they have actually written to me to ask for facts or explanations contained in the notes.

Of the Highlanders little more need be said here. The fact that they belonged to the Celtic (or Keltic) race has already been mentioned — the race which occupied the British Isles when we first know about them through the Roman Conquest in the first century of the Christian era; as in earlier times they formed the main population of Gaul (France) and Spain. The language of the Highlanders belonged to the Gaelic (or Goidelic) branch of the Celtic tongues, like that of the natives of Ireland and the Isle of Man; while that of the southern part of the island belonged to the British (or Brythonic) branch, represented later by the Welsh, the Cornish (which became extinct at the end of the eighteenth century) and the Breton, still spoken by about a million people in Brittany, on the other side of the English Channel. The Highland language had been somewhat affected by that of the ancient Picts, who were the earlier inhabitants of the country, but whose history and speech are still matter of dispute among the learned.

James V, King of Scotland at the time of the poem, had inherited the throne in 1513, when only a year old. During his boyhood he was under the control of his mother, Margaret, the Queen Dowager and Regent of Scotland, and under that of Douglas, Earl of Angus, after her hasty and imprudent marriage with that powerful nobleman. The match was extremely unpopular with her people, and led to the recall of the Duke of Albany, the nearest male relative of James, who had been banished in the reign of James III. Albany was generally accepted as Regent, but, after long conflict with opposing factions and being twice compelled to flee to France, finally left Scotland in May, 1524, never to return. Queen Margaret then endeavored to call the twelve-year-old James to the sovereignty, but the Earl of Angus regained his old supremacy, got possession of the person of the young king, and became Regent of Scotland without assuming the name. James, however, escaped from the restraint of Angus and took refuge in Stirling Castle. The nobility gathered to his support, Angus was eventually driven into exile with all his friends and kinsmen, and James in 1528 assumed the throne. For further particulars of this period in his history, see Scott's notes on page 198 (line 142) and page 200 (line 229); and for the war with the Border robbers which followed in 1529, and his dealings later with the Highland chiefs, see pages 208, 209 (lines 615, 634). For a more detailed account of the entire period (from 1513 to 1540) see the *Tales of a Grandfather*, vol. i, chapters 25–27. This general view of Scottish history, originally written by Scott for his young relative, Hugh Littleton, ought to be accessible (in its complete or abridged form) to juvenile readers in every family and school.

CONTENTS.

ARGUMENT.

The scene of the following Poem is laid chiefly in the vicinity of Loch Katrine, in the Western Highlands of Perthshire. The time of Action includes Six Days, and the transactions of each Day occupy a Canto.

SAINT FILLAN'S HILL.

THE LADY OF THE LAKE.

CANTO FIRST.

THE CHASE.

Harp of the North! that mouldering long hast hung
  On the witch-elm that shades Saint Fillan's spring,
And down the fitful breeze thy numbers flung,
  Till envious ivy did around thee cling,
Muffling with verdant ringlet every string,—
  O Minstrel Harp, still must thine accents sleep?
Mid rustling leaves and fountains murmuring,
  Still must thy sweeter sounds their silence keep,
Nor bid a warrior smile, nor teach a maid to weep?

Not thus, in ancient days of Caledon, 10
  Was thy voice mute amid the festal crowd,
When lay of hopeless love, or glory won,
  Aroused the fearful or subdued the proud.
At each according pause was heard aloud
  Thine ardent symphony sublime and high!
Fair dames and crested chiefs attention bowed;
  For still the burden of thy minstrelsy
Was Knighthood's dauntless deed, and Beauty's matchless eye.

O, wake once more! how rude soe'er the hand
  That ventures o'er thy magic maze to stray; 20
O, wake once more! though scarce my skill command
  Some feeble echoing of thine earlier lay:
Though harsh and faint, and soon to die away,
  And all unworthy of thy nobler strain,
Yet if one heart throb higher at its sway,
  The wizard note has not been touched in vain.
Then silent be no more! Enchantress, wake again!

I.

The stag at eve had drunk his fill,
Where danced the moon on Monan's rill,
And deep his midnight lair had made 30
In lone Glenartney's hazel shade;
But when the sun his beacon red
Had kindled on Benvoirlich's head,
The deep-mouthed bloodhound's heavy bay
Resounded up the rocky way,
And faint, from farther distance borne,
Were heard the clanging hoof and horn.

II.

As Chief, who hears his warder call,
'To arms! the foemen storm the wall,'
The antlered monarch of the waste 40
Sprung from his heathery couch in haste.
But ere his fleet career he took,
The dew-drops from his flanks he shook;
Like crested leader proud and high
Tossed his beamed frontlet to the sky;
A moment gazed adown the dale,
A moment snuffed the tainted gale,
A moment listened to the cry,
That thickened as the chase drew nigh;
Then, as the headmost foes appeared, 50
With one brave bound the copse he cleared,
And, stretching forward free and far,
Sought the wild heaths of Uam-Var.

III.

Yelled on the view the opening pack;
Rock, glen, and cavern paid them back;
To many a mingled sound at once
The awakened mountain gave response.
A hundred dogs bayed deep and strong,
Clattered a hundred steeds along,
Their peal the merry horns rung out, 60
A hundred voices joined the shout;
With hark and whoop and wild halloo,
No rest Benvoirlich's echoes knew.
Far from the tumult fled the roe,
Close in her covert cowered the doe.
The falcon, from her cairn on high,
Cast on the rout a wondering eye,

Till far beyond her piercing ken
The hurricane had swept the glen.
Faint, and more faint, its failing din 70
Returned from cavern, cliff, and linn,
And silence settled, wide and still,
On the lone wood and mighty hill.

IV.

Less loud the sounds of sylvan war
Disturbed the heights of Uam-Var,
And roused the cavern where, 't is told,
A giant made his den of old;
For ere that steep ascent was won,
High in his pathway hung the sun,
And many a gallant, stayed perforce, 80
Was fain to breathe his faltering horse,
And of the trackers of the deer
Scarce half the lessening pack was near;
So shrewdly on the mountain-side
Had the bold burst their mettle tried.

V.

The noble stag was pausing now
Upon the mountain's southern brow,
Where broad extended, far beneath,
The varied realms of fair Menteith.
With anxious eye he wandered o'er 90
Mountain and meadow, moss and moor,
And pondered refuge from his toil,
By far Lochard or Aberfoyle.
But nearer was the copsewood gray
That waved and wept on Loch Achray,
And mingled with the pine-trees blue
On the bold cliffs of Benvenue.

Fresh vigor with the hope returned,
With flying foot the heath he spurned,
Held westward with unwearied race, 100
And left behind the panting chase.

VI.

'T were long to tell what steeds gave o'er,
As swept the hunt through Cambusmore;
What reins were tightened in despair,
When rose Benledi's ridge in air;
Who flagged upon Bochastle's heath,
Who shunned to stem the flooded Teith,—
For twice that day, from shore to shore,
The gallant stag swam stoutly o'er.
Few were the stragglers, following far, 110
That reached the lake of Vennachar;
And when the Brigg of Turk was won,
The headmost horseman rode alone.

VII.

Alone, but with unbated zeal,
That horseman plied the scourge and steel;
For jaded now, and spent with toil,
Embossed with foam, and dark with soil,
While every gasp with sobs he drew,
The laboring stag strained full in view.
Two dogs of black Saint Hubert's breed, 120
Unmatched for courage, breath, and speed,
Fast on his flying traces came,
And all but won that desperate game;
For, scarce a spear's length from his haunch,
Vindictive toiled the bloodhounds stanch;
Nor nearer might the dogs attain,
Nor farther might the quarry strain.

THE BRIGG OF TURK.

Thus up the margin of the lake,
Between the precipice and brake,
O'er stock and rock their race they take. 130

VIII.

The Hunter marked that mountain high,
The lone lake's western boundary,
And deemed the stag must turn to bay,
Where that huge rampart barred the way;
Already glorying in the prize,
Measured his antlers with his eyes;

For the death-wound and death-halloo
Mustered his breath, his whinyard drew; —
But thundering as he came prepared,
With ready arm and weapon bared, 140
The wily quarry shunned the shock,
And turned him from the opposing rock;
Then, dashing down a darksome glen,
Soon lost to hound and Hunter's ken,
In the deep Trosachs' wildest nook
His solitary refuge took.
There, while close couched the thicket shed
Cold dews and wild flowers on his head,
He heard the baffled dogs in vain
Rave through the hollow pass amain, 150
Chiding the rocks that yelled again.

IX.

Close on the hounds the Hunter came,
To cheer them on the vanished game;
But, stumbling in the rugged dell,
The gallant horse exhausted fell.
The impatient rider strove in vain
To rouse him with the spur and rein,
For the good steed, his labors o'er,
Stretched his stiff limbs, to rise no more;
Then, touched with pity and remorse, 160
He sorrowed o'er the expiring horse.
'I little thought, when first thy rein
I slacked upon the banks of Seine,
That Highland eagle e'er should feed
On thy fleet limbs, my matchless steed!
Woe worth the chase, woe worth the day,
That costs thy life, my gallant gray!'

X.

Then through the dell his horn resounds,
From vain pursuit to call the hounds.
Back limped, with slow and crippled pace, 170
The sulky leaders of the chase;
Close to their master's side they pressed,
With drooping tail and humbled crest;
But still the dingle's hollow throat
Prolonged the swelling bugle-note.
The owlets started from their dream,
The eagles answered with their scream,
Round and around the sounds were cast,
Till echo seemed an answering blast;
And on the Hunter hied his way, 180
To join some comrades of the day,
Yet often paused, so strange the road,
So wondrous were the scenes it showed.

XI.

The western waves of ebbing day
Rolled o'er the glen their level way;
Each purple peak, each flinty spire,
Was bathed in floods of living fire.
But not a setting beam could glow
Within the dark ravines below,
Where twined the path in shadow hid, 190
Round many a rocky pyramid,
Shooting abruptly from the dell
Its thunder-splintered pinnacle;
Round many an insulated mass,
The native bulwarks of the pass,
Huge as the tower which builders vain
Presumptuous piled on Shinar's plain.

The rocky summits, split and rent,
Formed turret, dome, or battlement,
Or seemed fantastically set 200
With cupola or minaret,
Wild crests as pagod ever decked,
Or mosque of Eastern architect.
Nor were these earth-born castles bare,
Nor lacked they many a banner fair;
For, from their shivered brows displayed,
Far o'er the unfathomable glade,
All twinkling with the dewdrop sheen,
The brier-rose fell in streamers green,
And creeping shrubs of thousand dyes 210
Waved in the west-wind's summer sighs.

XII.

Boon nature scattered, free and wild,
Each plant or flower, the mountain's child.
Here eglantine embalmed the air,
Hawthorn and hazel mingled there;
The primrose pale and violet flower
Found in each clift a narrow bower;
Foxglove and nightshade, side by side,
Emblems of punishment and pride,
Grouped their dark hues with every stain 220
The weather-beaten crags retain.
With boughs that quaked at every breath,
Gray birch and aspen wept beneath;
Aloft, the ash and warrior oak
Cast anchor in the rifted rock;
And, higher yet, the pine-tree hung
His shattered trunk, and frequent flung,
Where seemed the cliffs to meet on high,
His boughs athwart the narrowed sky.

Highest of all, where white peaks glanced, 230
Where glistening streamers waved and danced,
The wanderer's eye could barely view
The summer heaven's delicious blue;
So wondrous wild, the whole might seem
The scenery of a fairy dream.

XIII.

Onward, amid the copse 'gan peep
A narrow inlet, still and deep,
Affording scarce such breadth of brim
As served the wild duck's brood to swim.
Lost for a space, through thickets veering. 240
But broader when again appearing,
Tall rocks and tufted knolls their face
Could on the dark-blue mirror trace;
And farther as the Hunter strayed,
Still broader sweep its channels made.
The shaggy mounds no longer stood,
Emerging from entangled wood,
But, wave-encircled, seemed to float,
Like castle girdled with its moat;
Yet broader floods extending still 250
Divide them from their parent hill,
Till each, retiring, claims to be
An islet in an inland sea.

XIV.

And now, to issue from the glen,
No pathway meets the wanderer's ken,
Unless he climb with footing nice
A far-projecting precipice.
The broom's tough roots his ladder made,
The hazel saplings lent their aid;

And thus an airy point he won, 260
Where, gleaming with the setting sun,
One burnished sheet of living gold,
Loch Katrine lay beneath him rolled,
In all her length far winding lay,
With promontory, creek, and bay,
And islands that, empurpled bright,
Floated amid the livelier light,
And mountains that like giants stand
To sentinel enchanted land.
High on the south, huge Benvenue 270
Down to the lake in masses threw
Crags, knolls, and mounds, confusedly hurled,
The fragments of an earlier world ;
A wildering forest feathered o'er
His ruined sides and summit hoar,
While on the north, through middle air,
Ben-an heaved high his forehead bare.

XV.

From the steep promontory gazed
The stranger, raptured and amazed,
And, 'What a scene were here,' he cried, 280
'For princely pomp or churchman's pride !
On this bold brow, a lordly tower ;
In that soft vale, a lady's bower ;
On yonder meadow far away,
The turrets of a cloister gray ;
How blithely might the bugle-horn
Chide on the lake the lingering morn !
How sweet at eve the lover's lute
Chime when the groves were still and mute !
And when the midnight moon should lave 290
Her forehead in the silver wave,

How solemn on the ear would come
The holy matins' distant hum,
While the deep peal's commanding tone
Should wake, in yonder islet lone,
A sainted hermit from his cell,
To drop a bead with every knell!
And bugle, lute, and bell, and all,
Should each bewildered stranger call
To friendly feast and lighted hall. 300

XVI.

'Blithe were it then to wander here!
But now — beshrew yon nimble deer —
Like that same hermit's, thin and spare,
The copse must give my evening fare;
Some mossy bank my couch must be,
Some rustling oak my canopy.
Yet pass we that; the war and chase
Give little choice of resting-place; —
A summer night in greenwood spent
Were but to-morrow's merriment: 310
But hosts may in these wilds abound,
Such as are better missed than found;
To meet with Highland plunderers here
Were worse than loss of steed or deer. —
I am alone; — my bugle-strain
May call some straggler of the train;
Or, fall the worst that may betide,
Ere now this falchion has been tried.'

XVII.

But scarce again his horn he wound,
When lo! forth starting at the sound. 320
From underneath an aged oak
That slanted from the islet rock,

A damsel guider of its way,
A little skiff shot to the bay,
That round the promontory steep
Led its deep line in graceful sweep,
Eddying, in almost viewless wave,
The weeping willow twig to lave,
And kiss, with whispering sound and slow,
The beach of pebbles bright as snow. 330
The boat had touched this silver strand
Just as the Hunter left his stand,
And stood concealed amid the brake,
To view this Lady of the Lake.
The maiden paused, as if again
She thought to catch the distant strain.
With head upraised, and look intent,
And eye and ear attentive bent,
And locks flung back, and lips apart,
Like monument of Grecian art, 340
In listening mood, she seemed to stand,
The guardian Naiad of the strand.

XVIII.

And ne'er did Grecian chisel trace
A Nymph, a Naiad, or a Grace,
Of finer form or lovelier face!
What though the sun, with ardent frown,
Had slightly tinged her cheek with brown,
The sportive toil, which, short and light,
Had dyed her glowing hue so bright,
Served too in hastier swell to show 350
Short glimpses of a breast of snow:
What though no rule of courtly grace
To measured mood had trained her pace,—
A foot more light, a step more true,
Ne'er from the heath-flower dashed the dew;

E'en the slight harebell raised its head,
Elastic from her airy tread :
What though upon her speech there hung
The accents of the mountain tongue,—
Those silver sounds, so soft, so dear, 360
The listener held his breath to hear !

XIX.

A chieftain's daughter seemed the maid ;
Her satin snood, her silken plaid,
Her golden brooch, such birth betrayed.
And seldom was a snood amid
Such wild luxuriant ringlets hid,
Whose glossy black to shame might bring
The plumage of the raven's wing ;
And seldom o'er a breast so fair
Mantled a plaid with modest care, 370
And never brooch the folds combined
Above a heart more good and kind.
Her kindness and her worth to spy,
You need but gaze on Ellen's eye ;
Not Katrine in her mirror blue
Gives back the shaggy banks more true,
Than every free-born glance confessed
The guileless movements of her breast ;
Whether joy danced in her dark eye,
Or woe or pity claimed a sigh, 380
Or filial love was glowing there,
Or meek devotion poured a prayer,
Or tale of injury called forth
The indignant spirit of the North.
One only passion unrevealed
With maiden pride the maid concealed,
Yet not less purely felt the flame ;—
O, need I tell that passion's name ?

XX.

Impatient of the silent horn,
Now on the gale her voice was borne:— 390
'Father!' she cried; the rocks around
Loved to prolong the gentle sound.
Awhile she paused, no answer came;—
'Malcolm, was thine the blast?' the name
Less resolutely uttered fell,
The echoes could not catch the swell.
'A stranger I,' the Huntsman said,
Advancing from the hazel shade.
The maid, alarmed, with hasty oar
Pushed her light shallop from the shore, 400
And when a space was gained between,
Closer she drew her bosom's screen;—
So forth the startled swan would swing,
So turn to prune his ruffled wing.
Then safe, though fluttered and amazed,
She paused, and on the stranger gazed.
Not his the form, nor his the eye,
That youthful maidens wont to fly.

XXI.

On his bold visage middle age
Had slightly pressed its signet sage, 410
Yet had not quenched the open truth
And fiery vehemence of youth;
Forward and frolic glee was there,
The will to do, the soul to dare,
The sparkling glance, soon blown to fire,
Of hasty love or he dlong ire.
His limbs were cast in manly mould
For hardy sports or contest bold;

And though in peaceful garb arrayed,
And weaponless except his blade, 420
His stately mien as well implied
A high-born heart, a martial pride,
As if a baron's crest he wore,
And sheathed in armor trode the shore.
Slighting the petty need he showed,
He told of his benighted road;
His ready speech flowed fair and free,
In phrase of gentlest courtesy,
Yet seemed that tone and gesture bland
Less used to sue than to command. 430

XXII.

Awhile the maid the stranger eyed,
And, reassured, at length replied,
That Highland halls were open still
To wildered wanderers of the hill.
'Nor think you unexpected come
To yon lone isle, our desert home;
Before the heath had lost the dew,
This morn, a couch was pulled for you;
On yonder mountain's purple head
Have ptarmigan and heath-cock bled, 440
And our broad nets have swept the mere,
To furnish forth your evening cheer.'—
'Now, by the rood, my lovely maid,
Your courtesy has erred,' he said;
'No right have I to claim, misplaced,
The welcome of expected guest.
A wanderer, here by fortune tost,
My way, my friends, my courser lost,
I ne'er before, believe me, fair,
Have ever drawn your mountain air, 450
Till on this lake's romantic strand
I found a fay in fairy land!'—

THE SILVER STRAND, LOCH KATRINE.

XXIII.

'I well believe,' the maid replied,
As her light skiff approached the side,—
'I well believe, that ne'er before
Your foot has trod Loch Katrine's shore;
But yet, as far as yesternight,
Old Allan-bane foretold your plight,—
A gray-haired sire, whose eye intent
Was on the visioned future bent. 460
He saw your steed, a dappled gray,
Lie dead beneath the birchen way;

Painted exact your form and mien,
Your hunting-suit of Lincoln green,
That tasselled horn so gayly gilt,
That falchion's crooked blade and hilt,
That cap with heron plumage trim,
And yon two hounds so dark and grim.
He bade that all should ready be
To grace a guest of fair degree; 470
But light I held his prophecy,
And deemed it was my father's horn
Whose echoes o'er the lake were borne.'

XXIV.

The stranger smiled: — 'Since to your home
A destined errant-knight I come,
Announced by prophet sooth and old,
Doomed, doubtless, for achievement bold,
I 'll lightly front each high emprise
For one kind glance of those bright eyes.
Permit me first the task to guide 480
Your fairy frigate o'er the tide.'
The maid, with smile suppressed and sly,
The toil unwonted saw him try;
For seldom, sure, if e'er before,
His noble hand had grasped an oar:
Yet with main strength his strokes he drew,
And o'er the lake the shallop flew;
With heads erect and whimpering cry,
The hounds behind their passage ply.
Nor frequent does the bright oar break 490
The darkening mirror of the lake,
Until the rocky isle they reach,
And moor their shallop on the beach.

XXV.

The stranger viewed the shore around;
'T was all so close with copsewood bound,
Nor track nor pathway might declare
That human foot frequented there,
Until the mountain maiden showed
A clambering unsuspected road,
That winded through the tangled screen, 500
And opened on a narrow green,
Where weeping birch and willow round
With their long fibres swept the ground.
Here, for retreat in dangerous hour,
Some chief had framed a rustic bower.

XXVI.

It was a lodge of ample size,
But strange of structure and device;
Of such materials as around
The workman's hand had readiest found.
Lopped of their boughs, their hoar trunks bared 510
And by the hatchet rudely squared,
To give the walls their destined height,
The sturdy oak and ash unite;
While moss and clay and leaves combined
To fence each crevice from the wind.
The lighter pine-trees overhead
Their slender length for rafters spread,
And withered heath and rushes dry
Supplied a russet canopy.
Due westward, fronting to the green, 520
A rural portico was seen,
Aloft on native pillars borne,
Of mountain fir with bark unshorn,
Where Ellen's hand had taught to twine
The ivy and Idæan vine.

The clematis, the favored flower
Which boasts the name of virgin-bower,
And every hardy plant could bear
Loch Katrine's keen and searching air.
An instant in this porch she stayed, 530
And gayly to the stranger said:
'On heaven and on thy lady call,
And enter the enchanted hall!'

XXVII.

'My hope, my heaven, my trust must be,
My gentle guide, in following thee!'—
He crossed the threshold,—and a clang
Of angry steel that instant rang.
To his bold brow his spirit rushed,
But soon for vain alarm he blushed,
When on the floor he saw displayed, 540
Cause of the din, a naked blade
Dropped from the sheath, that careless flung
Upon a stag's huge antlers swung;
For all around, the walls to grace,
Hung trophies of the fight or chase:
A target there, a bugle here,
A battle-axe, a hunting-spear,
And broadswords, bows, and arrows store,
With the tusked trophies of the boar.
Here grins the wolf as when he died, 550
And there the wild-cat's brindled hide
The frontlet of the elk adorns,
Or mantles o'er the bison's horns;
Pennons and flags defaced and stained,
That blackening streaks of blood retained,
And deer-skins, dappled, dun, and white,
With otter's fur and seal's unite,
In rude and uncouth tapestry all,
To garnish forth the sylvan hall.

XXVIII.

The wondering stranger round him gazed, 560
And next the fallen weapon raised: —
Few were the arms whose sinewy strength
Sufficed to stretch it forth at length.
And as the brand he poised and swayed,
'I never knew but one,' he said,
'Whose stalwart arm might brook to wield
A blade like this in battle-field.'
She sighed, then smiled and took the word:
'You see the guardian champion's sword;
As light it trembles in his hand 570
As in my grasp a hazel wand:
My sire's tall form might grace the part
Of Ferragus or Ascabart,
But in the absent giant's hold
Are women now, and menials old.'

XXIX.

The mistress of the mansion came,
Mature of age, a graceful dame,
Whose easy step and stately port
Had well become a princely court,
To whom, though more than kindred knew, 580
Young Ellen gave a mother's due.
Meet welcome to her guest she made,
And every courteous rite was paid
That hospitality could claim,
Though all unasked his birth and name.
Such then the reverence to a guest,
That fellest foe might join the feast,
And from his deadliest foeman's door
Unquestioned turn, the banquet o'er.

At length his rank the stranger names, 590
'The Knight of Snowdoun, James Fitz-James;
Lord of a barren heritage,
Which his brave sires, from age to age,
By their good swords had held with toil;
His sire had fallen in such turmoil,
And he, God wot, was forced to stand
Oft for his right with blade in hand.
This morning with Lord Moray's train
He chased a stalwart stag in vain,
Outstripped his comrades, missed the deer, 600
Lost his good steed, and wandered here.'

XXX.

Fain would the Knight in turn require
The name and state of Ellen's sire.
Well showed the elder lady's mien
That courts and cities she had seen;
Ellen, though more her looks displayed
The simple grace of sylvan maid,
In speech and gesture, form and face,
Showed she was come of gentle race.
'T were strange in ruder rank to find 610
Such looks, such manners, and such mind.
Each hint the Knight of Snowdoun gave,
Dame Margaret heard with silence grave;
Or Ellen, innocently gay,
Turned all inquiry light away:—
'Weird women we! by dale and down
We dwell, afar from tower and town.
We stem the flood, we ride the blast,
On wandering knights our spells we cast;
While viewless minstrels touch the string, 620
'T is thus our charmed rhymes we sing.'
She sung, and still a harp unseen
Filled up the symphony between.

XXXI.

SONG.

'Soldier, rest! thy warfare o'er,
  Sleep the sleep that knows not breaking;
Dream of battled fields no more,
  Days of danger, nights of waking.
In our isle's enchanted hall,
  Hands unseen thy couch are strewing,
Fairy strains of music fall, 630
  Every sense in slumber dewing.
Soldier, rest! thy warfare o'er,
Dream of fighting fields no more;
Sleep the sleep that knows not breaking,
Morn of toil, nor night of waking.

'No rude sound shall reach thine ear,
  Armor's clang or war-steed champing,
Trump nor pibroch summon here
  Mustering clan or squadron tramping.
Yet the lark's shrill fife may come 640
  At the daybreak from the fallow,
And the bittern sound his drum,
  Booming from the sedgy shallow.
Ruder sounds shall none be near,
Guards nor warders challenge here,
Here 's no war-steed's neigh and champing,
Shouting clans or squadrons stamping.'

XXXII.

She paused, — then, blushing, led the lay,
To grace the stranger of the day.
Her mellow notes awhile prolong 650
The cadence of the flowing song,
Till to her lips in measured frame
The minstrel verse spontaneous came.

SONG CONTINUED.

'Huntsman, rest! thy chase is done;
While our slumbrous spells assail ye,
Dream not, with the rising sun,
Bugles here shall sound reveillé.
Sleep! the deer is in his den;
Sleep! thy hounds are by thee lying;
Sleep! nor dream in yonder glen 660
How thy gallant steed lay dying.
Huntsman, rest! thy chase is done;
Think not of the rising sun,
For at dawning to assail ye
Here no bugles sound reveillé.'

XXXIII.

The hall was cleared, — the stranger's bed,
Was there of mountain heather spread,
Where oft a hundred guests had lain,
And dreamed their forest sports again.
But vainly did the heath-flower shed 670
Its moorland fragrance round his head;
Not Ellen's spell had lulled to rest
The fever of his troubled breast.
In broken dreams the image rose
Of varied perils, pains, and woes:
His steed now flounders in the brake,
Now sinks his barge upon the lake;
Now leader of a broken host,
His standard falls, his honor 's lost.
Then, — from my couch may heavenly might 680
Chase that worst phantom of the night! —
Again returned the scenes of youth,
Of confident, undoubting truth;

Again his soul he interchanged
With friends whose hearts were long estranged.
They come, in dim procession led,
The cold, the faithless, and the dead;
As warm each hand, each brow as gay,
As if they parted yesterday.
And doubt distracts him at the view,— 690
O were his senses false or true?
Dreamed he of death or broken vow,
Or is it all a vision now?

XXXIV.

At length, with Ellen in a grove
He seemed to walk and speak of love;
She listened with a blush and sigh,
His suit was warm, his hopes were high.
He sought her yielded hand to clasp,
And a cold gauntlet met his grasp:
The phantom's sex was changed and gone, 700
Upon its head a helmet shone;
Slowly enlarged to giant size,
With darkened cheek and threatening eyes,
The grisly visage, stern and hoar,
To Ellen still a likeness bore.—
He woke, and, panting with affright,
Recalled the vision of the night.
The hearth's decaying brands were red,
And deep and dusky lustre shed,
Half showing, half concealing, all 710
The uncouth trophies of the hall.
Mid those the stranger fixed his eye
Where that huge falchion hung on high,
And thoughts on thoughts, a countless throng,
Rushed, chasing countless thoughts along,
Until, the giddy whirl to cure,
He rose and sought the moonshine pure.

XXXV.

The wild rose, eglantine, and broom
Wasted around their rich perfume;
The birch-trees wept in fragrant balm; 720
The aspens slept beneath the calm;
The silver light, with quivering glance,
Played on the water's still expanse,—
Wild were the heart whose passion's sway
Could rage beneath the sober ray!
He felt its calm, that warrior guest,
While thus he communed with his breast:—
'Why is it, at each turn I trace
Some memory of that exiled race?
Can I not mountain maiden spy, 730
But she must bear the Douglas eye?
Can I not view a Highland brand,
But it must match the Douglas hand?
Can I not frame a fevered dream,
But still the Douglas is the theme?
I 'll dream no more,—by manly mind
Not even in sleep is will resigned.
My midnight orisons said o'er,
I 'll turn to rest, and dream no more.'
His midnight orisons he told, 740
A prayer with every bead of gold,
Consigned to heaven his cares and woes,
And sunk in undisturbed repose,
Until the heath-cock shrilly crew,
And morning dawned on Benvenue.

LOCH LOMOND AND BEN LOMOND, FROM BALLOCH.

CANTO SECOND.

THE ISLAND.

I.

At morn the black-cock trims his jetty wing,
'T is morning prompts the linnet's blithest lay,
All Nature's children feel the matin spring
Of life reviving, with reviving day;
And while yon little bark glides down the bay,
Wafting the stranger on his way again,
Morn's genial influence roused a minstrel gray,
And sweetly o'er the lake was heard thy strain,
Mixed with the sounding harp, O white-haired Allan-bane!

II.

SONG.

'Not faster yonder rowers' might 10
Flings from their oars the spray,
Not faster yonder rippling bright,
That tracks the shallop's course in light,
Melts in the lake away,
Than men from memory erase
The benefits of former days;
Then, stranger, go! good speed the while.
Nor think again of the lonely isle.

'High place to thee in royal court,
High place in battled line, 20
Good hawk and hound for sylvan sport!
Where beauty sees the brave resort,
The honored meed be thine!
True be thy sword, thy friend sincere,
Thy lady constant, kind, and dear,
And lost in love's and friendship's smile
Be memory of the lonely isle!

III.

SONG CONTINUED.

'But if beneath yon southern sky
A plaided stranger roam,
Whose drooping crest and stifled sigh, 30
And sunken cheek and heavy eye,
Pine for his Highland home;
Then, warrior, then be thine to show
The care that soothes a wanderer's woe;
Remember then thy hap erewhile,
A stranger in the lonely isle.

'Or if on life's uncertain main
  Mishap shall mar thy sail;
If faithful, wise, and brave in vain,
Woe, want, and exile thou sustain 40
  Beneath the fickle gale;
Waste not a sigh on fortune changed,
On thankless courts, or friends estranged,
But come where kindred worth shall smile,
To greet thee in the lonely isle.'

IV.

As died the sounds upon the tide,
The shallop reached the mainland side,
And ere his onward way he took,
The stranger cast a lingering look,
Where easily his eye might reach 50
The Harper on the islet beach,
Reclined against a blighted tree,
As wasted, gray, and worn as he.
To minstrel meditation given,
His reverend brow was raised to heaven,
As from the rising sun to claim
A sparkle of inspiring flame.
His hand, reclined upon the wire,
Seemed watching the awakening fire;
So still he sat as those who wait 60
Till judgment speak the doom of fate;
So still, as if no breeze might dare
To lift one lock of hoary hair;
So still, as life itself were fled
In the last sound his harp had sped.

V.

Upon a rock with lichens wild,
Beside him Ellen sat and smiled.—

Smiled she to see the stately drake
Lead forth his fleet upon the lake,
While her vexed spaniel from the beach 70
Bayed at the prize beyond his reach?
Yet tell me, then, the maid who knows,
Why deepened on her cheek the rose?—
Forgive, forgive, Fidelity!
Perchance the maiden smiled to see
Yon parting lingerer wave adieu,
And stop and turn to wave anew;
And, lovely ladies, ere your ire
Condemn the heroine of my lyre,
Show me the fair would scorn to spy 80
And prize such conquest of her eye!

VI.

While yet he loitered on the spot,
It seemed as Ellen marked him not;
But when he turned him to the glade,
One courteous parting sign she made;
And after, oft the knight would say,
That not when prize of festal day
Was dealt him by the brightest fair
Who e'er wore jewel in her hair,
So highly did his bosom swell 90
As at that simple mute farewell.
Now with a trusty mountain-guide,
And his dark stag-hounds by his side,
He parts,—the maid, unconscious still,
Watched him wind slowly round the hill:
But when his stately form was hid,
The guardian in her bosom chid,—
'Thy Malcolm! vain and selfish maid!'
'T was thus upbraiding conscience said,—
'Not so had Malcolm idly hung 100
On the smooth phrase of Southern tongue;

Not so had Malcolm strained his eye
Another step than thine to spy.' —
'Wake, Allan-bane,' aloud she cried
To the old minstrel by her side, —
'Arouse thee from thy moody dream!
I 'll give thy harp heroic theme,
And warm thee with a noble name;
Pour forth the glory of the Græme!'
Scarce from her lip the word had rushed, 110
When deep the conscious maiden blushed;
For of his clan, in hall and bower,
Young Malcolm Græme was held the flower.

VII.

The minstrel waked his harp, — three times
Arose the well-known martial chimes,
And thrice their high heroic pride
In melancholy murmurs died.
'Vainly thou bidst, O noble maid,'
Clasping his withered hands, he said,
'Vainly thou bidst me wake the strain, 120
Though all unwont to bid in vain.
Alas! than mine a mightier hand
Has tuned my harp, my strings has spanned!
I touch the chords of joy, but low
And mournful answer notes of woe;
And the proud march which victors tread
Sinks in the wailing for the dead.
O, well for me, if mine alone
That dirge's deep prophetic tone!
If, as my tuneful fathers said, 130
This harp, which erst Saint Modan swayed,
Can thus its master's fate foretell,
Then welcome be the minstrel's knell!

VIII.

'But ah! dear lady, thus it sighed,
The eve thy sainted mother died;
And such the sounds which, while I strove
To wake a lay of war or love,
Came marring all the festal mirth,
Appalling me who gave them birth,
And, disobedient to my call, 140
Wailed loud through Bothwell's bannered hall,
Ere Douglases, to ruin driven,
Were exiled from their native heaven.—
O! if yet worse mishap and woe
My master's house must undergo,
Or aught but weal to Ellen fair
Brood in these accents of despair,
No future bard, sad Harp! shall fling
Triumph or rapture from thy string;
One short, one final strain shall flow, 150
Fraught with unutterable woe,
Then shivered shall thy fragments lie,
Thy master cast him down and die!'

IX.

Soothing she answered him: 'Assuage,
Mine honored friend, the fears of age;
All melodies to thee are known
That harp has rung or pipe has blown,
In Lowland vale or Highland glen,
From Tweed to Spey—what marvel, then,
At times unbidden notes should rise, 160
Confusedly bound in memory's ties,
Entangling, as they rush along,
The war-march with the funeral song?—

Small ground is now for boding fear;
Obscure, but safe, we rest us here.
My sire, in native virtue great,
Resigning lordship, lands, and state,
Not then to fortune more resigned
Than yonder oak might give the wind;
The graceful foliage storms may reave, 170
The noble stem they cannot grieve.
For me' — she stooped, and, looking round,
Plucked a blue harebell from the ground, —
'For me, whose memory scarce conveys
An image of more splendid days,
This little flower that loves the lea
May well my simple emblem be;
It drinks heaven's dew as blithe as rose
That in the King's own garden grows;
And when I place it in my hair, 180
Allan, a bard is bound to swear
He ne'er saw coronet so fair.'
Then playfully the chaplet wild
She wreathed in her dark locks, and smiled.

X.

Her smile, her speech, with winning sway,
Wiled the old Harper's mood away.
With such a look as hermits throw,
When angels stoop to soothe their woe,
He gazed, till fond regret and pride
Thrilled to a tear, then thus replied: 190
'Loveliest and best! thou little know'st
The rank, the honors, thou hast lost!
O, might I live to see thee grace,
In Scotland's court, thy birthright place,
To see my favorite's step advance
The lightest in the courtly dance.

The cause of every gallant's sigh,
And leading star of every eye,
And theme of every minstrel's art,
The Lady of the Bleeding Heart!' 200

XI.

'Fair dreams are these,' the maiden cried,—
Light was her accent, yet she sighed,—
'Yet is this mossy rock to me
Worth splendid chair and canopy;
Nor would my footstep spring more gay
In courtly dance than blithe strathspey,
Nor half so pleased mine ear incline
To royal minstrel's lay as thine.
And then for suitors proud and high,
To bend before my conquering eye,— 210
Thou, flattering bard! thyself wilt say,
That grim Sir Roderick owns its sway.
The Saxon scourge, Clan-Alpine's pride,
The terror of Loch Lomond's side,
Would, at my suit, thou know'st, delay
A Lennox foray—for a day.'—

XII.

The ancient bard her glee repressed:
'Ill hast thou chosen theme for jest!
For who, through all this western wild,
Named Black Sir Roderick e'er, and smiled? 220
In Holy-Rood a knight he slew;
I saw, when back the dirk he drew,
Courtiers give place before the stride
Of the undaunted homicide;
And since, though outlawed, hath his hand
Full sternly kept his mountain land.

Who else dared give — ah ! woe the day,
That I such hated truth should say ! —
The Douglas, like a stricken deer,
Disowned by every noble peer, 230
Even the rude refuge we have here ?
Alas, this wild marauding Chief
Alone might hazard our relief,
And now thy maiden charms expand,
Looks for his guerdon in thy hand ;
Full soon may dispensation sought,
To back his suit, from Rome be brought.
Then, though an exile on the hill,
Thy father, as the Douglas, still
Be held in reverence and fear ; 240
And though to Roderick thou 'rt so dear
That thou mightst guide with silken thread,
Slave of thy will, this chieftain dread,
Yet, O loved maid, thy mirth refrain !
Thy hand is on a lion's mane.' —

XIII.

'Minstrel,' the maid replied, and high
Her father's soul glanced from her eye,
'My debts to Roderick's house I know :
All that a mother could bestow
To Lady Margaret's care I owe, 250
Since first an orphan in the wild
She sorrowed o'er her sister's child ;
To her brave chieftain son, from ire
Of Scotland's king who shrouds my sire,
A deeper, holier debt is owed ;
And, could I pay it with my blood,
Allan ! Sir Roderick should command
My blood, my life, — but not my hand.

Rather will Ellen Douglas dwell
A votaress in Maronnan's cell; 260
Rather through realms beyond the sea,
Seeking the world's cold charity,
Where ne'er was spoke a Scottish word,
And ne'er the name of Douglas heard,
An outcast pilgrim will she rove,
Than wed the man she cannot love.

XIV.

'Thou shak'st, good friend, thy tresses gray,—
That pleading look, what can it say
But what I own? — I grant him brave,
But wild as Bracklinn's thundering wave; 270
And generous, — save vindictive mood
Or jealous transport chafe his blood:
I grant him true to friendly band,
As his claymore is to his hand;
But O! that very blade of steel
More mercy for a foe would feel:
I grant him liberal, to fling
Among his clan the wealth they bring,
When back by lake and glen they wind,
And in the Lowland leave behind, 280
Where once some pleasant hamlet stood,
A mass of ashes slaked with blood.
The hand that for my father fought
I honor, as his daughter ought;
But can I clasp it reeking red
From peasants slaughtered in their shed?
No! wildly while his virtues gleam,
They make his passions darker seem,
And flash along his spirit high,
Like lightning o'er the midnight sky. 290

BRACKLINN FALLS.

While yet a child, — and children know,
Instinctive taught, the friend and foe, —
I shuddered at his brow of gloom,
His shadowy plaid and sable plume;
A maiden grown, I ill could bear
His haughty mien and lordly air:
But, if thou join'st a suitor's claim,
In serious mood, to Roderick's name,

I thrill with anguish! or, if e'er
A Douglas knew the word, with fear. 300
To change such odious theme were best, —
What think'st thou of our stranger guest?' —

XV.

'What think I of him? — woe the while
That brought such wanderer to our isle!
Thy father's battle-brand, of yore
For Tine-man forged by fairy lore,
What time he leagued, no longer foes,
His Border spears with Hotspur's bows,
Did, self-unscabbarded, foreshow
The footstep of a secret foe. 310
If courtly spy hath harbored here,
What may we for the Douglas fear?
What for this island, deemed of old
Clan-Alpine's last and surest hold?
If neither spy nor foe, I pray
What yet may jealous Roderick say? —
Nay, wave not thy disdainful head!
Bethink thee of the discord dread
That kindled when at Beltane game
Thou ledst the dance with Malcolm Græme; 320
Still, though thy sire the peace renewed,
Smoulders in Roderick's breast the feud:
Beware! — But hark! what sounds are these?
My dull ears catch no faltering breeze,
No weeping birch nor aspens wake,
Nor breath is dimpling in the lake;
Still is the canna's hoary beard,
Yet, by my minstrel faith, I heard —
And hark again! some pipe of war
Sends the bold pibroch from afar.' 330

XVI.

Far up the lengthened lake were spied
Four darkening specks upon the tide,
That, slow enlarging on the view,
Four manned and masted barges grew,
And, bearing downwards from Glengyle,
Steered full upon the lonely isle;
The point of Brianchoil they passed,
And, to the windward as they cast,
Against the sun they gave to shine
The bold Sir Roderick's bannered Pine. 340
Nearer and nearer as they bear,
Spears, pikes, and axes flash in air.
Now might you see the tartans brave,
And plaids and plumage dance and wave:
Now see the bonnets sink and rise,
As his tough oar the rower plies;
See, flashing at each sturdy stroke,
The wave ascending into smoke;
See the proud pipers on the bow,
And mark the gaudy streamers flow 350
From their loud chanters down, and sweep
The furrowed bosom of the deep,
As, rushing through the lake amain,
They plied the ancient Highland strain.

XVII.

Ever, as on they bore, more loud
And louder rung the pibroch proud.
At first the sounds, by distance tame,
Mellowed along the waters came,
And, lingering long by cape and bay,
Wailed every harsher note away, 360

Then bursting bolder on the ear,
The clan's shrill Gathering they could hear,
Those thrilling sounds that call the might
Of old Clan-Alpine to the fight.
Thick beat the rapid notes, as when
The mustering hundreds shake the glen,
And hurrying at the signal dread,
The battered earth returns their tread.
Then prelude light, of livelier tone,
Expressed their merry marching on, 370
Ere peal of closing battle rose,
With mingled outcry, shrieks, and blows;
And mimic din of stroke and ward,
As broadsword upon target jarred;
And groaning pause, ere yet again,
Condensed, the battle yelled amain:
The rapid charge, the rallying shout,
Retreat borne headlong into rout,
And bursts of triumph, to declare
Clan-Alpine's conquest — all were there. 380
Nor ended thus the strain, but slow
Sunk in a moan prolonged and low,
And changed the conquering clarion swell
For wild lament o'er those that fell.

XVIII.

The war-pipes ceased, but lake and hill
Were busy with their echoes still;
And, when they slept, a vocal strain
Bade their hoarse chorus wake again,
While loud a hundred clansmen raise
Their voices in their Chieftain's praise. 390
Each boatman, bending to his oar,
With measured sweep the burden bore,

In such wild cadence as the breeze
Makes through December's leafless trees.
The chorus first could Allan know,
'Roderick Vich Alpine, ho! iro!'
And near, and nearer as they rowed,
Distinct the martial ditty flowed.

XIX.

BOAT SONG.

Hail to the Chief who in triumph advances!
Honored and blessed be the ever-green Pine! 400
Long may the tree, in his banner that glances,
Flourish, the shelter and grace of our line!
Heaven send it happy dew,
Earth lend it sap anew,
Gayly to bourgeon and broadly to grow,
While every Highland glen
Sends our shout back again,
'Roderigh Vich Alpine dhu, ho! ieroe!'

Ours is no sapling, chance-sown by the fountain,
Blooming at Beltane, in winter to fade; 410
When the whirlwind has stripped every leaf on the mountain,
The more shall Clan-Alpine exult in her shade.
Moored in the rifted rock,
Proof to the tempest's shock,
Firmer he roots him the ruder it blow;
Menteith and Breadalbane, then,
Echo his praise again,
'Roderigh Vich Alpine dhu, ho! ieroe!'

XX.

Proudly our pibroch has thrilled in Glen Fruin,
And Bannochar's groans to our slogan replied; 420
Glen Luss and Ross-dhu, they are smoking in ruin,
And the best of Loch Lomond lie dead on her side

Widow and Saxon maid
Long shall lament our raid,
Think of Clan-Alpine with fear and with woe;
Lennox and Leven-glen
Shake when they hear again,
'Roderigh Vich Alpine dhu, ho! ieroe!'

Row, vassals, row, for the pride of the Highlands!
Stretch to your oars for the ever-green Pine! 430
O that the rosebud that graces yon islands
Were wreathed in a garland around him to twine!
O that some seedling gem,
Worthy such noble stem,
Honored and blessed in their shadow might grow!
Loud should Clan-Alpine then
Ring from her deepmost glen,
'Roderigh Vich Alpine dhu, ho! ieroe!'

XXI.

With all her joyful female band
Had Lady Margaret sought the strand. 440
Loose on the breeze their tresses flew,
And high their snowy arms they threw,
As echoing back with shrill acclaim,
And chorus wild, the Chieftain's name;
While, prompt to please, with mother's art,
The darling passion of his heart,
The Dame called Ellen to the strand,
To greet her kinsman ere he land:
'Come, loiterer, come! a Douglas thou,
And shun to wreathe a victor's brow?' 450
Reluctantly and slow, the maid
The unwelcome summoning obeyed,
And when a distant bugle rung,
In the mid-path aside she sprung:—

'List, Allan-bane! From mainland cast
I hear my father's signal blast.
Be ours,' she cried, 'the skiff to guide,
And waft him from the mountain-side.'
Then, like a sunbeam, swift and bright,
She darted to her shallop light, 460
And, eagerly while Roderick scanned,
For her dear form, his mother's band,
The islet far behind her lay,
And she had landed in the bay.

XXII.

Some feelings are to mortals given
With less of earth in them than heaven;
And if there be a human tear
From passion's dross refined and clear,
A tear so limpid and so meek
It would not stain an angel's cheek, 470
'T is that which pious fathers shed
Upon a duteous daughter's head!
And as the Douglas to his breast
His darling Ellen closely pressed,
Such holy drops her tresses steeped,
Though 't was an hero's eye that weeped.
Nor while on Ellen's faltering tongue
Her filial welcomes crowded hung,
Marked she that fear — affection's proof —
Still held a graceful youth aloof; 480
No! not till Douglas named his name,
Although the youth was Malcolm Græme.

XXIII.

Allan, with wistful look the while,
Marked Roderick landing on the isle;
His master piteously he eyed,
Then gazed upon the Chieftain's pride.

Then dashed with hasty hand away
From his dimmed eye the gathering spray;
And Douglas, as his hand he laid
On Malcolm's shoulder, kindly said: 490
'Canst thou, young friend, no meaning spy
In my poor follower's glistening eye?
I 'll tell thee: — he recalls the day
When in my praise he led the lay
O'er the arched gate of Bothwell proud,
While many a minstrel answered loud,
When Percy's Norman pennon, won
In bloody field, before me shone,
And twice ten knights, the least a name
As mighty as yon Chief may claim, 500
Gracing my pomp, behind me came.
Yet trust me, Malcolm, not so proud
Was I of all that marshalled crowd,
Though the waned crescent owned my might,
And in my train trooped lord and knight,
Though Blantyre hymned her holiest lays,
And Bothwell's bards flung back my praise,
As when this old man's silent tear,
And this poor maid's affection dear,
A welcome give more kind and true 510
Than aught my better fortunes knew.
Forgive, my friend, a father's boast, —
O, it out-beggars all I lost!'

XXIV.

Delightful praise! — like summer rose,
That brighter in the dew-drop glows,
The bashful maiden's cheek appeared,
For Douglas spoke, and Malcolm heard.
The flush of shame-faced joy to hide,
The hounds, the hawk, her cares divide;

The loved caresses of the maid 520
The dogs with crouch and whimper paid;
And, at her whistle, on her hand
The falcon took his favorite stand,
Closed his dark wing, relaxed his eye,
Nor, though unhooded, sought to fly.
And, trust, while in such guise she stood,
Like fabled Goddess of the wood,
That if a father's partial thought
O'erweighed her worth and beauty aught,
Well might the lover's judgment fail 530
To balance with a juster scale;
For with each secret glance he stole,
The fond enthusiast sent his soul.

XXV.

Of stature fair, and slender frame,
But firmly knit, was Malcolm Græme.
The belted plaid and tartan hose
Did ne'er more graceful limbs disclose:
His flaxen hair, of sunny hue,
Curled closely round his bonnet blue.
Trained to the chase, his eagle eye 540
The ptarmigan in snow could spy;
Each pass, by mountain, lake, and heath,
He knew, through Lennox and Menteith;
Vain was the bound of dark-brown doe
When Malcolm bent his sounding bow,
And scarce that doe, though winged with fear,
Outstripped in speed the mountaineer:
Right up Ben Lomond could he press,
And not a sob his toil confess.
His form accorded with a mind 550
Lively and ardent, frank and kind:

A blither heart, till Ellen came,
Did never love nor sorrow tame;
It danced as lightsome in his breast
As played the feather on his crest.
Yet friends, who nearest knew the youth,
His scorn of wrong, his zeal for truth,
And bards, who saw his features bold
When kindled by the tales of old,
Said, were that youth to manhood grown, 560
Not long should Roderick Dhu's renown
Be foremost voiced by mountain fame,
But quail to that of Malcolm Græme.

XXVI.

Now back they wend their watery way,
And, 'O my sire!' did Ellen say,
'Why urge thy chase so far astray?
And why so late returned? And why'—
The rest was in her speaking eye.
'My child, the chase I follow far,
'T is mimicry of noble war; 570
And with that gallant pastime reft
Were all of Douglas I have left.
I met young Malcolm as I strayed
Far eastward, in Glenfinlas' shade;
Nor strayed I safe, for all around
Hunters and horsemen scoured the ground.
This youth, though still a royal ward,
Risked life and land to be my guard,
And through the passes of the wood
Guided my steps, not unpursued; 580
And Roderick shall his welcome make,
Despite old spleen, for Douglas' sake.
Then must he seek Strath-Endrick glen,
Nor peril aught for me again.'

XXVII.

Sir Roderick, who to meet them came,
Reddened at sight of Malcolm Græme,
Yet, not in action, word, or eye,
Failed aught in hospitality.
In talk and sport they whiled away
The morning of that summer day; 590
But at high noon a courier light
Held secret parley with the knight,
Whose moody aspect soon declared
That evil were the news he heard.
Deep thought seemed toiling in his head;
Yet was the evening banquet made
Ere he assembled round the flame
His mother, Douglas, and the Græme,
And Ellen too; then cast around
His eyes, then fixed them on the ground, 600
As studying phrase that might avail
Best to convey unpleasant tale.
Long with his dagger's hilt he played,
Then raised his haughty brow, and said:—

XXVIII.

'Short be my speech;—nor time affords,
Nor my plain temper, glozing words.
Kinsman and father,—if such name
Douglas vouchsafe to Roderick's claim;
Mine honored mother;—Ellen,—why,
My cousin, turn away thine eye?— 610
And Græme, in whom I hope to know
Full soon a noble friend or foe,
When age shall give thee thy command,
And leading in thy native land,—

BENVENUE, FROM ELLEN'S ISLE.

List all! — The King's vindictive pride
Boasts to have tamed the Border-side,
Where chiefs, with hound and hawk who came
To share their monarch's sylvan game,
Themselves in bloody toils were snared,
And when the banquet they prepared, 620
And wide their loyal portals flung,
O'er their own gateway struggling hung.
Loud cries their blood from Meggat's mead,
From Yarrow braes and banks of Tweed,
Where the lone streams of Ettrick glide,
And from the silver Teviot's side;
The dales, where martial clans did ride,
Are now one sheep-walk, waste and wide.
This tyrant of the Scottish throne,
So faithless and so ruthless known, 630
Now hither comes; his end the same,
The same pretext of sylvan game.

What grace for Highland Chiefs, judge ye
By fate of Border chivalry.
Yet more; amid Glenfinlas' green,
Douglas, thy stately form was seen.
This by espial sure I know:
Your counsel in the streight I show.'

XXIX.

Ellen and Margaret fearfully
Sought comfort in each other's eye, 640
Then turned their ghastly look, each one.
This to her sire, that to her son.
The hasty color went and came
In the bold cheek of Malcolm Græme,
But from his glance it well appeared
'T was but for Ellen that he feared;
While, sorrowful, but undismayed,
The Douglas thus his counsel said:
'Brave Roderick, though the tempest roar
It may but thunder and pass o'er; 650
Nor will I here remain an hour,
To draw the lightning on thy bower;
For well thou know'st, at this gray head
The royal bolt were fiercest sped.
For thee, who, at thy King's command,
Canst aid him with a gallant band,
Submission, homage, humbled pride,
Shall turn the Monarch's wrath aside.
Poor remnants of the Bleeding Heart,
Ellen and I will seek apart 660
The refuge of some forest cell,
There, like the hunted quarry, dwell,
Till on the mountain and the moor
The stern pursuit be passed and o'er.'

XXX.

'No, by mine honor,' Roderick said,
'So help me Heaven, and my good blade!
No, never! Blasted be yon Pine,
My father's ancient crest and mine,
If from its shade in danger part
The lineage of the Bleeding Heart! 670
Hear my blunt speech: grant me this maid
To wife, thy counsel to mine aid;
To Douglas, leagued with Roderick Dhu,
Will friends and allies flock enow;
Like cause of doubt, distrust, and grief,
Will bind to us each Western Chief.
When the loud pipes my bridal tell,
The Links of Forth shall hear the knell,
The guards shall start in Stirling's porch;
And when I light the nuptial torch, 680
A thousand villages in flames
Shall scare the slumbers of King James! —
Nay, Ellen, blench not thus away,
And, mother, cease these signs, I pray;
I meant not all my heat might say. —
Small need of inroad or of fight,
When the sage Douglas may unite
Each mountain clan in friendly band,
To guard the passes of their land,
Till the foiled King from pathless glen 690
Shall bootless turn him home again.'

XXXI.

There are who have, at midnight hour,
In slumber scaled a dizzy tower,
And, on the verge that beetled o'er
The ocean tide's incessant roar,

Dreamed calmly out their dangerous dream,
Till wakened by the morning beam;
When, dazzled by the eastern glow,
Such startler cast his glance below,
And saw unmeasured depth around, 700
And heard unintermitted sound,
And thought the battled fence so frail,
It waved like cobweb in the gale;—
Amid his senses' giddy wheel,
Did he not desperate impulse feel,
Headlong to plunge himself below,
And meet the worst his fears foreshow?—
Thus Ellen, dizzy and astound,
As sudden ruin yawned around,
By crossing terrors wildly tossed, 710
Still for the Douglas fearing most,
Could scarce the desperate thought withstand,
To buy his safety with her hand.

XXXII.

Such purpose dread could Malcolm spy
In Ellen's quivering lip and eye,
And eager rose to speak,—but ere
His tongue could hurry forth his fear,
Had Douglas marked the hectic strife,
Where death seemed combating with life;
For to her cheek, in feverish flood, 720
One instant rushed the throbbing blood,
Then ebbing back, with sudden sway,
Left its domain as wan as clay.
'Roderick, enough! enough!' he cried,
'My daughter cannot be thy bride;
Not that the blush to wooer dear,
Nor paleness that of maiden fear.

It may not be, — forgive her, Chief,
Nor hazard aught for our relief.
Against his sovereign, Douglas ne'er 730
Will level a rebellious spear.
'T was I that taught his youthful hand
To rein a steed and wield a brand;
I see him yet, the princely boy!
Not Ellen more my pride and joy;
I love him still, despite my wrongs
By hasty wrath and slanderous tongues.
O, seek the grace you well may find,
Without a cause to mine combined!'

XXXIII.

Twice through the hall the Chieftain strode; 740
The waving of his tartans broad,
And darkened brow, where wounded pride
With ire and disappointment vied,
Seemed, by the torch's gloomy light,
Like the ill Demon of the night,
Stooping his pinions' shadowy sway
Upon the nighted pilgrim's way:
But, unrequited Love! thy dart
Plunged deepest its envenomed smart,
And Roderick, with thine anguish stung, 750
At length the hand of Douglas wrung,
While eyes that mocked at tears before
With bitter drops were running o'er.
The death-pangs of long-cherished hope
Scarce in that ample breast had scope,
But, struggling with his spirit proud,
Convulsive heaved its checkered shroud,
While every sob — so mute were all —
Was heard distinctly through the hall.

The son's despair, the mother's look, 760
Ill might the gentle Ellen brook ;
She rose, and to her side there came,
To aid her parting steps, the Græme.

XXXIV.

Then Roderick from the Douglas broke —
As flashes flame through sable smoke,
Kindling its wreaths, long, dark, and low,
To one broad blaze of ruddy glow,
So the deep anguish of despair
Burst, in fierce jealousy, to air.
With stalwart grasp his hand he laid 770
On Malcolm's breast and belted plaid :
'Back, beardless boy ! ' he sternly said,
'Back, minion ! holdst thou thus at naught
The lesson I so lately taught ?
This roof, the Douglas, and that maid,
Thank thou for punishment delayed.'
Eager as greyhound on his game,
Fiercely with Roderick grappled Græme.
'Perish my name, if aught afford
Its Chieftain safety save his sword ! ' 780
Thus as they strove their desperate hand
Griped to the dagger or the brand,
And death had been — but Douglas rose,
And thrust between the struggling foes
His giant strength : — ' Chieftains, forego !
I hold the first who strikes my foe. —
Madmen, forbear your frantic jar !
What ! is the Douglas fallen so far,
His daughter's hand is deemed the spoil
Of such dishonorable broil ? ' 790

Sullen and slowly they unclasp,
As struck with shame, their desperate grasp,
And each upon his rival glared,
With foot advanced and blade half bared.

XXXV.

Ere yet the brands aloft were flung,
Margaret on Roderick's mantle hung,
And Malcolm heard his Ellen's scream,
As faltered through terrific dream.
Then Roderick plunged in sheath his sword,
And veiled his wrath in scornful word: 800
'Rest safe till morning; pity 't were
Such cheek should feel the midnight air!
Then mayst thou to James Stuart tell,
Roderick will keep the lake and fell,
Nor lackey with his freeborn clan
The pageant pomp of earthly man.
More would he of Clan-Alpine know,
Thou canst our strength and passes show.—
Malise, what ho!'—his henchman came:
'Give our safe-conduct to the Græme.' 810
Young Malcolm answered, calm and bold:
'Fear nothing for thy favorite hold;
The spot an angel deigned to grace
Is blessed, though robbers haunt the place.
Thy churlish courtesy for those
Reserve, who fear to be thy foes.
As safe to me the mountain way
At midnight as in blaze of day,
Though with his boldest at his back
Even Roderick Dhu beset the track.— 820
Brave Douglas,—lovely Ellen,—nay,
Naught here of parting will I say.

Earth does not hold a lonesome glen
So secret but we meet again. —
Chieftain ! we too shall find an hour,' —
He said, and left the sylvan bower.

XXXVI.

Old Allan followed to the strand —
Such was the Douglas's command —
And anxious told, how, on the morn,
The stern Sir Roderick deep had sworn, 830
The Fiery Cross should circle o'er
Dale, glen, and valley, down and moor.
Much were the peril to the Græme
From those who to the signal came ;
Far up the lake 't were safest land,
Himself would row him to the strand.
He gave his counsel to the wind,
While Malcolm did, unheeding, bind,
Round dirk and pouch and broadsword rolled,
His ample plaid in tightened fold, 840
And stripped his limbs to such array
As best might suit the watery way, —

XXXVII.

Then spoke abrupt : ' Farewell to thee,
Pattern of old fidelity ! '
The Minstrel's hand he kindly pressed, —
' O, could I point a place of rest !
My sovereign holds in ward my land,
My uncle leads my vassal band ;
To tame his foes, his friends to aid,
Poor Malcolm has but heart and blade. 850
Yet, if there be one faithful Græme
Who loves the chieftain of his name,

Not long shall honored Douglas dwell
Like hunted stag in mountain cell;
Nor, ere yon pride-swollen robber dare, —
I may not give the rest to air!
Tell Roderick Dhu I owed him naught,
Not the poor service of a boat,
To waft me to yon mountain-side.'
Then plunged he in the flashing tide. 860
Bold o'er the flood his head he bore,
And stoutly steered him from the shore;
And Allan strained his anxious eye,
Far mid the lake his form to spy,
Darkening across each puny wave,
To which the moon her silver gave.
Fast as the cormorant could skim,
The swimmer plied each active limb;
Then landing in the moonlight dell,
Loud shouted of his weal to tell. 870
The Minstrel heard the far halloo,
And joyful from the shore withdrew.

THE PASS OF BEALA-NAM-BO.

CANTO THIRD.

THE GATHERING.

I.

TIME rolls his ceaseless course. The race of yore,
Who danced our infancy upon their knee,
And told our marvelling boyhood legends store
Of their strange ventures happed by land or sea,
How are they blotted from the things that be!

How few, all weak and withered of their force,
Wait on the verge of dark eternity,
Like stranded wrecks, the tide returning hoarse,
To sweep them from our sight! Time rolls his ceaseless
course.

Yet live there still who can remember well, 10
How, when a mountain chief his bugle blew,
Both field and forest, dingle, cliff, and dell,
And solitary heath, the signal knew;
And fast the faithful clan around him drew,
What time the warning note was keenly wound,
What time aloft their kindred banner flew,
While clamorous war-pipes yelled the gathering sound,
And while the Fiery Cross glanced, like a meteor, round.

II.

The Summer dawn's reflected hue
To purple changed Loch Katrine's blue; 20
Mildly and soft the western breeze
Just kissed the lake, just stirred the trees,
And the pleased lake, like maiden coy,
Trembled but dimpled not for joy:
The mountain-shadows on her breast
Were neither broken nor at rest;
In bright uncertainty they lie,
Like future joys to Fancy's eye.
The water-lily to the light
Her chalice reared of silver bright; 30
The doe awoke, and to the lawn,
Begemmed with dew-drops, led her fawn;
The gray mist left the mountain-side,
The torrent showed its glistening pride;
Invisible in flecked sky
The lark sent down her revelry;

The blackbird and the speckled thrush
Good-morrow gave from brake and bush;
In answer cooed the cushat dove
Her notes of peace and rest and love. 40

III.

No thought of peace, no thought of rest,
Assuaged the storm in Roderick's breast.
With sheathed broadsword in his hand,
Abrupt he paced the islet strand,
And eyed the rising sun, and laid
His hand on his impatient blade.
Beneath a rock, his vassals' care
Was prompt the ritual to prepare,
With deep and deathful meaning fraught;
For such Antiquity had taught 50
Was preface meet, ere yet abroad
The Cross of Fire should take its road.
The shrinking band stood oft aghast
At the impatient glance he cast;—
Such glance the mountain eagle threw,
As, from the cliffs of Benvenue,
She spread her dark sails on the wind,
And, high in middle heaven reclined,
With her broad shadow on the lake,
Silenced the warblers of the brake. 60

IV.

A heap of withered boughs was piled,
Of juniper and rowan wild,
Mingled with shivers from the oak,
Rent by the lightning's recent stroke.
Brian the Hermit by it stood,
Barefooted, in his frock and hood.

His grizzled beard and matted hair
Obscured a visage of despair;
His naked arms and legs, seamed o'er,
The scars of frantic penance bore.
That monk, of savage form and face,
The impending danger of his race
Had drawn from deepest solitude,
Far in Benharrow's bosom rude.
Not his the mien of Christian priest,
But Druid's, from the grave released,
Whose hardened heart and eye might brook
On human sacrifice to look;
And much, 't was said, of heathen lore
Mixed in the charms he muttered o'er. 80
The hallowed creed gave only worse
And deadlier emphasis of curse.
No peasant sought that Hermit's prayer,
His cave the pilgrim shunned with care;
The eager huntsman knew his bound,
And in mid chase called off his hound;
Or if, in lonely glen or strath,
The desert-dweller met his path,
He prayed, and signed the cross between,
While terror took devotion's mien. 90

V.

Of Brian's birth strange tales were told.
His mother watched a midnight fold,
Built deep within a dreary glen,
Where scattered lay the bones of men
In some forgotten battle slain,
And bleached by drifting wind and rain.
It might have tamed a warrior's heart
To view such mockery of his art!

The knot-grass fettered there the hand
Which once could burst an iron band; 100
Beneath the broad and ample bone,
That bucklered heart to fear unknown,
A feeble and a timorous guest,
The fieldfare framed her lowly nest;
There the slow blindworm left his slime
On the fleet limbs that mocked at time;
And there, too, lay the leader's skull,
Still wreathed with chaplet, flushed and full,
For heath-bell with her purple bloom
Supplied the bonnet and the plume. 110
All night, in this sad glen, the maid
Sat shrouded in her mantle's shade:
She said no shepherd sought her side,
No hunter's hand her snood untied,
Yet ne'er again to braid her hair
The virgin snood did Alice wear;
Gone was her maiden glee and sport,
Her maiden girdle all too short,
Nor sought she, from that fatal night,
Or holy church or blessed rite, 120
But locked her secret in her breast,
And died in travail, unconfessed.

VI.

Alone, among his young compeers,
Was Brian from his infant years;
A moody and heart-broken boy,
Estranged from sympathy and joy,
Bearing each taunt which careless tongue
On his mysterious lineage flung.
Whole nights he spent by moonlight pale,
To wood and stream his hap to wail. 130

Till, frantic, he as truth received
What of his birth the crowd believed,
And sought, in mist and meteor fire,
To meet and know his Phantom Sire!
In vain, to soothe his wayward fate,
The cloister oped her pitying gate;
In vain the learning of the age
Unclasped the sable-lettered page;
Even in its treasures he could find
Food for the fever of his mind. 140
Eager he read whatever tells
Of magic, cabala, and spells,
And every dark pursuit allied
To curious and presumptuous pride;
Till with fired brain and nerves o'erstrung,
And heart with mystic horrors wrung,
Desperate he sought Benharrow's den,
And hid him from the haunts of men.

VII.

The desert gave him visions wild,
Such as might suit the spectre's child. 150
Where with black cliffs the torrents toil,
He watched the wheeling eddies boil,
Till from their foam his dazzled eyes
Beheld the River Demon rise:
The mountain mist took form and limb
Of noontide hag or goblin grim;
The midnight wind came wild and dread,
Swelled with the voices of the dead;
Far on the future battle-heath
His eye beheld the ranks of death: 160
Thus the lone Seer, from mankind hurled,
Shaped forth a disembodied world.

One lingering sympathy of mind
Still bound him to the mortal kind;
The only parent he could claim
Of ancient Alpine's lineage came.
Late had he heard, in prophet's dream,
The fatal Ben-Shie's boding scream;
Sounds, too, had come in midnight blast
Of charging steeds, careering fast 170
Along Benharrow's shingly side,
Where mortal horseman ne'er might ride;
The thunderbolt had split the pine, —
All augured ill to Alpine's line.
He girt his loins, and came to show
The signals of impending woe,
And now stood prompt to bless or ban,
As bade the Chieftain of his clan.

VIII.

'T was all prepared; — and from the rock
A goat, the patriarch of the flock, 180
Before the kindling pile was laid,
And pierced by Roderick's ready blade.
Patient the sickening victim eyed
The life-blood ebb in crimson tide
Down his clogged beard and shaggy limb,
Till darkness glazed his eyeballs dim.
The grisly priest, with murmuring prayer,
A slender crosslet framed with care,
A cubit's length in measure due;
The shaft and limbs were rods of yew, 190
Whose parents in Inch-Cailliach wave
Their shadows o'er Clan-Alpine's grave,
And, answering Lomond's breezes deep,
Soothe many a chieftain's endless sleep.

The Cross thus formed he held on high,
With wasted hand and haggard eye,
And strange and mingled feelings woke,
While his anathema he spoke : —

IX.

'Woe to the clansman who shall view
This symbol of sepulchral yew, 200
Forgetful that its branches grew
Where weep the heavens their holiest dew
On Alpine's dwelling low !
Deserter of his Chieftain's trust,
He ne'er shall mingle with their dust,
But, from his sires and kindred thrust,
Each clansman's execration just
Shall doom him wrath and woe.'
He paused ; — the word the vassals took,
With forward step and fiery look, 210
On high their naked brands they shook,
Their clattering targets wildly strook ;
And first in murmur low,
Then, like the billow in his course,
That far to seaward finds his source,
And flings to shore his mustered force,
Burst with loud roar their answer hoarse,
'Woe to the traitor, woe !'
Ben-an's gray scalp the accents knew,
The joyous wolf from covert drew, 220
The exulting eagle screamed afar, —
They knew the voice of Alpine's war.

X.

The shout was hushed on lake and fell,
The Monk resumed his muttered spell :

Dismal and low its accents came,
The while he scathed the Cross with flame;
And the few words that reached the air,
Although the holiest name was there,
Had more of blasphemy than prayer.
But when he shook above the crowd 230
Its kindled points, he spoke aloud: —
'Woe to the wretch who fails to rear
At this dread sign the ready spear!
For, as the flames this symbol sear,
His home, the refuge of his fear,
  A kindred fate shall know;
Far o'er its roof the volumed flame
Clan-Alpine's vengeance shall proclaim,
While maids and matrons on his name
Shall call down wretchedness and shame, 240
  And infamy and woe.'
Then rose the cry of females, shrill
As goshawk's whistle on the hill,
Denouncing misery and ill,
Mingled with childhood's babbling trill
  Of curses stammered slow;
Answering with imprecation dread,
'Sunk be his home in embers red!
And cursed be the meanest shed
That e'er shall hide the houseless head 250
  We doom to want and woe!'
A sharp and shrieking echo gave,
Coir-Uriskin, thy goblin cave!
And the gray pass where birches wave
  On Beala-nam-bo.

XI.

Then deeper paused the priest anew,
And hard his laboring breath he drew,

While, with set teeth and clenched hand,
And eyes that glowed like fiery brand,
He meditated curse more dread, 260
And deadlier, on the clansman's head
Who, summoned to his chieftain's aid,
The signal saw and disobeyed.
The crosslet's points of sparkling wood
He quenched among the bubbling blood,
And, as again the sign he reared,
Hollow and hoarse his voice was heard:
'When flits this Cross from man to man,
Vich-Alpine's summons to his clan,
Burst be the ear that fails to heed! 270
Palsied the foot that shuns to speed!
May ravens tear the careless eyes,
Wolves make the coward heart their prize!
As sinks that blood-stream in the earth,
So may his heart's-blood drench his hearth!
As dies in hissing gore the spark,
Quench thou his light, Destruction dark!
And be the grace to him denied,
Bought by this sign to all beside!'
He ceased; no echo gave again 280
The murmur of the deep Amen.

XII.

Then Roderick with impatient look
From Brian's hand the symbol took:
'Speed, Malise, speed!' he said, and gave
The crosslet to his henchman brave.
'The muster-place be Lanrick mead —
Instant the time — speed, Malise, speed!'
Like heath-bird, when the hawks pursue,
A barge across Loch Katrine flew:

High stood the henchman on the prow; 290
So rapidly the barge-men row,
The bubbles, where they launched the boat,
Were all unbroken and afloat,
Dancing in foam and ripple still,
When it had neared the mainland hill;
And from the silver beach's side
Still was the prow three fathom wide,
When lightly bounded to the land
The messenger of blood and brand.

XIII.

Speed, Malise, speed! the dun deer's hide 300
On fleeter foot was never tied.
Speed, Malise, speed! such cause of haste
Thine active sinews never braced.
Bend 'gainst the steepy hill thy breast,
Burst down like torrent from its crest;
With short and springing footstep pass
The trembling bog and false morass;
Across the brook like roebuck bound,
And thread the brake like questing hound;
The crag is high, the scaur is deep, 310
Yet shrink not from the desperate leap:
Parched are thy burning lips and brow,
Yet by the fountain pause not now;
Herald of battle, fate, and fear,
Stretch onward in thy fleet career!
The wounded hind thou track'st not now,
Pursuest not maid through greenwood bough,
Nor pliest thou now thy flying pace
With rivals in the mountain race;
But danger, death, and warrior deed 320
Are in thy course — speed, Malise, speed!

XIV.

Fast as the fatal symbol flies,
In arms the huts and hamlets rise;
From winding glen, from upland brown,
They poured each hardy tenant down.
Nor slacked the messenger his pace;
He showed the sign, he named the place,
And, pressing forward like the wind,
Left clamor and surprise behind.
The fisherman forsook the strand, 330
The swarthy smith took dirk and brand;
With changed cheer, the mower blithe
Left in the half-cut swath his scythe;
The herds without a keeper strayed,
The plough was in mid-furrow stayed,
The falconer tossed his hawk away,
The hunter left the stag at bay;
Prompt at the signal of alarms,
Each son of Alpine rushed to arms;
So swept the tumult and affray 340
Along the margin of Achray.
Alas, thou lovely lake! that e'er
Thy banks should echo sounds of fear!
The rocks, the bosky thickets, sleep
So stilly on thy bosom deep,
The lark's blithe carol from the cloud
Seems for the scene too gayly loud.

XV.

Speed, Malise, speed! The lake is past,
Duncraggan's huts appear at last,
And peep, like moss-grown rocks, half seen, 350
Half hidden in the copse so green;

There mayst thou rest, thy labor done
Their lord shall speed the signal on. —
As stoops the hawk upon his prey,
The henchman shot him down the way.
What woful accents load the gale?
The funeral yell, the female wail!
A gallant hunter's sport is o'er,
A valiant warrior fights no more.
Who, in the battle or the chase, 360
At Roderick's side shall fill his place! —
Within the hall, where torch's ray
Supplies the excluded beams of day,
Lies Duncan on his lowly bier,
And o'er him streams his widow's tear.
His stripling son stands mournful by,
His youngest weeps, but knows not why,
The village maids and matrons round
The dismal coronach resound.

XVI.

CORONACH.

He is gone on the mountain, 370
He is lost to the forest,
Like a summer-dried fountain,
When our need was the sorest.
The font, reappearing,
From the rain-drops shall borrow,
But to us comes no cheering,
To Duncan no morrow!

The hand of the reaper
Takes the ears that are hoary
But the voice of the weeper 380
Wails manhood in glory

The autumn winds rushing
  Waft the leaves that are searest,
But our flower was in flushing,
  When blighting was nearest.

Fleet foot on the correi,
  Sage counsel in cumber,
Red hand in the foray,
  How sound is thy slumber!
Like the dew on the mountain, 390
  Like the foam on the river,
Like the bubble on the fountain,
  Thou art gone, and forever!

XVII.

See Stumah, who, the bier beside,
His master's corpse with wonder eyed,
Poor Stumah! whom his least halloo
Could send like lightning o'er the dew
Bristles his crest, and points his ears,
As if some stranger step he hears.
'T is not a mourner's muffled tread, 400
Who comes to sorrow o'er the dead,
But headlong haste or deadly fear
Urge the precipitate career.
All stand aghast: — unheeding all,
The henchman bursts into the hall;
Before the dead man's bier he stood,
Held forth the Cross besmeared with blood;
'The muster-place is Lanrick mead;
Speed forth the signal! clansmen, speed!'

XVIII.

Angus, the heir of Duncan's line, 410
Sprung forth and seized the fatal sign.

In haste the stripling to his side
His father's dirk and broadsword tied;
But when he saw his mother's eye
Watch him in speechless agony,
Back to her opened arms he flew,
Pressed on her lips a fond adieu, —
'Alas!' she sobbed, — 'and yet be gone,
And speed thee forth, like Duncan's son!'
One look he cast upon the bier, 420
Dashed from his eye the gathering tear,
Breathed deep to clear his laboring breast,
And tossed aloft his bonnet crest,
Then, like the high-bred colt when, freed,
First he essays his fire and speed,
He vanished, and o'er moor and moss
Sped forward with the Fiery Cross.
Suspended was the widow's tear
While yet his footsteps she could hear;
And when she marked the henchman's eye 430
Wet with unwonted sympathy,
'Kinsman,' she said, 'his race is run
That should have sped thine errand on;
The oak has fallen, — the sapling bough
Is all Duncraggan's shelter now.
Yet trust I well, his duty done,
The orphan's God will guard my son. —
And you, in many a danger true,
At Duncan's hest your blades that drew,
To arms, and guard that orphan's head! 440
Let babes and women wail the dead.'
Then weapon-clang and martial call
Resounded through the funeral hall,
While from the walls the attendant band
Snatched sword and targe with hurried hand;

And short and flitting energy
Glanced from the mourner's sunken eye,
As if the sounds to warrior dear
Might rouse her Duncan from his bier.
But faded soon that borrowed force; 450
Grief claimed his right, and tears their course.

XIX.

Benledi saw the Cross of Fire,
It glanced like lightning up Strath-Ire.
O'er dale and hill the summons flew,
Nor rest nor pause young Angus knew;
The tear that gathered in his eye
He left the mountain-breeze to dry;
Until, where Teith's young waters roll
Betwixt him and a wooded knoll
That graced the sable strath with green, 460
The chapel of Saint Bride was seen.
Swoln was the stream, remote the bridge,
But Angus paused not on the edge;
Though the dark waves danced dizzily,
Though reeled his sympathetic eye,
He dashed amid the torrent's roar:
His right hand high the crosslet bore,
His left the pole-axe grasped, to guide
And stay his footing in the tide.
He stumbled twice, — the foam splashed high, 470
With hoarser swell the stream raced by;
And had he fallen, — forever there,
Farewell Duncraggan's orphan heir!
But still, as if in parting life,
Firmer he grasped the Cross of strife,
Until the opposing bank he gained,
And up the chapel pathway strained.

XX.

A blithesome rout that morning-tide
Had sought the chapel of Saint Bride.
Her troth Tombea's Mary gave 480
To Norman, heir of Armandave,
And, issuing from the Gothic arch,
The bridal now resumed their march.
In rude but glad procession came
Bonneted sire and coif-clad dame;
And plaided youth, with jest and jeer,
Which snooded maiden would not hear;
And children, that, unwitting why,
Lent the gay shout their shrilly cry;
And minstrels, that in measures vied 490
Before the young and bonny bride,
Whose downcast eye and cheek disclose
The tear and blush of morning rose.
With virgin step and bashful hand
She held the kerchief's snowy band.
The gallant bridegroom by her side
Beheld his prize with victor's pride,
And the glad mother in her ear
Was closely whispering word of cheer.

XXI.

Who meets them at the churchyard gate? 500
The messenger of fear and fate!
Haste in his hurried accent lies,
And grief is swimming in his eyes.
All dripping from the recent flood,
Panting and travel-soiled he stood,
The fatal sign of fire and sword
Held forth, and spoke the appointed word:

'The muster-place is Lanrick mead;
Speed forth the signal! Norman, speed!'
And must he change so soon the hand 510
Just linked to his by holy band,
For the fell Cross of blood and brand?
And must the day so blithe that rose,
And promised rapture in the close,
Before its setting hour, divide
The bridegroom from the plighted bride?
O fatal doom! — it must! it must!
Clan-Alpine's cause, her Chieftain's trust,
Her summons dread, brook no delay;
Stretch to the race, — away! away! 520

XXII.

Yet slow he laid his plaid aside,
And lingering eyed his lovely bride,
Until he saw the starting tear
Speak woe he might not stop to cheer;
Then, trusting not a second look,
In haste he sped him up the brook,
Nor backward glanced till on the heath
Where Lubnaig's lake supplies the Teith. —
What in the racer's bosom stirred?
The sickening pang of hope deferred, 530
And memory with a torturing train
Of all his morning visions vain.
Mingled with love's impatience, came
The manly thirst for martial fame;
The stormy joy of mountaineers
Ere yet they rush upon the spears;
And zeal for Clan and Chieftain burning,
And hope, from well-fought field returning,
With war's red honors on his crest,
To clasp his Mary to his breast. 540

Stung by such thoughts, o'er bank and brae,
Like fire from flint he glanced away,
While high resolve and feeling strong
Burst into voluntary song.

XXIII.

SONG.

The heath this night must be my bed,
The bracken curtain for my head,
My lullaby the warder's tread,
  Far, far, from love and thee, Mary;
To-morrow eve, more stilly laid,
My couch may be my bloody plaid, 550
My vesper song thy wail, sweet maid!
  It will not waken me, Mary!

I may not, dare not, fancy now
The grief that clouds thy lovely brow,
I dare not think upon thy vow,
  And all it promised me, Mary.
No fond regret must Norman know;
When bursts Clan-Alpine on the foe,
His heart must be like bended bow,
  His foot like arrow free, Mary. 560

A time will come with feeling fraught,
For, if I fall in battle fought,
Thy hapless lover's dying thought
  Shall be a thought on thee, Mary.
And if returned from conquered foes,
How blithely will the evening close,
How sweet the linnet sing repose,
  To my young bride and me, Mary!

XXIV.

Not faster o'er thy heathery braes,
Balquidder, speeds the midnight blaze, 570
Rushing in conflagration strong
Thy deep ravines and dells along,
Wrapping thy cliffs in purple glow,
And reddening the dark lakes below;
Nor faster speeds it, nor so far,
As o'er thy heaths the voice of war.
The signal roused to martial coil
The sullen margin of Loch Voil,
Waked still Loch Doine, and to the source
Alarmed, Balvaig, thy swampy course; 580
Thence southward turned its rapid road
Adown Strath-Gartney's valley broad,
Till rose in arms each man might claim
A portion in Clan-Alpine's name,
From the gray sire, whose trembling hand
Could hardly buckle on his brand,
To the raw boy, whose shaft and bow
Were yet scarce terror to the crow.
Each valley, each sequestered glen,
Mustered its little horde of men, 590
That met as torrents from the height
In Highland dales their streams unite,
Still gathering, as they pour along,
A voice more loud, a tide more strong,
Till at the rendezvous they stood
By hundreds prompt for blows and blood,
Each trained to arms since life began,
Owning no tie but to his clan,
No oath but by his chieftain's hand,
No law but Roderick Dhu's command. 600

XXV.

That summer morn had Roderick Dhu
Surveyed the skirts of Benvenue,
And sent his scouts o'er hill and heath,
To view the frontiers of Menteith.
All backward came with news of truce;
Still lay each martial Græme and Bruce,
In Rednock courts no horsemen wait,
No banner waved on Cardross gate,
On Duchray's towers no beacon shone,
Nor scared the herons from Loch Con; 610
All seemed at peace. — Now wot ye why
The Chieftain with such anxious eye,
Ere to the muster he repair,
This western frontier scanned with care? —
In Benvenue's most darksome cleft,
A fair though cruel pledge was left;
For Douglas, to his promise true,
That morning from the isle withdrew,
And in a deep sequestered dell
Had sought a low and lonely cell. 620
By many a bard in Celtic tongue
Has Coir-nan-Uriskin been sung;
A softer name the Saxons gave,
And called the grot the Goblin Cave.

XXVI.

It was a wild and strange retreat,
As e'er was trod by outlaw's feet.
The dell, upon the mountain's crest,
Yawned like a gash on warrior's breast;
Its trench had stayed full many a rock,
Hurled by primeval earthquake shock 630

THE GOBLIN'S CAVE.

From Benvenue's gray summit wild,
And here, in random ruin piled,
They frowned incumbent o'er the spot,
And formed the rugged sylvan grot.
The oak and birch with mingled shade
At noontide there a twilight made,
Unless when short and sudden shone
Some straggling beam on cliff or stone,
With such a glimpse as prophet's eye
Gains on thy depth, Futurity. 640

No murmur waked the solemn still,
Save tinkling of a fountain rill;
But when the wind chafed with the lake,
A sullen sound would upward break,
With dashing hollow voice, that spoke
The incessant war of wave and rock.
Suspended cliffs with hideous sway
Seemed nodding o'er the cavern gray.
From such a den the wolf had sprung,
In such the wild-cat leaves her young; 650
Yet Douglas and his daughter fair
Sought for a space their safety there.
Gray Superstition's whisper dread
Debarred the spot to vulgar tread;
For there, she said, did fays resort,
And satyrs hold their sylvan court,
By moonlight tread their mystic maze,
And blast the rash beholder's gaze.

XXVII.

Now eve, with western shadows long,
Floated on Katrine bright and strong, 660
When Roderick with a chosen few
Repassed the heights of Benvenue.
Above the Goblin Cave they go,
Through the wild pass of Beal-nam-bo;
The prompt retainers speed before,
To launch the shallop from the shore,
For 'cross Loch Katrine lies his way
To view the passes of Achray,
And place his clansmen in array.
Yet lags the Chief in musing mind, 670
Unwonted sight, his men behind.
A single page, to bear his sword,
Alone attended on his lord;

The rest their way through thickets break,
And soon await him by the lake.
It was a fair and gallant sight,
To view them from the neighboring height,
By the low-levelled sunbeam's light!
For strength and stature, from the clan
Each warrior was a chosen man, 680
As even afar might well be seen,
By their proud step and martial mien.
Their feathers dance, their tartans float,
Their targets gleam, as by the boat
A wild and warlike group they stand,
That well became such mountain-strand.

XXVIII.

Their Chief with step reluctant still
Was lingering on the craggy hill,
Hard by where turned apart the road
To Douglas's obscure abode. 690
It was but with that dawning morn
That Roderick Dhu had proudly sworn
To drown his love in war's wild roar,
Nor think of Ellen Douglas more;
But he who stems a stream with sand,
And fetters flame with flaxen band,
Has yet a harder task to prove,—
By firm resolve to conquer love!
Eve finds the Chief, like restless ghost,
Still hovering near his treasure lost; 700
For though his haughty heart deny
A parting meeting to his eye,
Still fondly strains his anxious ear
The accents of her voice to hear,
And inly did he curse the breeze
That waked to sound the rustling trees.

But hark! what mingles in the strain?
It is the harp of Allan-bane,
That wakes its measure slow and high,
Attuned to sacred minstrelsy. 71
What melting voice attends the strings?
'Tis Ellen, or an angel, sings.

XXIX.

HYMN TO THE VIRGIN.

Ave Maria! maiden mild!
  Listen to a maiden's prayer!
Thou canst hear though from the wild,
  Thou canst save amid despair.
Safe may we sleep beneath thy care,
  Though banished, outcast, and reviled —
Maiden! hear a maiden's prayer;
  Mother, hear a suppliant child! 720
Ave Maria!

Ave Maria! undefiled!
  The flinty couch we now must share
Shall seem with down of eider piled,
  If thy protection hover there.
The murky cavern's heavy air
  Shall breathe of balm if thou hast smiled;
Then, Maiden! hear a maiden's prayer,
  Mother, list a suppliant child!
Ave Maria!

Ave Maria! stainless styled!
  Foul demons of the earth and air, 730
From this their wonted haunt exiled,
  Shall flee before thy presence fair.

We bow us to our lot of care,
Beneath thy guidance reconciled.
Hear for a maid a maiden's prayer,
And for a father hear a child!
Ave Maria!

XXX.

Died on the harp the closing hymn, —
Unmoved in attitude and limb,
As listening still, Clan-Alpine's lord
Stood leaning on his heavy sword, 740
Until the page with humble sign
Twice pointed to the sun's decline.
Then while his plaid he round him cast,
'It is the last time — 't is the last,'
He muttered thrice, — 'the last time e'er
That angel-voice shall Roderick hear!'
It was a goading thought, — his stride
Hied hastier down the mountain-side;
Sullen he flung him in the boat,
An instant 'cross the lake it shot. 750
They landed in that silvery bay,
And eastward held their hasty way,
Till, with the latest beams of light,
The band arrived on Lanrick height,
Where mustered in the vale below
Clan-Alpine's men in martial show.

XXXI.

A various scene the clansmen made:
Some sat, some stood, some slowly strayed;
But most, with mantles folded round,
Were couched to rest upon the ground,
Scarce to be known by curious eye
From the deep heather where they lie.

LANRICK HEIGHTS, FROM LANRICK MEAD.

So well was matched the tartan screen
With heath-bell dark and brackens green;
Unless where, here and there, a blade
Or lance's point a glimmer made,
Like glow-worm twinkling through the shade.
But when, advancing through the gloom,
They saw the Chieftain's eagle plume,
Their shout of welcome, shrill and wide, 770
Shook the steep mountain's steady side.
Thrice it arose, and lake and fell
Three times returned the martial yell;
It died upon Bochastle's plain,
And Silence claimed her evening reign.

FALLS AT HERO'S TARGE.

CANTO FOURTH.

THE PROPHECY.

I.

'THE rose is fairest when 't is budding new,
  And hope is brightest when it dawns from fears;
The rose is sweetest washed with morning dew,
  And love is loveliest when embalmed in tears.

O wilding rose, whom fancy thus endears,
I bid your blossoms in my bonnet wave,
Emblem of hope and love through future years!'
Thus spoke young Norman, heir of Armandave,
What time the sun arose on Vennachar's broad wave.

II.

Such fond conceit, half said, half sung, 10
Love prompted to the bridegroom's tongue.
All while he stripped the wild-rose spray,
His axe and bow beside him lay,
For on a pass 'twixt lake and wood
A wakeful sentinel he stood.
Hark! — on the rock a footstep rung,
And instant to his arms he sprung.
'Stand, or thou diest! — What, Malise? — soon
Art thou returned from Braes of Doune.
By thy keen step and glance I know, 20
Thou bring'st us tidings of the foe.' —
For while the Fiery Cross hied on,
On distant scout had Malise gone. —
'Where sleeps the Chief?' the henchman said.
'Apart, in yonder misty glade;
To his lone couch I'll be your guide.' —
Then called a slumberer by his side,
And stirred him with his slackened bow, —
'Up, up, Glentarkin! rouse thee, ho!
We seek the Chieftain; on the track 30
Keep eagle watch till I come back.'

III.

Together up the pass they sped:
'What of the foeman?' Norman said. —
'Varying reports from near and far;
This certain, — that a band of war

Has for two days been ready boune,
At prompt command to march from Doune;
King James the while, with princely powers,
Holds revelry in Stirling towers.
Soon will this dark and gathering cloud 40
Speak on our glens in thunder loud.
Inured to bide such bitter bout,
The warrior's plaid may bear it out;
But, Norman, how wilt thou provide
A shelter for thy bonny bride?'—
'What! know ye not that Roderick's care
To the lone isle hath caused repair
Each maid and matron of the clan,
And every child and aged man
Unfit for arms; and given his charge, 50
Nor skiff nor shallop, boat nor barge,
Upon these lakes shall float at large,
But all beside the islet moor,
That such dear pledge may rest secure?'—

IV.

''T is well advised,—the Chieftain's plan
Bespeaks the father of his clan.
But wherefore sleeps Sir Roderick Dhu
Apart from all his followers true?'
'It is because last evening-tide
Brian an augury hath tried, 60
Of that dread kind which must not be
Unless in dread extremity,
The Taghairm called; by which, afar,
Our sires foresaw the events of war.
Duncraggan's milk-white bull they slew,'—

MALISE.

'Ah! well the gallant brute I knew!
The choicest of the prey we had

When swept our merrymen Gallangad.
His hide was snow, his horns were dark,
His red eye glowed like fiery spark; 70
So fierce, so tameless, and so fleet,
Sore did he cumber our retreat,
And kept our stoutest kerns in awe,
Even at the pass of Beal 'maha.
But steep and flinty was the road,
And sharp the hurrying pikeman's goad,
And when we came to Dennan's Row
A child might scathless stroke his brow.'

V.

NORMAN.

'That bull was slain; his reeking hide
They stretched the cataract beside, 80
Whose waters their wild tumult toss
Adown the black and craggy boss
Of that huge cliff whose ample verge
Tradition calls the Hero's Targe.
Couched on a shelf beneath its brink,
Close where the thundering torrents sink,
Rocking beneath their headlong sway,
And drizzled by the ceaseless spray,
Midst groan of rock and roar of stream,
The wizard waits prophetic dream. 90
Nor distant rests the Chief; — but hush!
See, gliding slow through mist and bush,
The hermit gains yon rock, and stands
To gaze upon our slumbering bands.
Seems he not, Malise, like a ghost,
That hovers o'er a slaughtered host?
Or raven on the blasted oak,
That, watching while the deer is broke,
His morsel claims with sullen croak?'

MALISE.

'Peace! peace! to other than to me 100
Thy words were evil augury;
But still I hold Sir Roderick's blade
Clan-Alpine's omen and her aid,
Not aught that, gleaned from heaven or hell,
Yon fiend-begotten Monk can tell.
The Chieftain joins him, see — and now
Together they descend the brow.'

VI.

And, as they came, with Alpine's Lord
The Hermit Monk held solemn word: —
'Roderick! it is a fearful strife, 110
For man endowed with mortal life,
Whose shroud of sentient clay can still
Feel feverish pang and fainting chill,
Whose eye can stare in stony trance,
Whose hair can rouse like warrior's lance, —
'T is hard for such to view, unfurled,
The curtain of the future world.
Yet, witness every quaking limb,
My sunken pulse, mine eyeballs dim,
My soul with harrowing anguish torn, 120
This for my Chieftain have I borne! —
The shapes that sought my fearful couch
A human tongue may ne'er avouch;
No mortal man — save he, who, bred
Between the living and the dead,
Is gifted beyond nature's law —
Had e'er survived to say he saw.
At length the fateful answer came
In characters of living flame!

Not spoke in word, nor blazed in scroll, 130
But borne and branded on my soul:—
WHICH SPILLS THE FOREMOST FOEMAN'S LIFE,
THAT PARTY CONQUERS IN THE STRIFE.

VII.

'Thanks, Brian, for thy zeal and care!
Good is thine augury, and fair.
Clan-Alpine ne'er in battle stood
But first our broadswords tasted blood.
A surer victim still I know,
Self-offered to the auspicious blow:
A spy has sought my land this morn,— 140
No eve shall witness his return!
My followers guard each pass's mouth,
To east, to westward, and to south;
Red Murdoch, bribed to be his guide,
Has charge to lead his steps aside,
Till in deep path or dingle brown
He light on those shall bring him down.—
But see, who comes his news to show!
Malise! what tidings of the foe?'

VIII.

'At Doune, o'er many a spear and glaive 150
Two Barons proud their banners wave.
I saw the Moray's silver star,
And marked the sable pale of Mar.'
'By Alpine's soul, high tidings those!
I love to hear of worthy foes.
When move they on?' 'To-morrow's noon
Will see them here for battle boune.'
'Then shall it see a meeting stern!
But, for the place,—say, couldst thou learn
Nought of the friendly clans of Earn? 160

Strengthened by them, we well might bide
The battle on Benledi's side.
Thou couldst not? — well! Clan-Alpine's men
Shall man the Trosachs' shaggy glen;
Within Loch Katrine's gorge we 'll fight,
All in our maids' and matrons' sight,
Each for his hearth and household fire,
Father for child, and son for sire,
Lover for maid beloved! — But why —
Is it the breeze affects mine eye? 170
Or dost thou come, ill-omened tear!
A messenger of doubt or fear?
No! sooner may the Saxon lance
Unfix Benledi from his stance,
Than doubt or terror can pierce through
The unyielding heart of Roderick Dhu!
'T is stubborn as his trusty targe.
Each to his post! — all know their charge.'
The pibroch sounds, the bands advance,
The broadswords gleam, the banners dance, 180
Obedient to the Chieftain's glance. —
I turn me from the martial roar,
And seek Coir-Uriskin once more.

IX.

Where is the Douglas? — he is gone;
And Ellen sits on the gray stone
Fast by the cave, and makes her moan,
While vainly Allan's words of cheer
Are poured on her unheeding ear.
'He will return — dear lady, trust! —
With joy return; — he will — he must 190
Well was it time to seek afar
Some refuge from impending war,

When e'en Clan-Alpine's rugged swarm
Are cowed by the approaching storm.
I saw their boats with many a light,
Floating the livelong yesternight,
Shifting like flashes darted forth
By the red streamers of the north;
I marked at morn how close they ride,
Thick moored by the lone islet's side, 200
Like wild ducks couching in the fen
When stoops the hawk upon the glen.
Since this rude race dare not abide
The peril on the mainland side,
Shall not thy noble father's care
Some safe retreat for thee prepare?'

X.

ELLEN.

'No, Allan, no! Pretext so kind
My wakeful terrors could not blind.
When in such tender tone, yet grave,
Douglas a parting blessing gave, 210
The tear that glistened in his eye
Drowned not his purpose fixed and high.
My soul, though feminine and weak,
Can image his; e'en as the lake,
Itself disturbed by slightest stroke,
Reflects the invulnerable rock.
He hears report of battle rife,
He deems himself the cause of strife.
I saw him redden when the theme
Turned, Allan, on thine idle dream 220
Of Malcolm Græme in fetters bound,
Which I, thou saidst, about him wound.
Think'st thou he trowed thine omen aught?
O no! 't was apprehensive thought

For the kind youth, — for Roderick too —
Let me be just — that friend so true;
In danger both, and in our cause!
Minstrel, the Douglas dare not pause.
Why else that solemn warning given,
'If not on earth, we meet in heaven!' 230
Why else, to Cambus-kenneth's fane,
If eve return him not again,
Am I to hie and make me known?
Alas! he goes to Scotland's throne,
Buys his friends' safety with his own;
He goes to do — what I had done,
Had Douglas' daughter been his son!'

XI.

'Nay, lovely Ellen! — dearest, nay!
If aught should his return delay,
He only named yon holy fane 240
As fitting place to meet again.
Be sure he 's safe; and for the Græme, —
Heaven's blessing on his gallant name! —
My visioned sight may yet prove true,
Nor bode of ill to him or you.
When did my gifted dream beguile?
Think of the stranger at the isle,
And think upon the harpings slow
That presaged this approaching woe!
Sooth was my prophecy of fear; 250
Believe it when it augurs cheer.
Would we had left this dismal spot!
Ill luck still haunts a fairy grot.
Of such a wondrous tale I know —
Dear lady, change that look of woe,
My harp was wont thy grief to cheer.'

ELLEN.

'Well, be it as thou wilt; I hear,
But cannot stop the bursting tear.'
The Minstrel tried his simple art,
But distant far was Ellen's heart. 260

XII.

BALLAD.

ALICE BRAND.

Merry it is in the good greenwood,
When the mavis and merle are singing,
When the deer sweeps by, and the hounds are in cry,
And the hunter's horn is ringing.

'O Alice Brand, my native land
Is lost for love of you;
And we must hold by wood and wold,
As outlaws wont to do.

'O Alice, 't was all for thy locks so bright,
And 't was all for thine eyes so blue, 270
That on the night of our luckless flight
Thy brother bold I slew.

'Now must I teach to hew the beech
The hand that held the glaive,
For leaves to spread our lowly bed,
And stakes to fence our cave.

'And for vest of pall, thy fingers small,
That wont on harp to stray,
A cloak must shear from the slaughtered deer,
To keep the cold away.' 280

IN THE GREENWOOD.

'O Richard! if my brother died,
'T was but a fatal chance;
For darkling was the battle tried,
And fortune sped the lance.

'If pall and vair no more I wear,
Nor thou the crimson sheen,
As warm, we 'll say, is the russet gray,
As gay the forest-green.

'And, Richard, if our lot be hard,
And lost thy native land,
Still Alice has her own Richard,
And he his Alice Brand.'

290

XIII.

BALLAD CONTINUED.

'T is merry, 't is merry, in good greenwood;
So blithe Lady Alice is singing;
On the beech's pride, and oak's brown side
Lord Richard's axe is ringing.

Up spoke the moody Elfin King,
Who woned within the hill,—
Like wind in the porch of a ruined church,
His voice was ghostly shrill. 300

'Why sounds yon stroke on beech and oak,
Our moonlight circle's screen?
Or who comes here to chase the deer,
Beloved of our Elfin Queen?
Or who may dare on wold to wear
The fairies' fatal green?

'Up, Urgan, up! to yon mortal hie,
For thou wert christened man;
For cross or sign thou wilt not fly,
For muttered word or ban. 310

'Lay on him the curse of the withered heart,
The curse of the sleepless eye;
Till he wish and pray that his life would part,
Nor yet find leave to die.'

XIV.

BALLAD CONTINUED.

'T is merry, 't is merry, in good greenwood,
Though the birds have stilled their singing;
The evening blaze doth Alice raise,
And Richard is fagots bringing.

Up Urgan starts, that hideous dwarf,
 Before Lord Richard stands, 320
And, as he crossed and blessed himself,
'I fear not sign,' quoth the grisly elf,
 'That is made with bloody hands.'

But out then spoke she, Alice Brand,
 That woman void of fear, —
'And if there 's blood upon his hand,
 'T is but the blood of deer.'

'Now loud thou liest, thou bold of mood!
 It cleaves unto his hand,
The stain of thine own kindly blood, 330
 The blood of Ethert Brand.'

Then forward stepped she, Alice Brand,
 And made the holy sign, —
'And if there 's blood on Richard's hand,
 A spotless hand is mine.

'And I conjure thee, demon elf,
 By Him whom demons fear,
To show us whence thou art thyself,
 And what thine errand here?'

XV

BALLAD CONTINUED.

''T is merry, 't is merry, in Fairy-land, 340
 When fairy birds are singing,
When the court doth ride by their monarch's side,
 With bit and bridle ringing:

'And gayly shines the Fairy-land —
But all is glistening show,
Like the idle gleam that December's beam
Can dart on ice and snow.

'And fading, like that varied gleam,
Is our inconstant shape,
Who now like knight and lady seem, 350
And now like dwarf and ape.

'It was between the night and day,
When the Fairy King has power,
That I sunk down in a sinful fray,
And 'twixt life and death was snatched away
To the joyless Elfin bower.

'But wist I of a woman bold,
Who thrice my brow durst sign,
I might regain my mortal mould,
As fair a form as thine.' 360

She crossed him once — she crossed him twice —
That lady was so brave;
The fouler grew his goblin hue,
The darker grew the cave.

She crossed him thrice, that lady bold;
He rose beneath her hand
The fairest knight on Scottish mould,
Her brother, Ethert Brand!

Merry it is in good greenwood,
When the mavis and merle are singing, 370
But merrier were they in Dunfermline gray,
When all the bells were ringing.

XVI.

Just as the minstrel sounds were stayed,
A stranger climbed the steepy glade;
His martial step, his stately mien,
His hunting-suit of Lincoln green,
His eagle glance, remembrance claims —
'T is Snowdoun's Knight, 't is James Fitz-James.
Ellen beheld as in a dream,
Then, starting, scarce suppressed a scream: 380
'O stranger! in such hour of fear
What evil hap has brought thee here?'
'An evil hap how can it be
That bids me look again on thee?
By promise bound, my former guide
Met me betimes this morning-tide,
And marshalled over bank and bourne
The happy path of my return.'
'The happy path! — what! said he naught
Of war, of battle to be fought, 390
Of guarded pass?' 'No, by my faith!
Nor saw I aught could augur scathe.'
'O haste thee, Allan, to the kern:
Yonder his tartans I discern;
Learn thou his purpose, and conjure
That he will guide the stranger sure! —
What prompted thee, unhappy man?
The meanest serf in Roderick's clan
Had not been bribed, by love or fear,
Unknown to him to guide thee here.' 400

XVII.

'Sweet Ellen, dear my life must be,
Since it is worthy care from thee;

Yet life I hold but idle breath
When love or honor 's weighed with death.
Then let me profit by my chance,
And speak my purpose bold at once.
I come to bear thee from a wild
Where ne'er before such blossom smiled,
By this soft hand to lead thee far
From frantic scenes of feud and war. 410
Near Bochastle my horses wait;
They bear us soon to Stirling gate.
I 'll place thee in a lovely bower,
I 'll guard thee like a tender flower —'
'O hush, Sir Knight! 't were female art,
To say I do not read thy heart;
Too much, before, my selfish ear
Was idly soothed my praise to hear.
That fatal bait hath lured thee back,
In deathful hour, o'er dangerous track; 42
And how, O how, can I atone
The wreck my vanity brought on! —
One way remains — I 'll tell him all —
Yes! struggling bosom, forth it shall!
Thou, whose light folly bears the blame,
Buy thine own pardon with thy shame!
But first — my father is a man
Outlawed and exiled, under ban;
The price of blood is on his head,
With me 't were infamy to wed. 430
Still wouldst thou speak? — then hear the truth!
Fitz-James, there is a noble youth —
If yet he is! — exposed for me
And mine to dread extremity —
Thou hast the secret of my heart;
Forgive, be generous, and depart!'

XVIII.

Fitz-James knew every wily train
A lady's fickle heart to gain,
But here he knew and felt them vain.
There shot no glance from Ellen's eye, 440
To give her steadfast speech the lie;
In maiden confidence she stood,
Though mantled in her cheek the blood,
And told her love with such a sigh
Of deep and hopeless agony,
As death had sealed her Malcolm's doom
And she sat sorrowing on his tomb.
Hope vanished from Fitz-James's eye,
But not with hope fled sympathy.
He proffered to attend her side, 450
As brother would a sister guide.
'O little know'st thou Roderick's heart!
Safer for both we go apart.
O haste thee, and from Allan learn
If thou mayst trust yon wily kern.'
With hand upon his forehead laid,
The conflict of his mind to shade,
A parting step or two he made;
Then, as some thought had crossed his brain,
He paused, and turned, and came again. 460

XIX.

'Hear, lady, yet a parting word!—
It chanced in fight that my poor sword
Preserved the life of Scotland's lord.
This ring the grateful Monarch gave,
And bade, when I had boon to crave,
To bring it back, and boldly claim
The recompense that I would name.

Ellen, I am no courtly lord,
But one who lives by lance and sword,
Whose castle is his helm and shield, 470
His lordship the embattled field.
What from a prince can I demand,
Who neither reck of state nor land?
Ellen, thy hand — the ring is thine;
Each guard and usher knows the sign.
Seek thou the King without delay;
This signet shall secure thy way:
And claim thy suit, whate'er it be,
As ransom of his pledge to me.'
He placed the golden circlet on, 480
Paused — kissed her hand — and then was gone.
The aged Minstrel stood aghast,
So hastily Fitz-James shot past.
He joined his guide, and wending down
The ridges of the mountain brown,
Across the stream they took their way
That joins Loch Katrine to Achray.

XX.

All in the Trosachs' glen was still,
Noontide was sleeping on the hill:
Sudden his guide whooped loud and high — 490
'Murdoch! was that a signal cry?' —
He stammered forth. 'I shout to scare
Yon raven from his dainty fare.'
He looked — he knew the raven's prey,
His own brave steed: 'Ah! gallant gray!
For thee — for me, perchance — 't were well
We ne'er had seen the Trosachs' dell. —
Murdoch, move first — but silently;
Whistle or whoop, and thou shalt die!'
Jealous and sullen on they fared, 500
Each silent, each upon his guard.

ON THE BORDER OF LOCH ACHRAY.

XXI.

Now wound the path its dizzy ledge
Around a precipice's edge,
When lo! a wasted female form,
Blighted by wrath of sun and storm,
In tattered weeds and wild array,
Stood on a cliff beside the way,
And glancing round her restless eye,
Upon the wood, the rock, the sky,
Seemed naught to mark, yet all to spy. 510
Her brow was wreathed with gaudy broom;
With gesture wild she waved a plume
Of feathers, which the eagles fling
To crag and cliff from dusky wing;
Such spoils her desperate step had sought,
Where scarce was footing for the goat.

The tartan plaid she first descried,
And shrieked till all the rocks replied;
As loud she laughed when near they drew,
For then the Lowland garb she knew; 520
And then her hands she wildly wrung,
And then she wept, and then she sung —
She sung! — the voice, in better time,
Perchance to harp or lute might chime;
And now, though strained and roughened, still
Rung wildly sweet to dale and hill.

XXII.

SONG.

They bid me sleep, they bid me pray,
  They say my brain is warped and wrung —
I cannot sleep on Highland brae,
  I cannot pray in Highland tongue. 530
But were I now where Allan glides,
Or heard my native Devan's tides,
So sweetly would I rest, and pray
That Heaven would close my wintry day!

'T was thus my hair they bade me braid,
  They made me to the church repair;
It was my bridal morn they said,
  And my true love would meet me there.
But woe betide the cruel guile
That drowned in blood the morning smile! 540
And woe betide the fairy dream!
I only waked to sob and scream.

XXIII.

'Who is this maid? what means her lay?
She hovers o'er the hollow way,
And flutters wide her mantle gray,

As the lone heron spreads his wing,
By twilight, o'er a haunted spring.'
''T is Blanche of Devan,' Murdoch said,
'A crazed and captive Lowland maid,
Ta'en on the morn she was a bride, 550
When Roderick forayed Devan-side.
The gay bridegroom resistance made,
And felt our Chief's unconquered blade.
I marvel she is now at large,
But oft she 'scapes from Maudlin's charge. —
Hence, brain-sick fool!' — He raised his bow:—
'Now, if thou strik'st her but one blow,
I'll pitch thee from the cliff as far
As ever peasant pitched a bar!'
'Thanks, champion, thanks!' the Maniac cried, 560
And pressed her to Fitz-James's side.
'See the gray pennons I prepare,
To seek my true love through the air!
I will not lend that savage groom,
To break his fall, one downy plume!
No! — deep amid disjointed stones,
The wolves shall batten on his bones,
And then shall his detested plaid,
By bush and brier in mid-air stayed,
Wave forth a banner fair and free, 570
Meet signal for their revelry.'

XXIV

'Hush thee, poor maiden, and be still!'
'O! thou look'st kindly, and I will.
Mine eye has dried and wasted been,
But still it loves the Lincoln green;
And, though mine ear is all unstrung,
Still, still it loves the Lowland tongue.

'For O my sweet William was forester true,
He stole poor Blanche's heart away!
His coat it was all of the greenwood hue, 580
And so blithely he trilled the Lowland lay!

'It was not that I meant to tell . . .
But thou art wise and guessest well.'
Then, in a low and broken tone,
And hurried note, the song went on.
Still on the Clansman fearfully
She fixed her apprehensive eye,
Then turned it on the Knight, and then
Her look glanced wildly o'er the glen.

XXV.

'The toils are pitched, and the stakes are set,— 590
Ever sing merrily, merrily;
The bows they bend, and the knives they whet,
Hunters live so cheerily.

'It was a stag, a stag of ten,
Bearing its branches sturdily;
He came stately down the glen,—
Ever sing hardily, hardily.

'It was there he met with a wounded doe,
She was bleeding deathfully;
She warned him of the toils below, 600
O, so faithfully, faithfully!

'He had an eye, and he could heed,—
Ever sing warily, warily;
He had a foot, and he could speed,—
Hunters watch so narrowly.'

XXVI.

Fitz-James's mind was passion-tossed,
When Ellen's hints and fears were lost;
But Murdoch's shout suspicion wrought,
And Blanche's song conviction brought.
Not like a stag that spies the snare, 610
But lion of the hunt aware,
He waved at once his blade on high,
'Disclose thy treachery, or die!'
Forth at full speed the Clansman flew,
But in his race his bow he drew.
The shaft just grazed Fitz-James's crest,
And thrilled in Blanche's faded breast.—
Murdoch of Alpine! prove thy speed,
For ne'er had Alpine's son such need;
With heart of fire, and foot of wind, 620
The fierce avenger is behind!
Fate judges of the rapid strife—
The forfeit death—the prize is life;
Thy kindred ambush lies before,
Close couched upon the heathery moor;
Them couldst thou reach!—it may not be—
Thine ambushed kin thou ne'er shalt see,
The fiery Saxon gains on thee!—
Resistless speeds the deadly thrust,
As lightning strikes the pine to dust; 630
With foot and hand Fitz-James must strain
Ere he can win his blade again.
Bent o'er the fallen with falcon eye,
He grimly smiled to see him die,
Then slower wended back his way,
Where the poor maiden bleeding lay.

XXVII.

She sat beneath the birchen tree,
Her elbow resting on her knee;
She had withdrawn the fatal shaft,
And gazed on it, and feebly laughed; 640
Her wreath of broom and feathers gray,
Daggled with blood, beside her lay.
The Knight to stanch the life-stream tried, —
'Stranger, it is in vain!' she cried.
'This hour of death has given me more
Of reason's power than years before;
For, as these ebbing veins decay,
My frenzied visions fade away.
A helpless injured wretch I die,
And something tells me in thine eye 650
That thou wert mine avenger born.
Seest thou this tress? — O, still I've worn
This little tress of yellow hair,
Through danger, frenzy, and despair!
It once was bright and clear as thine,
But blood and tears have dimmed its shine.
I will not tell thee when 't was shred,
Nor from what guiltless victim's head, —
My brain would turn! — but it shall wave
Like plumage on thy helmet brave, 660
Till sun and wind shall bleach the stain,
And thou wilt bring it me again.
I waver still. — O God! more bright
Let reason beam her parting light! —
O, by thy knighthood's honored sign,
And for thy life preserved by mine,
When thou shalt see a darksome man,
Who boasts him Chief of Alpine's Clan,

With tartans broad and shadowy plume,
And hand of blood, and brow of gloom, 670
Be thy heart bold, thy weapon strong,
And wreak poor Blanche of Devan's wrong! —
They watch for thee by pass and fell . . .
Avoid the path . . . O God! . . . farewell.'

XXVIII.

A kindly heart had brave Fitz-James;
Fast poured his eyes at pity's claims;
And now, with mingled grief and ire,
He saw the murdered maid expire.
'God, in my need, be my relief,
As I wreak this on yonder Chief!' 680
A lock from Blanche's tresses fair
He blended with her bridegroom's hair;
The mingled braid in blood he dyed,
And placed it on his bonnet-side:
'By Him whose word is truth, I swear,
No other favor will I wear,
Till this sad token I imbrue
In the best blood of Roderick Dhu! —
But hark! what means yon faint halloo?
The chase is up, — but they shall know, 690
The stag at bay 's a dangerous foe.'
Barred from the known but guarded way,
Through copse and cliffs Fitz-James must stray,
And oft must change his desperate track,
By stream and precipice turned back.
Heartless, fatigued, and faint, at length,
From lack of food and loss of strength,
He couched him in a thicket hoar,
And thought his toils and perils o'er: —

'Of all my rash adventures past, 700
This frantic feat must prove the last!
Who e'er so mad but might have guessed
That all this Highland hornet's nest
Would muster up in swarms so soon
As e'er they heard of bands at Doune?—
Like bloodhounds now they search me out,—
Hark, to the whistle and the shout!—
If farther through the wilds I go,
I only fall upon the foe:
I 'll couch me here till evening gray, 710
Then darkling try my dangerous way.'

XXIX.

The shades of eve come slowly down,
The woods are wrapt in deeper brown,
The owl awakens from her dell,
The fox is heard upon the fell;
Enough remains of glimmering light
To guide the wanderer's steps aright,
Yet not enough from far to show
His figure to the watchful foe.
With cautious step and ear awake, 720
He climbs the crag and threads the brake;
And not the summer solstice there
Tempered the midnight mountain air,
But every breeze that swept the wold
Benumbed his drenched limbs with cold.
In dread, in danger, and alone,
Famished and chilled, through ways unknown,
Tangled and steep, he journeyed on;
Till, as a rock's huge point he turned,
A watch-fire close before him burned. 730

XXX.

Beside its embers red and clear,
Basked in his plaid a mountaineer;
And up he sprung with sword in hand, —
'Thy name and purpose! Saxon, stand!'
'A stranger.' 'What dost thou require?'
'Rest and a guide, and food and fire.
My life 's beset, my path is lost,
The gale has chilled my limbs with frost.'
'Art thou a friend to Roderick?' 'No.'
'Thou dar'st not call thyself a foe?' 740
'I dare! to him and all the band
He brings to aid his murderous hand.'
'Bold words! — but, though the beast of game
The privilege of chase may claim,
Though space and law the stag we lend,
Ere hound we slip or bow we bend,
Who ever recked, where, how, or when,
The prowling fox was trapped or slain?
Thus treacherous scouts, — yet sure they lie,
Who say thou cam'st a secret spy!' — 750
'They do, by heaven! — come Roderick Dhu,
And of his clan the boldest two,
And let me but till morning rest,
I write the falsehood on their crest.'
'If by the blaze I mark aright,
Thou bear'st the belt and spur of Knight.'
'Then by these tokens mayst thou know
Each proud oppressor's mortal foe.'
'Enough, enough; sit down and share
A soldier's couch, a soldier's fare.' 760

XXXI.

He gave him of his Highland cheer,
The hardened flesh of mountain deer;

Dry fuel on the fire he laid,
And bade the Saxon share his plaid.
He tended him like welcome guest,
Then thus his further speech addressed:—
'Stranger, I am to Roderick Dhu
A clansman born, a kinsman true;
Each word against his honor spoke
Demands of me avenging stroke; 770
Yet more,—upon thy fate, 't is said,
A mighty augury is laid.
It rests with me to wind my horn,—
Thou art with numbers overborne;
It rests with me, here, brand to brand,
Worn as thou art, to bid thee stand:
But, not for clan, nor kindred's cause,
Will I depart from honor's laws;
To assail a wearied man were shame,
And stranger is a holy name; 780
Guidance and rest, and food and fire,
In vain he never must require.
Then rest thee here till dawn of day;
Myself will guide thee on the way,
O'er stock and stone, through watch and ward,
Till past Clan-Alpine's outmost guard.
As far as Coilantogle's ford;
From thence thy warrant is thy sword.'
'I take thy courtesy, by heaven,
As freely as 't is nobly given!' 790
'Well, rest thee; for the bittern's cry
Sings us the lake's wild lullaby.'
With that he shook the gathered heath,
And spread his plaid upon the wreath;
And the brave foemen, side by side,
Lay peaceful down like brothers tried,
And slept until the dawning beam
Purpled the mountain and the stream.

BETWEEN DUNCRAGGAN AND LANRICK.

CANTO FIFTH.

THE COMBAT.

I.

FAIR as the earliest beam of eastern light,
  When first, by the bewildered pilgrim spied,
It smiles upon the dreary brow of night,
  And silvers o'er the torrent's foaming tide,
And lights the fearful path on mountain-side, —
  Fair as that beam, although the fairest far,
Giving to horror grace, to danger pride,
  Shine martial Faith, and Courtesy's bright star,
Through all the wreckful storms that cloud the brow of War.

II.

That early beam, so fair and sheen, 10
Was twinkling through the hazel screen,

When, rousing at its glimmer red,
The warriors left their lowly bed,
Looked out upon the dappled sky,
Muttered their soldier matins by,
And then awaked their fire, to steal,
As short and rude, their soldier meal.
That o'er, the Gael around him threw
His graceful plaid of varied hue,
And, true to promise, led the way, 20
By thicket green and mountain gray.
A wildering path ! — they winded now
Along the precipice's brow,
Commanding the rich scenes beneath,
The windings of the Forth and Teith,
And all the vales between that lie,
Till Stirling's turrets melt in sky ;
Then, sunk in copse, their farthest glance
Gained not the length of horseman's lance.
'T was oft so steep, the foot was fain 30
Assistance from the hand to gain ;
So tangled oft that, bursting through,
Each hawthorn shed her showers of dew, —
That diamond dew, so pure and clear,
It rivals all but Beauty's tear !

III.

At length they came where, stern and steep,
The hill sinks down upon the deep.
Here Vennachar in silver flows,
There, ridge on ridge, Benledi rose ;
Ever the hollow path twined on, 40
Beneath steep bank and threatening stone ;
A hundred men might hold the post
With hardihood against a host.

The rugged mountain's scanty cloak
Was dwarfish shrubs of birch and oak,
With shingles bare, and cliffs between,
And patches bright of bracken green,
And heather black, that waved so high,
It held the copse in rivalry.
But where the lake slept deep and still, 50
Dank osiers fringed the swamp and hill;
And oft both path and hill were torn,
Where wintry torrent down had borne,
And heaped upon the cumbered land
Its wreck of gravel, rocks, and sand.
So toilsome was the road to trace,
The guide, abating of his pace,
Led slowly through the pass's jaws,
And asked Fitz-James by what strange cause
He sought these wilds, traversed by few, 60
Without a pass from Roderick Dhu.

IV.

'Brave Gael, my pass, in danger tried,
Hangs in my belt and by my side;
Yet, sooth to tell,' the Saxon said,
'I dreamt not now to claim its aid.
When here, but three days since, I came,
Bewildered in pursuit of game,
All seemed as peaceful and as still
As the mist slumbering on yon hill;
Thy dangerous Chief was then afar, 70
Nor soon expected back from war.
Thus said, at least, my mountain-guide,
Though deep perchance the villain lied.'
'Yet why a second venture try?'
'A warrior thou, and ask me why!—

Moves our free course by such fixed cause
As gives the poor mechanic laws?
Enough, I sought to drive away
The lazy hours of peaceful day;
Slight cause will then suffice to guide 80
A Knight's free footsteps far and wide,—
A falcon flown, a greyhound strayed,
The merry glance of mountain maid;
Or, if a path be dangerous known,
The danger's self is lure alone.'

V.

'Thy secret keep, I urge thee not;—
Yet, ere again ye sought this spot,
Say, heard ye naught of Lowland war,
Against Clan-Alpine, raised by Mar?'
'No, by my word;—of bands prepared 90
To guard King James's sports I heard;
Nor doubt I aught, but, when they hear
This muster of the mountaineer,
Their pennons will abroad be flung,
Which else in Doune had peaceful hung.'
'Free be they flung! for we were loath
Their silken folds should feast the moth.
Free be they flung!—as free shall wave
Clan-Alpine's pine in banner brave.
But, stranger, peaceful since you came, 100
Bewildered in the mountain-game,
Whence the bold boast by which you show
Vich-Alpine's vowed and mortal foe?'
'Warrior, but yester-morn I knew
Naught of thy Chieftain, Roderick Dhu,
Save as an outlawed desperate man,
The chief of a rebellious clan,

Who, in the Regent's court and sight,
With ruffian dagger stabbed a knight;
Yet this alone might from his part 110
Sever each true and loyal heart.'

VI.

Wrathful at such arraignment foul,
Dark lowered the clansman's sable scowl.
A space he paused, then sternly said,
'And heardst thou why he drew his blade?
Heardst thou that shameful word and blow
Brought Roderick's vengeance on his foe?
What recked the Chieftain if he stood
On Highland heath or Holy-Rood?
He rights such wrong where it is given, 120
If it were in the court of heaven.'
'Still was it outrage; — yet, 't is true,
Not then claimed sovereignty his due;
While Albany with feeble hand
Held borrowed truncheon of command,
The young King, mewed in Stirling tower,
Was stranger to respect and power.
But then, thy Chieftain's robber life! —
Winning mean prey by causeless strife,
Wrenching from ruined Lowland swain 130
His herds and harvest reared in vain, —
Methinks a soul like thine should scorn
The spoils from such foul foray borne.'

VII.

The Gael beheld him grim the while,
And answered with disdainful smile:
'Saxon, from yonder mountain high,
I marked thee send delighted eye

Far to the south and east, where lay,
Extended in succession gay,
Deep waving fields and pastures green, 140
With gentle slopes and groves between:—
These fertile plains, that softened vale,
Were once the birthright of the Gael;
The stranger came with iron hand,
And from our fathers reft the land.
Where dwell we now? See, rudely swell
Crag over crag, and fell o'er fell.
Ask we this savage hill we tread
For fattened steer or household bread,
Ask we for flocks these shingles dry, 150
And well the mountain might reply,—
"To you, as to your sires of yore,
Belong the target and claymore!
I give you shelter in my breast,
Your own good blades must win the rest."
Pent in this fortress of the North,
Think'st thou we will not sally forth,
To spoil the spoiler as we may,
And from the robber rend the prey?
Ay, by my soul!—While on yon plain 160
The Saxon rears one shock of grain,
While of ten thousand herds there strays
But one along yon river's maze,—
The Gael, of plain and river heir,
Shall with strong hand redeem his share.
Where live the mountain Chiefs who hold
That plundering Lowland field and fold
Is aught but retribution true?
Seek other cause 'gainst Roderick Dhu.'

VIII.

Answered Fitz-James: 'And, if I sought, 170
Think'st thou no other could be brought?

What deem ye of my path waylaid?
My life given o'er to ambuscade?'
'As of a meed to rashness due:
Hadst thou sent warning fair and true,—
I seek my hound or falcon strayed,
I seek, good faith, a Highland maid,—
Free hadst thou been to come and go;
But secret path marks secret foe.
Nor yet for this, even as a spy, 180
Hadst thou, unheard, been doomed to die,
Save to fulfil an augury.'
'Well, let it pass; nor will I now
Fresh cause of enmity avow,
To chafe thy mood and cloud thy brow.
Enough, I am by promise tied
To match me with this man of pride:
Twice have I sought Clan-Alpine's glen
In peace; but when I come again,
I come with banner, brand, and bow, 190
As leader seeks his mortal foe.
For love-lorn swain in lady's bower
Ne'er panted for the appointed hour,
As I, until before me stand
This rebel Chieftain and his band!'

IX.

'Have then thy wish!'—He whistled shrill,
And he was answered from the hill;
Wild as the scream of the curlew,
From crag to crag the signal flew.
Instant, through copse and heath, arose 200
Bonnets and spears and bended bows;
On right, on left, above, below,
Sprung up at once the lurking foe;

From shingles gray their lances start,
The bracken bush sends forth the dart,
The rushes and the willow-wand
Are bristling into axe and brand,
And every tuft of broom gives life
To plaided warrior armed for strife.
That whistle garrisoned the glen 210
At once with full five hundred men,
As if the yawning hill to heaven
A subterranean host had given.
Watching their leader's beck and will,
All silent there they stood and still.
Like the loose crags whose threatening mass
Lay tottering o'er the hollow pass,
As if an infant's touch could urge
Their headlong passage down the verge,
With step and weapon forward flung, 220
Upon the mountain-side they hung.
The Mountaineer cast glance of pride
Along Benledi's living side,
Then fixed his eye and sable brow
Full on Fitz-James: 'How say'st thou now?
These are Clan-Alpine's warriors true;
And, Saxon, — I am Roderick Dhu!'

X.

Fitz-James was brave: — though to his heart
The life-blood thrilled with sudden start,
He manned himself with dauntless air, 230
Returned the Chief his haughty stare,
His back against a rock he bore,
And firmly placed his foot before: —
'Come one, come all! this rock shall fly
From its firm base as soon as I.'

Sir Roderick marked, — and in his eyes
Respect was mingled with surprise,
And the stern joy which warriors feel
In foeman worthy of their steel.
Short space he stood — then waved his hand: 240
Down sunk the disappearing band;
Each warrior vanished where he stood,
In broom or bracken, heath or wood;
Sunk brand and spear and bended bow,
In osiers pale and copses low;
It seemed as if their mother Earth
Had swallowed up her warlike birth.
The wind's last breath had tossed in air
Pennon and plaid and plumage fair, —
The next but swept a lone hill-side, 250
Where heath and fern were waving wide:
The sun's last glance was glinted back
From spear and glaive, from targe and jack, —
The next, all unreflected, shone
On bracken green and cold gray stone.

XI.

Fitz-James looked round, — yet scarce believed
The witness that his sight received;
Such apparition well might seem
Delusion of a dreadful dream.
Sir Roderick in suspense he eyed, 260
And to his look the Chief replied:
'Fear naught — nay, that I need not say —
But — doubt not aught from mine array.
Thou art my guest; — I pledged my word
As far as Coilantogle ford:
Nor would I call a clansman's brand
For aid against one valiant hand,

Though on our strife lay every vale
Rent by the Saxon from the Gael.
So move we on; — I only meant 270
To show the reed on which you leant,
Deeming this path you might pursue
Without a pass from Roderick Dhu.'
They moved; — I said Fitz-James was brave
As ever knight that belted glaive,
Yet dare not say that now his blood
Kept on its wont and tempered flood,
As, following Roderick's stride, he drew
That seeming lonesome pathway through,
Which yet by fearful proof was rife 280
With lances, that, to take his life,
Waited but signal from a guide,
So late dishonored and defied.
Ever, by stealth, his eye sought round
The vanished guardians of the ground,
And still from copse and heather deep
Fancy saw spear and broadsword peep,
And in the plover's shrilly strain
The signal whistle heard again.
Nor breathed he free till far behind 290
The pass was left; for then they wind
Along a wide and level green,
Where neither tree nor tuft was seen,
Nor rush nor bush of broom was near,
To hide a bonnet or a spear.

XII.

The Chief in silence strode before,
And reached that torrent's sounding shore,
Which, daughter of three mighty lakes,
From Vennachar in silver breaks.

Sweeps through the plain, and ceaseless mines 300
On Bochastle the mouldering lines,
Where Rome, the Empress of the world,
Of yore her eagle wings unfurled.
And here his course the Chieftain stayed,
Threw down his target and his plaid,
And to the Lowland warrior said:
'Bold Saxon! to his promise just,
Vich-Alpine has discharged his trust.
This murderous Chief, this ruthless man,
This head of a rebellious clan, 310
Hath led thee safe, through watch and ward,
Far past Clan-Alpine's outmost guard.
Now, man to man, and steel to steel,
A Chieftain's vengeance thou shalt feel.
See, here all vantageless I stand,
Armed like thyself with single brand;
For this is Coilantogle ford,
And thou must keep thee with thy sword.'

XIII.

The Saxon paused: 'I ne'er delayed,
When foeman bade me draw my blade; 320
Nay more, brave Chief, I vowed thy death;
Yet sure thy fair and generous faith,
And my deep debt for life preserved,
A better meed have well deserved:
Can naught but blood our feud atone?
Are there no means?' — 'No, stranger, none!
And hear, — to fire thy flagging zeal, —
The Saxon cause rests on thy steel;
For thus spoke Fate by prophet bred
Between the living and the dead: 330
"Who spills the foremost foeman's life,
His party conquers in the strife."'

'Then, by my word,' the Saxon said,
'The riddle is already read.
Seek yonder brake beneath the cliff, —
There lies Red Murdoch, stark and stiff.
Thus Fate hath solved her prophecy;
Then yield to Fate, and not to me.
To James at Stirling let us go,
When, if thou wilt be still his foe, 340
Or if the King shall not agree
To grant thee grace and favor free,
I plight mine honor, oath, and word
That, to thy native strengths restored,
With each advantage shalt thou stand
That aids thee now to guard thy land.'

XIV.

Dark lightning flashed from Roderick's eye:
'Soars thy presumption, then, so high,
Because a wretched kern ye slew,
Homage to name to Roderick Dhu? 350
He yields not, he, to man nor Fate!
Thou add'st but fuel to my hate; —
My clansman's blood demands revenge.
Not yet prepared? — By heaven, I change
My thought, and hold thy valor light
As that of some vain carpet knight,
Who ill deserved my courteous care,
And whose best boast is but to wear
A braid of his fair lady's hair.'
'I thank thee, Roderick, for the word! 360
It nerves my heart, it steels my sword;
For I have sworn this braid to stain
In the best blood that warms thy vein.
Now, truce, farewell! and, ruth, begone! —

Yet think not that by thee alone,
Proud Chief! can courtesy be shown;
Though not from copse, or heath, or cairn,
Start at my whistle clansmen stern,
Of this small horn one feeble blast
Would fearful odds against thee cast. 371
But fear not — doubt not — which thou wilt —
We try this quarrel hilt to hilt.'
Then each at once his falchion drew,
Each on the ground his scabbard threw,
Each looked to sun and stream and plain
As what they ne'er might see again;
Then foot and point and eye opposed,
In dubious strife they darkly closed.

XV.

Ill fared it then with Roderick Dhu,
That on the field his targe he threw, 380
Whose brazen studs and tough bull-hide
Had death so often dashed aside;
For, trained abroad his arms to wield,
Fitz-James's blade was sword and shield.
He practised every pass and ward,
To thrust, to strike, to feint, to guard;
While less expert, though stronger far,
The Gael maintained unequal war.
Three times in closing strife they stood,
And thrice the Saxon blade drank blood; 390
No stinted draught, no scanty tide,
The gushing flood the tartans dyed.
Fierce Roderick felt the fatal drain,
And showered his blows like wintry rain;
And, as firm rock or castle-roof
Against the winter shower is proof,

The foe, invulnerable still,
Foiled his wild rage by steady skill;
Till, at advantage ta'en, his brand
Forced Roderick's weapon from his hand, 400
And backward borne upon the lea,
Brought the proud Chieftain to his knee.

XVI.

'Now yield thee, or by Him who made
The world, thy heart's blood dyes my blade!'
'Thy threats, thy mercy, I defy!
Let recreant yield, who fears to die.'
Like adder darting from his coil,
Like wolf that dashes through the toil,
Like mountain-cat who guards her young,
Full at Fitz-James's throat he sprung; 410
Received, but recked not of a wound,
And locked his arms his foeman round.—
Now, gallant Saxon, hold thine own!
No maiden's hand is round thee thrown!
That desperate grasp thy frame might feel
Through bars of brass and triple steel!
They tug, they strain! down, down they go,
The Gael above, Fitz-James below.
The Chieftain's gripe his throat compressed,
His knee was planted on his breast; 420
His clotted locks he backward threw,
Across his brow his hand he drew,
From blood and mist to clear his sight,
Then gleamed aloft his dagger bright!
But hate and fury ill supplied
The stream of life's exhausted tide,
And all too late the advantage came,
To turn the odds of deadly game:

For, while the dagger gleamed on high,
Reeled soul and sense, reeled brain and eye. 430
Down came the blow! but in the heath
The erring blade found bloodless sheath.
The struggling foe may now unclasp
The fainting Chief's relaxing grasp;
Unwounded from the dreadful close,
But breathless all, Fitz-James arose.

XVII.

He faltered thanks to Heaven for life,
Redeemed, unhoped, from desperate strife;
Next on his foe his look he cast,
Whose every gasp appeared his last; 440
In Roderick's gore he dipped the braid, —
'Poor Blanche! thy wrongs are dearly paid;
Yet with thy foe must die, or live,
The praise that faith and valor give.'
With that he blew a bugle note,
Undid the collar from his throat,
Unbonneted, and by the wave
Sat down his brow and hands to lave.
Then faint afar are heard the feet
Of rushing steeds in gallop fleet; 450
The sounds increase, and now are seen
Four mounted squires in Lincoln green;
Two who bear lance, and two who lead
By loosened rein a saddled steed;
Each onward held his headlong course,
And by Fitz-James reined up his horse, —
With wonder viewed the bloody spot, —
'Exclaim not, gallants! question not. —
You, Herbert and Luffness, alight,
And bind the wounds of yonder knight; 460

Let the gray palfrey bear his weight,
We destined for a fairer freight,
And bring him on to Stirling straight;
I will before at better speed,
To seek fresh horse and fitting weed.
The sun rides high; — I must be boune
To see the archer-game at noon;
But lightly Bayard clears the lea. —
De Vaux and Herries, follow me.

XVIII.

'Stand, Bayard, stand!' — the steed obeyed, 470
With arching neck and bended head,
And glancing eye and quivering ear,
As if he loved his lord to hear.
No foot Fitz-James in stirrup stayed,
No grasp upon the saddle laid,
But wreathed his left hand in the mane,
And lightly bounded from the plain,
Turned on the horse his armed heel,
And stirred his courage with the steel.
Bounded the fiery steed in air, 480
The rider sat erect and fair,
Then like a bolt from steel crossbow
Forth launched, along the plain they go.
They dashed that rapid torrent through,
And up Carhonie's hill they flew;
Still at the gallop pricked the Knight,
His merrymen followed as they might.
Along thy banks, swift Teith! they ride,
And in the race they mock thy tide;
Torry and Lendrick now are past, 490
And Deanstown lies behind them cast;
They rise, the bannered towers of Doune,
They sink in distant woodland soon;

STIRLING CASTLE.

Blair-Drummond sees the hoofs strike fire,
They sweep like breeze through Ochtertyre;
They mark just glance and disappear
The lofty brow of ancient Kier;
They bathe their coursers' sweltering sides,
Dark Forth! amid thy sluggish tides,
And on the opposing shore take ground, 500
With plash, with scramble, and with bound.
Right-hand they leave thy cliffs, Craig-Forth!
And soon the bulwark of the North,
Gray Stirling, with her towers and town,
Upon their fleet career looked down.

XIX.

As up the flinty path they strained,
Sudden his steed the leader reined;
A signal to his squire he flung,
Who instant to his stirrup sprung:—
'Seest thou, De Vaux, yon woodsman gray, 510
Who townward holds the rocky way,
Of stature tall and poor array?
Mark'st thou the firm, yet active stride,
With which he scales the mountain-side?
Know'st thou from whence he comes, or whom?'
'No, by my word;—a burly groom
He seems, who in the field or chase
A baron's train would nobly grace—'
'Out, out, De Vaux! can fear supply,
And jealousy, no sharper eye? 520
Afar, ere to the hill he drew,
That stately form and step I knew;
Like form in Scotland is not seen,
Treads not such step on Scottish green.
'T is James of Douglas, by Saint Serle!
The uncle of the banished Earl.
Away, away, to court, to show
The near approach of dreaded foe:
The King must stand upon his guard;
Douglas and he must meet prepared.' 530
Then right-hand wheeled their steeds, and straight
They won the Castle's postern gate.

XX.

The Douglas, who had bent his way
From Cambus-kenneth's abbey gray,
Now, as he climbed the rocky shelf,
Held sad communion with himself:—

'Yes! all is true my fears could frame;
A prisoner lies the noble Græme,
And fiery Roderick soon will feel
The vengeance of the royal steel. 540
I, only I, can ward their fate,—
God grant the ransom come not late!
The Abbess hath her promise given,
My child shall be the bride of Heaven;—
Be pardoned one repining tear!
For He who gave her knows how dear,
How excellent!—but that is by,
And now my business is—to die.—
Ye towers! within whose circuit dread
A Douglas by his sovereign bled; 550
And thou, O sad and fatal mound!
That oft hast heard the death-axe sound,
As on the noblest of the land
Fell the stern headsman's bloody hand,—
The dungeon, block, and nameless tomb
Prepare—for Douglas seeks his doom!
But hark! what blithe and jolly peal
Makes the Franciscan steeple reel?
And see! upon the crowded street,
In motley groups what masquers meet! 560
Banner and pageant, pipe and drum,
And merry morrice-dancers come.
I guess, by all this quaint array,
The burghers hold their sports to-day.
James will be there; he loves such show,
Where the good yeoman bends his bow,
And the tough wrestler foils his foe,
As well as where, in proud career,
The high-born tilter shivers spear.
I 'll follow to the Castle-park, 570
And play my prize;—King James shall mark
If age has tamed these sinews stark.

Whose force so oft in happier days
His boyish wonder loved to praise.'

XXI.

The Castle gates were open flung,
The quivering drawbridge rocked and rung,
And echoed loud the flinty street
Beneath the coursers' clattering feet,
As slowly down the steep descent
Fair Scotland's King and nobles went, 580
While all along the crowded way
Was jubilee and loud huzza.
And ever James was bending low
To his white jennet's saddle-bow,
Doffing his cap to city dame,
Who smiled and blushed for pride and shame.
And well the simperer might be vain,—
He chose the fairest of the train.
Gravely he greets each city sire,
Commends each pageant's quaint attire, 590
Gives to the dancers thanks aloud,
And smiles and nods upon the crowd,
Who rend the heavens with their acclaims,—
'Long live the Commons' King, King James!'
Behind the King thronged peer and knight,
And noble dame and damsel bright,
Whose fiery steeds ill brooked the stay
Of the steep street and crowded way.
But in the train you might discern
Dark lowering brow and visage stern; 600
There nobles mourned their pride restrained,
And the mean burgher's joys disdained;
And chiefs, who, hostage for their clan,
Were each from home a banished man,
There thought upon their own gray tower,

Their waving woods, their feudal power,
And deemed themselves a shameful part
Of pageant which they cursed in heart.

XXII.

Now, in the Castle-park, drew out
Their checkered bands the joyous rout. 610
There morricers, with bell at heel
And blade in hand, their mazes wheel;
But chief, beside the butts, there stand
Bold Robin Hood and all his band, —
Friar Tuck with quarterstaff and cowl,
Old Scathelocke with his surly scowl,
Maid Marian, fair as ivory bone,
Scarlet, and Mutch, and Little John;
Their bugles challenge all that will,
In archery to prove their skill. 620
The Douglas bent a bow of might, —
His first shaft centred in the white,
And when in turn he shot again,
His second split the first in twain.
From the King's hand must Douglas take
A silver dart, the archers' stake;
Fondly he watched, with watery eye,
Some answering glance of sympathy, —
No kind emotion made reply!
Indifferent as to archer wight, 630
The monarch gave the arrow bright.

XXIII.

Now, clear the ring! for, hand to hand,
The manly wrestlers take their stand.
Two o'er the rest superior rose,
And proud demanded mightier foes, —

Nor called in vain, for Douglas came.—
For life is Hugh of Larbert lame;
Scarce better John of Alloa's fare,
Whom senseless home his comrades bare.
Prize of the wrestling match, the King 640
To Douglas gave a golden ring,
While coldly glanced his eye of blue,
As frozen drop of wintry dew.
Douglas would speak, but in his breast
His struggling soul his words suppressed;
Indignant then he turned him where
Their arms the brawny yeomen bare,
To hurl the massive bar in air.
When each his utmost strength had shown,
The Douglas rent an earth-fast stone 650
From its deep bed, then heaved it high,
And sent the fragment through the sky
A rood beyond the farthest mark;
And still in Stirling's royal park,
The gray-haired sires, who know the past,
To strangers point the Douglas cast,
And moralize on the decay
Of Scottish strength in modern day.

XXIV.

The vale with loud applauses rang,
The Ladies' Rock sent back the clang. 660
The King, with look unmoved, bestowed
A purse well filled with pieces broad.
Indignant smiled the Douglas proud,
And threw the gold among the crowd,
Who now with anxious wonder scan,
And sharper glance, the dark gray man;
Till whispers rose among the throng,
That heart so free, and hand so strong,
Must to the Douglas blood belong.

The old men marked and shook the head, 670
To see his hair with silver spread,
And winked aside, and told each son
Of feats upon the English done,
Ere Douglas of the stalwart hand
Was exiled from his native land.
The women praised his stately form,
Though wrecked by many a winter's storm;
The youth with awe and wonder saw
His strength surpassing Nature's law.
Thus judged, as is their wont, the crowd, 680
Till murmurs rose to clamors loud.
But not a glance from that proud ring
Of peers who circled round the King
With Douglas held communion kind,
Or called the banished man to mind;
No, not from those who at the chase
Once held his side the honored place,
Begirt his board, and in the field
Found safety underneath his shield;
For he whom royal eyes disown, 690
When was his form to courtiers known!

XXV.

The Monarch saw the gambols flag,
And bade let loose a gallant stag,
Whose pride, the holiday to crown,
Two favorite greyhounds should pull down,
That venison free and Bourdeaux wine
Might serve the archery to dine.
But Lufra, — whom from Douglas' side
Nor bribe nor threat could e'er divide,
The fleetest hound in all the North, — 700
Brave Lufra saw, and darted forth.

She left the royal hounds midway,
And dashing on the antlered prey,
Sunk her sharp muzzle in his flank,
And deep the flowing life-blood drank.
The King's stout huntsman saw the sport
By strange intruder broken short,
Came up, and with his leash unbound
In anger struck the noble hound.
The Douglas had endured, that morn, 710
The King's cold look, the nobles' scorn,
And last, and worst to spirit proud,
Had borne the pity of the crowd;
But Lufra had been fondly bred,
To share his board, to watch his bed,
And oft would Ellen Lufra's neck
In maiden glee with garlands deck;
They were such playmates that with name
Of Lufra Ellen's image came.
His stifled wrath is brimming high, 720
In darkened brow and flashing eye;
As waves before the bark divide,
The crowd gave way before his stride;
Needs but a buffet and no more,
The groom lies senseless in his gore.
Such blow no other hand could deal,
Though gauntleted in glove of steel.

XXVI.

Then clamored loud the royal train,
And brandished swords and staves amain.
But stern the Baron's warning: 'Back! 730
Back, on your lives, ye menial pack!
Beware the Douglas.—Yes! behold,
King James! The Douglas, doomed of old,

And vainly sought for near and far,
A victim to atone the war,
A willing victim, now attends,
Nor craves thy grace but for his friends.—'
'Thus is my clemency repaid?
Presumptuous Lord!' the Monarch said:
'Of thy misproud ambitious clan, 740
Thou, James of Bothwell, wert the man,
The only man, in whom a foe
My woman-mercy would not know;
But shall a Monarch's presence brook
Injurious blow and haughty look?—
What ho! the Captain of our Guard!
Give the offender fitting ward.—
Break off the sports!'—for tumult rose,
And yeomen 'gan to bend their bows,—
'Break off the sports!' he said and frowned, 750
'And bid our horsemen clear the ground.'

XXVII.

Then uproar wild and misarray
Marred the fair form of festal day.
The horsemen pricked among the crowd,
Repelled by threats and insult loud;
To earth are borne the old and weak,
The timorous fly, the women shriek;
With flint, with shaft, with staff, with bar,
The hardier urge tumultuous war.
At once round Douglas darkly sweep 760
The royal spears in circle deep,
And slowly scale the pathway steep,
While on the rear in thunder pour
The rabble with disordered roar.
With grief the noble Douglas saw
The Commons rise against the law.

And to the leading soldier said:
'Sir John of Hyndford, 't was my blade
That knighthood on thy shoulder laid;
For that good deed permit me then 770
A word with these misguided men.—

XXVIII.

'Hear, gentle friends, ere yet for me
Ye break the bands of fealty.
My life, my honor, and my cause,
I tender free to Scotland's laws.
Are these so weak as must require
The aid of your misguided ire?
Or if I suffer causeless wrong,
Is then my selfish rage so strong,
My sense of public weal so low, 780
That, for mean vengeance on a foe,
Those cords of love I should unbind
Which knit my country and my kind?
O no! Believe, in yonder tower
It will not soothe my captive hour,
To know those spears our foes should dread
For me in kindred gore are red:
To know, in fruitless brawl begun,
For me that mother wails her son,
For me that widow's mate expires, 790
For me that orphans weep their sires,
That patriots mourn insulted laws,
And curse the Douglas for the cause,
O let your patience ward such ill,
And keep your right to love me still!'

XXIX.

The crowd's wild fury sunk again
In tears, as tempests melt in rain.

With lifted hands and eyes, they prayed
For blessings on his generous head
Who for his country felt alone, 800
And prized her blood beyond his own.
Old men upon the verge of life
Blessed him who stayed the civil strife;
And mothers held their babes on high,
The self-devoted Chief to spy,
Triumphant over wrongs and ire,
To whom the prattlers owed a sire.
Even the rough soldier's heart was moved;
As if behind some bier beloved,
With trailing arms and drooping head, 810
The Douglas up the hill he led,
And at the Castle's battled verge,
With sighs resigned his honored charge.

XXX.

The offended Monarch rode apart,
With bitter thought and swelling heart,
And would not now vouchsafe again
Through Stirling streets to lead his train.
'O Lennox, who would wish to rule
This changeling crowd, this common fool?
Hear'st thou,' he said, 'the loud acclaim 820
With which they shout the Douglas name?
With like acclaim the vulgar throat
Strained for King James their morning note;
With like acclaim they hailed the day
When first I broke the Douglas sway;
And like acclaim would Douglas greet
If he could hurl me from my seat.
Who o'er the herd would wish to reign,
Fantastic, fickle, fierce, and vain?

Vain as the leaf upon the stream,
And fickle as a changeful dream;
Fantastic as a woman's mood,
And fierce as Frenzy's fevered blood.
Thou many-headed monster-thing,
O who would wish to be thy king?—

XXXI.

'But soft! what messenger of speed
Spurs hitherward his panting steed?
I guess his cognizance afar—
What from our cousin, John of Mar?'

'He prays, my liege, your sports keep bound 840
Within the safe and guarded ground;
For some foul purpose yet unknown,—
Most sure for evil to the throne,—
The outlawed Chieftain, Roderick Dhu,
Has summoned his rebellious crew;
'T is said, in James of Bothwell's aid
These loose banditti stand arrayed.
The Earl of Mar this morn from Doune
To break their muster marched, and soon
Your Grace will hear of battle fought; 850
But earnestly the Earl besought,
Till for such danger he provide,
With scanty train you will not ride.'

XXXII.

'Thou warn'st me I have done amiss,—
I should have earlier looked to this;
I lost it in this bustling day.—
Retrace with speed thy former way;
Spare not for spoiling of thy steed,
The best of mine shall be thy meed.
Say to our faithful Lord of Mar, 860
We do forbid the intended war;
Roderick this morn in single fight
Was made our prisoner by a knight,
And Douglas hath himself and cause
Submitted to our kingdom's laws.
The tidings of their leaders lost
Will soon dissolve the mountain host,
Nor would we that the vulgar feel,
For their Chief's crimes, avenging steel.
Bear Mar our message, Braco, fly!' 870
He turned his steed,—'My liege, I hie,

Yet ere I cross this lily lawn
I fear the broadswords will be drawn.'
The turf the flying courser spurned,
And to his towers the King returned.

XXXIII.

Ill with King James's mood that day
Suited gay feast and minstrel lay;
Soon were dismissed the courtly throng,
And soon cut short the festal song.
Nor less upon the saddened town 880
The evening sunk in sorrow down.
The burghers spoke of civil jar,
Of rumored feuds and mountain war,
Of Moray, Mar, and Roderick Dhu,
All up in arms; — the Douglas too,
They mourned him pent within the hold,
'Where stout Earl William was of old.' —
And there his word the speaker stayed,
And finger on his lip he laid,
Or pointed to his dagger blade. 890
But jaded horsemen from the west
At evening to the Castle pressed,
And busy talkers said they bore
Tidings of fight on Katrine's shore;
At noon the deadly fray begun,
And lasted till the set of sun.
Thus giddy rumor shook the town,
Till closed the Night her pennons brown.

THE OLD BRIDGE AT CALLANDER.

CANTO SIXTH.

THE GUARD-ROOM

I.

THE sun, awakening, through the smoky air
 Of the dark city casts a sullen glance,
Rousing each caitiff to his task of care,
 Of sinful man the sad inheritance;
Summoning revellers from the lagging dance,
 Scaring the prowling robber to his den;
Gilding on battled tower the warder's lance,
 And warning student pale to leave his pen,
And yield his drowsy eyes to the kind nurse of men.

What various scenes, and O, what scenes of woe. 10
Are witnessed by that red and struggling beam!
The fevered patient, from his pallet low,
Through crowded hospital beholds it stream;
The ruined maiden trembles at its gleam,
The debtor wakes to thought of gyve and jail,
The love-lorn wretch starts from tormenting dream;
The wakeful mother, by the glimmering pale,
Trims her sick infant's couch, and soothes his feeble wail.

II.

At dawn the towers of Stirling rang
With soldier-step and weapon-clang, 20
While drums with rolling note foretell
Relief to weary sentinel.
Through narrow loop and casement barred,
The sunbeams sought the Court of Guard,
And, struggling with the smoky air,
Deadened the torches' yellow glare.
In comfortless alliance shone
The lights through arch of blackened stone,
And showed wild shapes in garb of war,
Faces deformed with beard and scar, 30
All haggard from the midnight watch,
And fevered with the stern debauch;
For the oak table's massive board,
Flooded with wine, with fragments stored,
And beakers drained, and cups o'erthrown,
Showed in what sport the night had flown.
Some, weary, snored on floor and bench;
Some labored still their thirst to quench;
Some, chilled with watching, spread their hands
O'er the huge chimney's dying brands, 40
While round them, or beside them flung,
At every step their harness rung.

III.

These drew not for their fields the sword,
Like tenants of a feudal lord,
Nor owned the patriarchal claim
Of Chieftain in their leader's name;
Adventurers they, from far who roved,
To live by battle which they loved.
There the Italian's clouded face,
The swarthy Spaniard's there you trace; 50
The mountain-loving Switzer there
More freely breathed in mountain-air;
The Fleming there despised the soil
That paid so ill the laborer's toil;
Their rolls showed French and German name;
And merry England's exiles came,
To share, with ill-concealed disdain,
Of Scotland's pay the scanty gain.
All brave in arms, well trained to wield
The heavy halberd, brand, and shield; 60
In camps licentious, wild, and bold;
In pillage fierce and uncontrolled;
And now, by holytide and feast,
From rules of discipline released.

IV.

They held debate of bloody fray,
Fought 'twixt Loch Katrine and Achray.
Fierce was their speech, and mid their words
Their hands oft grappled to their swords;
Nor sunk their tone to spare the ear
Of wounde comrades groaning near, 70
Whose mangled limbs and bodies gored
Bore token of the mountain sword,

Though, neighboring to the Court of Guard,
Their prayers and feverish wails were heard, —
Sad burden to the ruffian joke,
And savage oath by fury spoke ! —
At length up started John of Brent,
A yeoman from the banks of Trent ;
A stranger to respect or fear,
In peace a chaser of the deer, 80
In host a hardy mutineer,
But still the boldest of the crew
When deed of danger was to do.
He grieved that day their games cut short,
And marred the dicer's brawling sport,
And shouted loud, 'Renew the bowl !
And, while a merry catch I troll,
Let each the buxom chorus bear,
Like brethren of the brand and spear.'

V.

SOLDIER'S SONG.

Our vicar still preaches that Peter and Poule 90
Laid a swinging long curse on the bonny brown bowl,
That there 's wrath and despair in the jolly black-jack,
And the seven deadly sins in a flagon of sack ;
Yet whoop, Barnaby ! off with thy liquor,
Drink upsees out, and a fig for the vicar !

Our vicar he calls it damnation to sip
The ripe ruddy dew of a woman's dear lip,
Says that Beelzebub lurks in her kerchief so sly,
And Apollyon shoots darts from her merry black eye ;
Yet whoop, Jack ! kiss Gillian the quicker, 100
Till she bloom like a rose, and a fig for the vicar !

Our vicar thus preaches, — and why should he not?
For the dues of his cure are the placket and pot;
And 't is right of his office poor laymen to lurch
Who infringe the domains of our good Mother Church.
Yet whoop, bully-boys! off with your liquor,
Sweet Marjorie 's the word, and a fig for the vicar!

VI.

The warder's challenge, heard without,
Stayed in mid-roar the merry shout.
A soldier to the portal went, — 110
'Here is old Bertram, sirs, of Ghent;
And — beat for jubilee the drum! —
A maid and minstrel with him come.'
Bertram, a Fleming, gray and scarred,
Was entering now the Court of Guard,
A harper with him, and, in plaid
All muffled close, a mountain maid,
Who backward shrunk to 'scape the view
Of the loose scene and boisterous crew.
'What news?' they roared: — 'I only know, 120
From noon till eve we fought with foe,
As wild and as untamable
As the rude mountains where they dwell;
On both sides store of blood is lost,
Nor much success can either boast.' —
'But whence thy captives, friend? such spoil
As theirs must needs reward thy toil.
Old dost thou wax, and wars grow sharp;
Thou now hast glee-maiden and harp!
Get thee an ape, and trudge the land, 130
The leader of a juggler band.'

VII.

'No, comrade; — no such fortune mine.
After the fight these sought our line.

That aged harper and the girl,
And, having audience of the Earl,
Mar bade I should purvey them steed,
And bring them hitherward with speed.
Forbear your mirth and rude alarm,
For none shall do them shame or harm.—'
'Hear ye his boast?' cried John of Brent, 140
Ever to strife and jangling bent;
'Shall he strike doe beside our lodge,
And yet the jealous niggard grudge
To pay the forester his fee?
I'll have my share howe'er it be,
Despite of Moray, Mar, or thee.'
Bertram his forward step withstood;
And, burning in his vengeful mood,
Old Allan, though unfit for strife,
Laid hand upon his dagger-knife; 150
But Ellen boldly stepped between,
And dropped at once the tartan screen:—
So, from his morning cloud, appears
The sun of May through summer tears.
The savage soldiery, amazed,
As on descended angel gazed;
Even hardy Brent, abashed and tamed,
Stood half admiring, half ashamed.

VIII.

Boldly she spoke: 'Soldiers, attend!
My father was the soldier's friend, 160
Cheered him in camps, in marches led,
And with him in the battle bled.
Not from the valiant or the strong
Should exile's daughter suffer wrong.'
Answered De Brent, most forward still
In every feat or good or ill:

'I shame me of the part I played;
And thou an outlaw's child, poor maid!
An outlaw I by forest laws,
And merry Needwood knows the cause. 170
Poor Rose, — if Rose be living now,' —
He wiped his iron eye and brow, —
'Must bear such age, I think, as thou. —
Hear ye, my mates! I go to call
The Captain of our watch to hall:
There lies my halberd on the floor;
And he that steps my halberd o'er,
To do the maid injurious part,
My shaft shall quiver in his heart!
Beware loose speech, or jesting rough; 180
Ye all know John de Brent. Enough.'

IX.

Their Captain came, a gallant young, —
Of Tullibardine's house he sprung, —
Nor wore he yet the spurs of knight;
Gay was his mien, his humor light,
And, though by courtesy controlled,
Forward his speech, his bearing bold.
The high-born maiden ill could brook
The scanning of his curious look
And dauntless eye: — and yet, in sooth, 190
Young Lewis was a generous youth;
But Ellen's lovely face and mien,
Ill suited to the garb and scene,
Might lightly bear construction strange,
And give loose fancy scope to range.
'Welcome to Stirling towers, fair maid!
Come ye to seek a champion's aid,
On palfrey white, with harper hoar,
Like errant damosel of yore?

Does thy high quest a knight require, 200
Or may the venture suit a squire?'
Her dark eye flashed; — she paused and sighed: —
'O what have I to do with pride! —
Through scenes of sorrow, shame, and strife,
A suppliant for a father's life,
I crave an audience of the King.
Behold, to back my suit, a ring,
The royal pledge of grateful claims,
Given by the Monarch to Fitz-James.'

X.

The signet-ring young Lewis took
With deep respect and altered look,
And said: 'This ring our duties own;
And pardon, if to worth unknown,
In semblance mean obscurely veiled,
Lady, in aught my folly failed.
Soon as the day flings wide his gates,
The King shall know what suitor waits.
Please you meanwhile in fitting bower
Repose you till his waking hour;
Female attendance shall obey 220
Your hest, for service or array.
Permit I marshal you the way.'
But, ere she followed, with the grace
And open bounty of her race,
She bade her slender purse be shared
Among the soldiers of the guard.
The rest with thanks their guerdon took,
But Brent, with shy and awkward look,
On the reluctant maiden's hold
Forced bluntly back the proffered gold: — 230
'Forgive a haughty English heart,
And O, forget its ruder part!

The vacant purse shall be my share,
Which in my barret-cap I 'll bear,
Perchance, in jeopardy of war,
Where gayer crests may keep afar.'
With thanks — 't was all she could — the maid
His rugged courtesy repaid.

XI.

When Ellen forth with Lewis went,
Allan made suit to John of Brent: — 240
'My lady safe, O let your grace
Give me to see my master's face!
His minstrel I, — to share his doom
Bound from the cradle to the tomb.
Tenth in descent, since first my sires
Waked for his noble house their lyres,
Nor one of all the race was known
But prized its weal above their own.
With the Chief's birth begins our care;
Our harp must soothe the infant heir, 250
Teach the youth tales of fight, and grace
His earliest feat of field or chase;
In peace, in war, our rank we keep,
We cheer his board, we soothe his sleep,
Nor leave him till we pour our verse —
A doleful tribute! — o'er his hearse.
Then let me share his captive lot;
It is my right, — deny it not!'
'Little we reck,' said John of Brent,
'We Southern men, of long descent; 260
Nor wot we how a name — a word —
Makes clansmen vassals to a lord:
Yet kind my noble landlord's part, —
God bless the house of Beaudesert!

And, but I loved to drive the deer
More than to guide the laboring steer,
I had not dwelt an outcast here.
Come, good old Minstrel, follow me;
Thy Lord and Chieftain shalt thou see.'

XII.

Then, from a rusted iron hook, 270
A bunch of ponderous keys he took,
Lighted a torch, and Allan led
Through grated arch and passage dread.
Portals they passed, where, deep within,
Spoke prisoner's moan and fetters' din;
Through rugged vaults, where, loosely stored,
Lay wheel, and axe, and headsman's sword,
And many a hideous engine grim,
For wrenching joint and crushing limb,
By artists formed who deemed it shame 280
And sin to give their work a name.
They halted at a low-browed porch,
And Brent to Allan gave the torch,
While bolt and chain he backward rolled,
And made the bar unhasp its hold.
They entered: — 't was a prison-room
Of stern security and gloom,
Yet not a dungeon; for the day
Through lofty gratings found its way,
And rude and antique garniture 290
Decked the sad walls and oaken floor,
Such as the rugged days of old
Deemed fit for captive noble's hold.
'Here,' said De Brent, 'thou mayst remain
Till the Leech visit him again.
Strict is his charge, the warders tell,
To tend the noble prisoner well.'

Retiring then the bolt he drew,
And the lock's murmurs growled anew.
Roused at the sound, from lowly bed 300
A captive feebly raised his head;
The wondering Minstrel looked, and knew—
Not his dear lord, but Roderick Dhu!
For, come from where Clan-Alpine fought,
They, erring, deemed the Chief he sought.

XIII.

As the tall ship, whose lofty prore
Shall never stem the billows more,
Deserted by her gallant band,
Amid the breakers lies astrand,—
So on his couch lay Roderick Dhu! 310
And oft his fevered limbs he threw
In toss abrupt, as when her sides
Lie rocking in the advancing tides,
That shake her frame with ceaseless beat,
Yet cannot heave her from her seat;—
O, how unlike her course at sea!
Or his free step on hill and lea!—
Soon as the Minstrel he could scan,—
'What of thy lady?—of my clan?—
My mother?—Douglas?—tell me all! 320
Have they been ruined in my fall?
Ah, yes! or wherefore art thou here?
Yet speak,—speak boldly,—do not fear.'—
For Allan, who his mood well knew,
Was choked with grief and terror too.—
'Who fought?—who fled?—Old man, be brief;—
Some might,—for they had lost their Chief.
Who basely live?—who bravely died?'
'O, calm thee, Chief!' the Minstrel cried,
'Ellen is safe!' 'For that thank Heaven!' 330
'And hopes are for the Douglas given;—

ALLAN-BANE AND RODERICK.

The Lady Margaret, too, is well;
And, for thy clan, — on field or fell,
Has never harp of minstrel told
Of combat fought so true and bold.
Thy stately Pine is yet unbent,
Though many a goodly bough is rent.'

XIV.

The Chieftain reared his form on high,
And fever's fire was in his eye;
But ghastly, pale, and livid streaks
Checkered his swarthy brow and cheeks.
'Hark, Minstrel! I have heard thee play,
With measure bold on festal day,

34

In yon lone isle, — again where ne'er
Shall harper play or warrior hear ! —
That stirring air that peals on high,
O'er Dermid's race our victory. —
Strike it ! — and then, — for well thou canst, —
Free from thy minstrel-spirit glanced,
Fling me the picture of the fight, 350
When met my clan the Saxon might.
I 'll listen, till my fancy hears
The clang of swords, the crash of spears !
These grates, these walls, shall vanish then
For the fair field of fighting men,
And my free spirit burst away,
As if it soared from battle fray.'
The trembling Bard with awe obeyed, —
Slow on the harp his hand he laid ;
But soon remembrance of the sight 360
He witnessed from the mountain's height,
With what old Bertram told at night,
Awakened the full power of song,
And bore him in career along ; —
As shallop launched on river's tide,
That slow and fearful leaves the side,
But, when it feels the middle stream,
Drives downward swift as lightning's beam.

XV.

BATTLE OF BEAL' AN DUINE.

'The Minstrel came once more to view
The eastern ridge of Benvenue, 370
For ere he parted he would say
Farewell to lovely Loch Achray —
Where shall he find, in foreign land,
So lone a lake, so sweet a strand ! —

There is no breeze upon the fern,
 No ripple on the lake,
Upon her eyry nods the erne,
 The deer has sought the brake;
The small birds will not sing aloud,
 The springing trout lies still, 380
So darkly glooms yon thunder-cloud,
That swathes, as with a purple shroud,
 Benledi's distant hill.
Is it the thunder's solemn sound
 That mutters deep and dread,
Or echoes from the groaning ground
 The warrior's measured tread?
Is it the lightning's quivering glance
 That on the thicket streams,
Or do they flash on spear and lance 390
 The sun's retiring beams?—
I see the dagger-crest of Mar,
I see the Moray's silver star,
Wave o'er the cloud of Saxon war,
That up the lake comes winding far!
 To hero boune for battle-strife,
 Or bard of martial lay,
 'T were worth ten years of peaceful life,
 One glance at their array!

XVI.

'Their light-armed archers far and near 400
 Surveyed the tangled ground,
Their centre ranks, with pike and spear,
 A twilight forest frowned,
Their barded horsemen in the rear
 The stern battalia crowned.
No cymbal clashed, no clarion rang,
 Still were the pipe and drum;

Save heavy tread, and armor's clang,
  The sullen march was dumb.
There breathed no wind their crests to shake, 410
  Or wave their flags abroad;
Scarce the frail aspen seemed to quake,
  That shadowed o'er their road.
Their vaward scouts no tidings bring,
  Can rouse no lurking foe,
Nor spy a trace of living thing,
  Save when they stirred the roe;
The host moves like a deep-sea wave,
Where rise no rocks its pride to brave,
  High-swelling, dark, and slow. 420
The lake is passed, and now they gain
A narrow and a broken plain,
Before the Trosachs' rugged jaws;
And here the horse and spearmen pause,
While, to explore the dangerous glen,
Dive through the pass the archer-men.

XVII.

'At once there rose so wild a yell
Within that dark and narrow dell,
As all the fiends from heaven that fell
Had pealed the banner-cry of hell! 430
  Forth from the pass in tumult driven,
  Like chaff before the wind of heaven,
    The archery appear:
  For life! for life! their flight they ply—
  And shriek, and shout, and battle-cry,
  And plaids and bonnets waving high,
  And broadswords flashing to the sky,
    Are maddening in the rear.
  Onward they drive in dreadful race,
    Pursuers and pursued: 440

Before that tide of flight and chase,
How shall it keep its rooted place,
The spearmen's twilight wood?—
"Down, down," cried Mar, "your lances down!
Bear back both friend and foe!"—
Like reeds before the tempest's frown,
That serried grove of lances brown
At once lay levelled low;
And closely shouldering side to side,
The bristling ranks the onset bide.— 4[illegible]
"We 'll quell the savage mountaineer.
As their Tinchel cows the game!
They come as fleet as forest deer,
We 'll drive them back as tame."

XVIII.

'Bearing before them in their course
The relics of the archer force,
Like wave with crest of sparkling foam,
Right onward did Clan-Alpine come.
Above the tide, each broadsword bright
Was brandishing like beam of light, 460
Each targe was dark below;
And with the ocean's mighty swing,
When heaving to the tempest's wing,
They hurled them on the foe.
I heard the lance's shivering crash,
As when the whirlwind rends the ash;
I heard the broadsword's deadly clang,
As if a hundred anvils rang!
But Moray wheeled his rearward rank
Of horsemen on Clan-Alpine's flank,—
"My banner-man, advance!
I see," he cried, "their column shake.
Now, gallants! for your ladies' sake,
Upon them with the lance!"—

The horsemen dashed among the rout,
  As deer break through the broom;
Their steeds are stout, their swords are out,
  They soon make lightsome room.
Clan-Alpine's best are backward borne —
  Where, where was Roderick then! 480
One blast upon his bugle-horn
  Were worth a thousand men.
And refluent through the pass of fear
  The battle's tide was poured;
Vanished the Saxon's struggling spear,
  Vanished the mountain-sword.
As Bracklinn's chasm, so black and steep,
  Receives her roaring linn,
As the dark caverns of the deep
  Suck the wild whirlpool in, 490
So did the deep and darksome pass
Devour the battle's mingled mass;
None linger now upon the plain,
Save those who ne'er shall fight again.

XIX.

'Now westward rolls the battle's din,
That deep and doubling pass within. —
Minstrel, away! the work of fate
Is bearing on; its issue wait,
Where the rude Trosachs' dread defile
Opens on Katrine's lake and isle. 500
Gray Benvenue I soon repassed,
Loch Katrine lay beneath me cast.
  The sun is set; — the clouds are met,
    The lowering scowl of heaven
  An inky hue of livid blue
    To the deep lake has given;

Strange gusts of wind from mountain glen
Swept o'er the lake, then sunk again.
I heeded not the eddying surge,
Mine eye but saw the Trosachs' gorge, 510
Mine ear but heard that sullen sound,
Which like an earthquake shook the ground,
And spoke the stern and desperate strife
That parts not but with parting life,
Seeming, to minstrel ear, to toll
The dirge of many a passing soul.
Nearer it comes — the dim-wood glen
The martial flood disgorged again,
But not in mingled tide;
The plaided warriors of the North 520
High on the mountain thunder forth
And overhang its side,
While by the lake below appears
The darkening cloud of Saxon spears.
At weary bay each shattered band,
Eying their foemen, sternly stand;
Their banners stream like tattered sail,
That flings its fragments to the gale,
And broken arms and disarray
Marked the fell havoc of the day. 530

XX.

'Viewing the mountain's ridge askance,
The Saxons stood in sullen trance,
Till Moray pointed with his lance,
And cried: "Behold yon isle! —
See! none are left to guard its strand
But women weak, that wring the hand:
'T is there of yore the robber band
Their booty wont to pile; —

My purse, with bonnet-pieces store,
To him will swim a bow-shot o'er, 540
And loose a shallop from the shore.
Lightly we 'll tame the war-wolf then,
Lords of his mate, and brood, and den."
Forth from the ranks a spearman sprung,
On earth his casque and corselet rung,
He plunged him in the wave :—
All saw the deed,—the purpose knew,
And to their clamors Benvenue
A mingled echo gave;
The Saxons shout, their mate to cheer, 550
The helpless females scream for fear,
And yells for rage the mountaineer.
'T was then, as by the outcry riven,
Poured down at once the lowering heaven:
A whirlwind swept Loch Katrine's breast,
Her billows reared their snowy crest.
Well for the swimmer swelled they high,
To mar the Highland marksman's eye;
For round him showered, mid rain and hail,
The vengeful arrows of the Gael. 560
In vain.—He nears the isle—and lo!
His hand is on a shallop's bow.
Just then a flash of lightning came,
It tinged the waves and strand with flame;
I marked Duncraggan's widowed dame,
Behind an oak I saw her stand,
A naked dirk gleamed in her hand:—
It darkened,—but amid the moan
Of waves I heard a dying groan;—
Another flash!—the spearman floats 570
A weltering corse beside the boats,
And the stern matron o'er him stood,
Her hand and dagger streaming blood.

ISLANDS IN LOCH KATRINE.

XXI.

"“Revenge! revenge!” the Saxons cried,
The Gaels' exulting shout replied.
Despite the elemental rage,
Again they hurried to engage;
But, ere they closed in desperate fight,
Bloody with spurring came a knight,
Sprung from his horse, and from a crag 580
Waved 'twixt the hosts a milk-white flag.
Clarion and trumpet by his side
Rung forth a truce-note high and wide.

While, in the Monarch's name, afar
A herald's voice forbade the war,
For Bothwell's lord and Roderick bold
Were both, he said, in captive hold.' —
But here the lay made sudden stand,
The harp escaped the Minstrel's hand!
Oft had he stolen a glance, to spy 590
How Roderick brooked his minstrelsy:
At first, the Chieftain, to the chime,
With lifted hand kept feeble time;
That motion ceased, — yet feeling strong
Varied his look as changed the song;
At length, no more his deafened ear
The minstrel melody can hear;
His face grows sharp, — his hands are clenched,
As if some pang his heart-strings wrenched;
Set are his teeth, his fading eye 600
Is sternly fixed on vacancy;
Thus, motionless and moanless, drew
His parting breath stout Roderick Dhu! —
Old Allan-bane looked on aghast,
While grim and still his spirit passed;
But when he saw that life was fled,
He poured his wailing o'er the dead.

XXII.

LAMENT.

'And art thou cold and lowly laid,
Thy foeman's dread, thy people's aid,
Breadalbane's boast, Clan-Alpine's shade! 610
For thee shall none a requiem say? —
For thee, who loved the minstrel's lay,
For thee, of Bothwell's house the stay,
The shelter of her exiled line,

E'en in this prison-house of thine,
I'll wail for Alpine's honored Pine!

'What groans shall yonder valleys fill!
What shrieks of grief shall rend yon hill!
What tears of burning rage shall thrill,
When mourns thy tribe thy battles done, 620
Thy fall before the race was won,
Thy sword ungirt ere set of sun!
There breathes not clansman of thy line,
But would have given his life for thine.
O, woe for Alpine's honored Pine!

'Sad was thy lot on mortal stage!—
The captive thrush may brook the cage,
The prisoned eagle dies for rage.
Brave spirit, do not scorn my strain!
And, when its notes awake again, 630
Even she, so long beloved in vain,
Shall with my harp her voice combine,
And mix her woe and tears with mine,
To wail Clan-Alpine's honored Pine.'

XXIII.

Ellen the while, with bursting heart,
Remained in lordly bower apart,
Where played, with many-colored gleams,
Through storied pane the rising beams.
In vain on gilded roof they fall,
And lightened up a tapestried wall,
And for her use a menial train
A rich collation spread in vain.
The banquet proud, the chamber gay,
Scarce drew one curious glance astray;

Or if she looked, 't was but to say,
With better omen dawned the day
In that lone isle, where waved on high
The dun-deer's hide for canopy;
Where oft her noble father shared
The simple meal her care prepared, 650
While Lufra, crouching by her side,
Her station claimed with jealous pride,
And Douglas, bent on woodland game,
Spoke of the chase to Malcolm Græme,
Whose answer, oft at random made,
The wandering of his thoughts betrayed.
Those who such simple joys have known
Are taught to prize them when they 're gone.
But sudden, see, she lifts her head,
The window seeks with cautious tread. 660
What distant music has the power
To win her in this woeful hour?
'T was from a turret that o'erhung
Her latticed bower, the strain was sung.

XXIV.

LAY OF THE IMPRISONED HUNTSMAN.

'My hawk is tired of perch and hood,
My idle greyhound loathes his food,
My horse is weary of his stall,
And I am sick of captive thrall.
I wish I were as I have been,
Hunting the hart in forest green, 670
With bended bow and bloodhound free,
For that 's the life is meet for me.

I hate to learn the ebb of time
From yon dull steeple's drowsy chime,

Or mark it as the sunbeams crawl,
Inch after inch, along the wall.
The lark was wont my matins ring,
The sable rook my vespers sing;
These towers, although a king's they be,
Have not a hall of joy for me. 680

No more at dawning morn I rise,
And sun myself in Ellen's eyes,
Drive the fleet deer the forest through,
And homeward wend with evening dew;
A blithesome welcome blithely meet,
And lay my trophies at her feet,
While fled the eve on wing of glee,—
That life is lost to love and me!'

XXV.

The heart-sick lay was hardly said,
The listener had not turned her head, 690
It trickled still, the starting tear,
When light a footstep struck her ear,
And Snowdoun's graceful Knight was near.
She turned the hastier, lest again
The prisoner should renew his strain.
'O welcome, brave Fitz-James!' she said;
'How may an almost orphan maid
Pay the deep debt—' 'O say not so!
To me no gratitude you owe.
Not mine, alas! the boon to give, 700
And bid thy noble father live;
I can but be thy guide, sweet maid,
With Scotland's King thy suit to aid.
No tyrant he, though ire and pride
May lay his better mood aside.
Come, Ellen, come! 't is more than time,
He holds his court at morning prime.'

With beating heart, and bosom wrung,
As to a brother's arm she clung.
Gently he dried the falling tear, 710
And gently whispered hope and cheer;
Her faltering steps half led, half stayed,
Through gallery fair and high arcade,
Till at his touch its wings of pride
A portal arch unfolded wide.

XXVI.

Within 't was brilliant all and light,
A thronging scene of figures bright;
It glowed on Ellen's dazzled sight,
As when the setting sun has given
Ten thousand hues to summer even, 720
And from their tissue fancy frames
Aerial knights and fairy dames.
Still by Fitz-James her footing staid;
A few faint steps she forward made,
Then slow her drooping head she raised,
And fearful round the presence gazed;
For him she sought who owned this state,
The dreaded Prince whose will was fate!—
She gazed on many a princely port
Might well have ruled a royal court; 730
On many a splendid garb she gazed,—
Then turned bewildered and amazed,
For all stood bare; and in the room
Fitz-James alone wore cap and plume.
To him each lady's look was lent,
On him each courtier's eye was bent;
Midst furs and silks and jewels sheen,
He stood, in simple Lincoln green,
The centre of the glittering ring,—
And Snowdoun's Knight is Scotland's King! 740

XXVII.

As wreath of snow on mountain-breast
Slides from the rock that gave it rest,
Poor Ellen glided from her stay,
And at the Monarch's feet she lay;
No word her choking voice commands, —
She showed the ring, — she clasped her hands.
O, not a moment could he brook,
The generous Prince, that suppliant look!
Gently he raised her, — and, the while,
Checked with a glance the circle's smile; 750
Graceful, but grave, her brow he kissed,
And bade her terrors be dismissed: —
'Yes, fair; the wandering poor Fitz-James
The fealty of Scotland claims.
To him thy woes, thy wishes, bring;
He will redeem his signet ring.
Ask naught for Douglas; — yester even,
His Prince and he have much forgiven;
Wrong hath he had from slanderous tongue,
I, from his rebel kinsmen, wrong. 760
We would not, to the vulgar crowd,
Yield what they craved with clamor loud;
Calmly we heard and judged his cause,
Our council aided and our laws.
I stanched thy father's death-feud stern
With stout De Vaux and gray Glencairn;
And Bothwell's Lord henceforth we own
The friend and bulwark of our throne. —
But, lovely infidel, how now?
What clouds thy misbelieving brow? 770
Lord James of Douglas, lend thine aid;
Thou must confirm this doubting maid.'

XXVIII.

Then forth the noble Douglas sprung,
And on his neck his daughter hung.
The Monarch drank, that happy hour,
The sweetest, holiest draught of Power, —
When it can say with godlike voice,
Arise, sad Virtue, and rejoice!
Yet would not James the general eye
On nature's raptures long should pry; 780
He stepped between — 'Nay, Douglas, nay,
Steal not my proselyte away!
The riddle 't is my right to read,
That brought this happy chance to speed.
Yes, Ellen, when disguised I stray
In life's more low but happier way,
'T is under name which veils my power,
Nor falsely veils, — for Stirling's tower
Of yore the name of Snowdoun claims,
And Normans call me James Fitz-James. 790
Thus watch I o'er insulted laws,
Thus learn to right the injured cause.'
Then, in a tone apart and low, —
'Ah, little traitress! none must know
What idle dream, what lighter thought,
What vanity full dearly bought,
Joined to thine eye's dark witchcraft, drew
My spell-bound steps to Benvenue
In dangerous hour, and all but gave
Thy Monarch's life to mountain glaive! 800
Aloud he spoke: 'Thou still dost hold
That little talisman of gold,
Pledge of my faith, Fitz-James's ring, —
What seeks fair Ellen of the King?'

XXIX.

Full well the conscious maiden guessed
He probed the weakness of her breast;
But with that consciousness there came
A lightening of her fears for Græme,
And more she deemed the Monarch's ire
Kindled 'gainst him who for her sire 810
Rebellious broadsword boldly drew;
And, to her generous feeling true,
She craved the grace of Roderick Dhu.
'Forbear thy suit; — the King of kings
Alone can stay life's parting wings.
I know his heart, I know his hand,
Have shared his cheer, and proved his brand; —
My fairest earldom would I give
To bid Clan-Alpine's Chieftain live! —
Hast thou no other boon to crave? 820
No other captive friend to save?'
Blushing, she turned her from the King,
And to the Douglas gave the ring,
As if she wished her sire to speak
The suit that stained her glowing cheek.
'Nay, then, my pledge has lost its force,
And stubborn justice holds her course.
Malcolm, come forth!' — and, at the word,
Down kneeled the Græme to Scotland's Lord.
'For thee, rash youth, no suppliant sues, 830
From thee may Vengeance claim her dues,
Who, nurtured underneath our smile,
Hast paid our care by treacherous wile,
And sought amid thy faithful clan
A refuge for an outlawed man,
Dishonoring thus thy loyal name. —
Fetters and warder for the Græme!'

His chain of gold the King unstrung,
The links o'er Malcolm's neck he flung,
Then gently drew the glittering band, 840
And laid the clasp on Ellen's hand.

HARP of the North, farewell! The hills grow dark,
On purple peaks a deeper shade descending;
In twilight copse the glow-worm lights her spark,
The deer, half seen, are to the covert wending.
Resume thy wizard elm! the fountain lending,
And the wild breeze, thy wilder minstrelsy;
Thy numbers sweet with nature's vespers blending,
With distant echo from the fold and lea,
And herd-boy's evening pipe, and hum of housing bee.

Yet, once again, farewell, thou Minstrel Harp! 851
Yet, once again, forgive my feeble sway,
And little reck I of the censure sharp
May idly cavil at an idle lay.
Much have I owed thy strains on life's long way,
Through secret woes the world has never known,
When on the weary night dawned wearier day,
And bitterer was the grief devoured alone.—
That I o'erlive such woes, Enchantress! is thine own.

Hark! as my lingering footsteps slow retire, 860
Some Spirit of the Air has waked thy string!
'T is now a seraph bold, with touch of fire,
'T is now the brush of Fairy's frolic wing.
Receding now, the dying numbers ring
Fainter and fainter down the rugged dell;
And now the mountain breezes scarcely bring
A wandering witch-note of the distant spell—
And now, 't is silent all!—Enchantress, fare thee well!

NOTES

ABBREVIATIONS USED IN THE NOTES.

Cf. (*confer*), compare.
F. Q., Spenser's *Faërie Queene*
Fol., following.
Id. (*idem*), the same.
Lockhart, J. G. Lockhart's edition of Scott's poems (various issues).
P. L., Milton's *Paradise Lost.*
Taylor, R. W. Taylor's edition of *The Lady of the Lake* (London, 1875).
Wb., Webster's Dictionary (revised quarto edition of 1879).
Worc., Worcester's Dictionary (quarto edition).

The abbreviations of the names of Shakespeare's plays will be readily understood The line-numbers are those of the "Globe" edition.

The references to Scott's *Lay of the Last Minstrel* are to canto and *line;* those to *Marmion* and other poems to canto and *stanza.*

NOTES.

THE EASTERN END OF LOCH KATRINE.

INTRODUCTION.

The Lady of the Lake was first published in 1810, when Scott was thirty-nine, and it was dedicated to "the most noble John James, Marquis of Abercorn." Eight thousand copies were sold between June 2d and September 22d, 1810, and repeated editions were subsequently called for. In 1830, the following "Introduction" was prefixed to the poem by the author:—

After the success of *Marmion*, I felt inclined to exclaim with Ulysses in the *Odyssey*:—

Οὗτος μὲν δὴ ἄεθλος ἀάατος ἐκτετέλεσται·
Νῦν αὖτε σκοπὸν ἄλλον.
Odys. χ. 5.

"One venturous game my hand has won to-day—
Another, gallants, yet remains to play."

The ancient manners, the habits and customs of the aboriginal race by whom the Highlands of Scotland were inhabited, had always appeared to me peculiarly adapted to poetry. The change in their manners, too, had taken place almost within my own time, or at least I had learned many particulars concerning the ancient state of the Highlands from the old men of the last generation. I had always thought the old Scottish Gael highly adapted for poetical composition. The feuds and political dissensions which, half a century earlier, would have rendered the richer and wealthier part of the kingdom indisposed to countenance a poem, the scene of which was laid in the Highlands, were now sunk in the generous compassion which the English, more than any other nation, feel for the misfortunes of an honorable foe. The Poems of Ossian had by their popularity sufficiently shown that, if writings on Highland subjects were qualified to interest the reader, mere national prejudices were, in the present day, very unlikely to interfere with their success.

I had also read a great deal, seen much, and heard more, of that romantic country where I was in the habit of spending some time every autumn; and the scenery of Loch Katrine was connected with the recollection of many a dear friend and merry expedition of former days. This poem, the action of which lay among scenes so beautiful and so deeply imprinted on my recollections, was a labor of love, and it was no less so to recall the manners and incidents introduced. The frequent custom of James IV., and particularly of James V., to walk through their kingdom in disguise, afforded me the hint of an incident which never fails to be interesting if managed with the slightest address or dexterity.

I may now confess, however, that the employment, though attended with great pleasure, was not without its doubts and anxieties. A lady, to whom I was nearly related, and with whom I lived, during her whole life, on the most brotherly terms of affection, was residing with me at the time when the work was in progress, and used to ask me, what I could possibly do to rise so early in the morning (that happening to be the most convenient to me for composition). At last I told her the subject of my meditations; and I can never forget the anxiety and affection expressed in her reply. "Do not be so rash," she said, "my dearest cousin.[1] You are already popular, — more so, perhaps, than you yourself will believe, or than even I, or other partial friends, can fairly allow to your merit. You stand high, — do not rashly attempt to climb higher, and incur the risk of a fall; for, depend upon it, a favorite will not be permitted even to stumble with impunity." I replied to this affectionate expostulation in the words of Montrose, —

> "'He either fears his fate too much,
> Or his deserts are small,
> Who dares not put it to the touch
> To gain or lose it all.'

"If I fail," I said, for the dialogue is strong in my recollection, "it is a sign that I ought never to have succeeded, and I will write prose for

[1] Lockhart says: "The lady with whom Sir Walter Scott held this conversation was, no doubt, his aunt, Miss Christian Rutherford; there was no other female relation *dead* when this Introduction was written, whom I can suppose him to have consulted on literary questions. Lady Capulet, on seeing the corpse of Tybalt, exclaims, —

'Tybalt, my cousin! O my brother's child!'"

life: you shall see no change in my temper, nor will I eat a single meal the worse. But if I succeed,

> 'Up with the bonnie blue bonnet,
> The dirk, and the feather, and a'!'"

Afterwards I showed my affectionate and anxious critic the first canto of the poem, which reconciled her to my imprudence. Nevertheless, although I answered thus confidently, with the obstinacy often said to be proper to those who bear my surname, I acknowledge that my confidence was considerably shaken by the warning of her excellent taste and unbiased friendship. Nor was I much comforted by her retractation of the unfavorable judgment, when I recollected how likely a natural partiality was to effect that change of opinion. In such cases, affection rises like a light on the canvas, improves any favorable tints which it formerly exhibited, and throws its defects into the shade.

I remember that about the same time a friend started in to "heeze up my hope," like the "sportsman with his cutty gun," in the old song. He was bred a farmer, but a man of powerful understanding, natural good taste, and warm poetical feeling, perfectly competent to supply the wants of an imperfect or irregular education. He was a passionate admirer of field-sports, which we often pursued together.

As this friend happened to dine with me at Ashestiel one day, I took the opportunity of reading to him the first canto of *The Lady of the Lake*, in order to ascertain the effect the poem was likely to produce upon a person who was but too favorable a representative of readers at large. It is of course to be supposed that I determined rather to guide my opinion by what my friend might appear to feel, than by what he might think fit to say. His reception of my recitation, or prelection, was rather singular. He placed his hand across his brow, and listened with great attention through the whole account of the stag-hunt, till the dogs threw themselves into the lake to follow their master, who embarks with Ellen Douglas. He then started up with a sudden exclamation, struck his hand on the table, and declared, in a voice of censure calculated for the occasion, that the dogs must have been totally ruined by being permitted to take the water after such a severe chase. I own I was much encouraged by the species of revery which had possessed so zealous a follower of the sports of the ancient Nimrod, who had been completely surprised out of all doubts of the reality of the tale. Another of his remarks gave me less pleasure. He detected the identity of the King with the wandering knight, Fitz-James, when he winds his bugle to summon his attendants. He was probably thinking of the lively, but somewhat licentious, old ballad, in which the *dénouement* of a royal intrigue takes place as follows:

> "He took a bugle frae his side,
> He blew both loud and shrill,
> And four and twenty belted knights
> Came skipping ower the hill;
> Then he took out a little knife,
> Let a' his duddies fa',
> And he was the brawest gentleman
> That was amang them a'.
> And we'll go no more a roving," etc.

This discovery, as Mr. Pepys says of the rent in his camlet cloak, was but a trifle, yet it troubled me; and I was at a good deal of pains to efface any marks by which I thought my secret could be traced before the conclusion, when I relied on it with the same hope of producing effect, with which the Irish post-boy is said to reserve a "trot for the avenue."

I took uncommon pains to verify the accuracy of the local circumstances of this story. I recollect, in particular, that to ascertain whether I was telling a probable tale, I went into Perthshire, to see whether King James could actually have ridden from the banks of Loch Vennachar to Stirling Castle within the time supposed in the poem, and had the pleasure to satisfy myself that it was quite practicable.

After a considerable delay, *The Lady of the Lake* appeared in June, 1810; and its success was certainly so extraordinary as to induce me for the moment to conclude that I had at last fixed a nail in the proverbially inconstant wheel of Fortune, whose stability in behalf of an individual who had so boldly courted her favors for three successive times had not as yet been shaken. I had attained, perhaps, that degree of reputation at which prudence, or certainly timidity, would have made a halt, and discontinued efforts by which I was far more likely to diminish my fame than to increase it. But, as the celebrated John Wilkes is said to have explained to his late Majesty, that he himself, amid his full tide of popularity, was never a Wilkite, so I can, with honest truth, exculpate myself from having been at any time a partisan of my own poetry, even when it was in the highest fashion with the million. It must not be supposed that I was either so ungrateful, or so superabundantly candid, as to despise or scorn the value of those whose voice had elevated me so much higher than my own opinion told me I deserved. I felt, on the contrary, the more grateful to the public, as receiving that from partiality to me, which I could not have claimed from merit; and I endeavored to deserve the partiality, by continuing such exertions as I was capable of for their amusement.

It may be that I did not, in this continued course of scribbling, consult either the interest of the public or my own. But the former had effectual means of defending themselves, and could, by their coldness, sufficiently check any approach to intrusion; and for myself, I had now for several years dedicated my hours so much to literary labor that I should have felt difficulty in employing myself otherwise; and so, like Dogberry, I generously bestowed all my tediousness on the public, comforting myself with the reflection that, if posterity should think me undeserving of the favor with which I was regarded by my contemporaries, "they could not but say I *had* the crown," and had enjoyed for a time that popularity which is so much coveted.

I conceived, however, that I held the distinguished situation I had obtained, however unworthily, rather like the champion of pugilism,[1]

[1] Lockhart quotes Byron, *Don Juan*, xi. 55:

"In twice five years the 'greatest living poet,'
Like to the champion in the fisty ring,
Is called on to support his claim, or show it,
Although 't is an imaginary thing," etc

on the condition of being always ready to show proofs of my skill, than in the manner of the champion of chivalry, who performs his duties only on rare and solemn occasions. I was in any case conscious that I could not long hold a situation which the caprice, rather than the judgment, of the public, had bestowed upon me, and preferred being deprived of my precedence by some more worthy rival, to sinking into contempt for my indolence, and losing my reputation by what Scottish lawyers call the *negative prescription.* Accordingly, those who choose to look at the Introduction to *Rokeby*, will be able to trace the steps by which I declined as a poet to figure as a novelist; as the ballad says, Queen Eleanor sunk at Charing Cross to rise again at Queenhithe.

It only remains for me to say that, during my short pre-eminence of popularity, I faithfully observed the rules of moderation which I had resolved to follow before I began my course as a man of letters. If a man is determined to make a noise in the world, he is as sure to encounter abuse and ridicule, as he who gallops furiously through a village must reckon on being followed by the curs in full cry. Experienced persons know that in stretching to flog the latter, the rider is very apt to catch a bad fall; nor is an attempt to chastise a malignant critic attended with less danger to the author. On this principle, I let parody, burlesque, and squibs find their own level; and while the latter hissed most fiercely, I was cautious never to catch them up, as schoolboys do, to throw them back against the naughty boy who fired them off, wisely remembering that they are in such cases apt to explode in the handling. Let me add, that my reign[1] (since Byron has so called it) was marked by some instances of good-nature as well as patience. I never refused a literary person of merit such services in smoothing his way to the public as were in my power; and I had the advantage, rather an uncommon one with our irritable race, to enjoy general favor without incurring permanent ill-will, so far as is known to me, among any of my contemporaries.

W. S.

ABBOTSFORD, *April*, 1830.

Our limits do not permit us to add any extended selections from the many critical notices of the poem. The verdict of Jeffrey, in the *Edinburgh Review*, on its first appearance, has been generally endorsed: —

"Upon the whole, we are inclined to think more highly of *The Lady of the Lake* than of either of its author's former publications [the *Lay* and *Marmion*]. We are more sure, however, that it has fewer faults than that it has greater beauties; and as its beauties bear a strong resemblance to those with which the public has been already made familiar in these celebrated works, we should not be surprised if its popularity were less splendid and remarkable. For our own parts, however, we are of opinion that it will be oftener read hereafter than either of them; and that, if it had appeared first in the series, their reception would have been less favorable than that which it has experienced. It is more

[1] "Sir Walter reigned before me," etc. (*Don Juan*, xi. 57)

polished in its diction, and more regular in its versification; the story is constructed with infinitely more skill and address; there is a greater proportion of pleasing and tender passages, with much less antiquarian detail; and, upon the whole, a larger variety of characters, more artfully and judiciously contrasted. There is nothing so fine, perhaps, as the battle in *Marmion*, or so picturesque as some of the scattered sketches in the *Lay;* but there is a richness and a spirit in the whole piece which does not pervade either of those poems, — a profusion of incident and a shifting brilliancy of coloring that reminds us of the witchery of Ariosto, and a constant elasticity and occasional energy which seem to belong more peculiarly to the author now before us."

CANTO FIRST.

Each canto is introduced by one or more Spenserian stanzas,[1] forming a kind of prelude to it. Those prefixed to the first canto serve as an introduction to the whole poem, which is "inspired by the spirit of the old Scottish minstrelsy."

2. *Witch-elm.* The broad-leaved or wych elm (*Ulmus montana*), indigenous to Scotland. Forked branches of the tree were used in the olden time as divining-rods, and riding switches from it were supposed to insure good luck on a journey. In the closing stanzas of the poem (vi. 846) it is called the "wizard elm." Tennyson (*In Memoriam*, 89) refers to

> "Witch-elms that counterchange the floor
> Of this flat lawn with dusk and bright."

Saint Fillan was a Scotch abbot of the seventh century who became famous as a saint. He had two *springs*, which appear to be confounded by some editors of the poem. One was at the eastern end of Loch Earn, where the pretty modern village of St. Fillans now stands, under the shadow of Dun Fillan, or *St. Fillan's Hill*, six hundred feet high, on the top of which the saint used to say his prayers, as the marks of his knees in the rock still testify to the credulous. The other spring is at another village called St. Fillans, nearly thirty miles to the westward, just outside the limits of our map, on the road to Tyndrum. In this *Holy Pool*, as it is called, insane folk were dipped with certain ceremonies, and then left bound all night in the open air. If they were found loose the next morning, they were supposed to have been cured. This treatment was practised as late as 1790, according to Pennant, who adds that the patients were generally found in the morning relieved of their troubles — by death. Another writer, in 1843, says that the pool is still visited, not by people of the vicinity, who have no faith in

[1] The *Spenserian stanza*, first used by Spenser in his *Faerie Queene*, consists of eight lines of ten syllables, followed by a line of twelve syllables, the accents throughout being on the even syllables (the so-called *iambic* measure). There are three sets of rhymes: one for the first and third lines; another for the second, fourth, fifth, and seventh; and a third for the sixth, eighth, and ninth.

its virtue, but by those from distant places. Scott alludes to this spring in *Marmion*, i. 29:

> "Thence to Saint Fillan's blessed well,
> Whose springs can frenzied dreams dispel,
> And the crazed brain restore."

3. *And down the fitful breeze*, etc. The original MS. reads:

> "And on the fitful breeze thy numbers flung,
> Till envious ivy, with her verdant ring,
> Mantled and muffled each melodious string, —
> O Wizard Harp, still must thine accents sleep?"

10. *Caledon.* Caledonia, the Roman name of Scotland.

14. *Each according pause.* That is, each pause in the singing. In *Marmion*, ii. 11, *according* is used of music that fills the intervals of other music:

> "Soon as they neared his turrets strong,
> The maidens raised Saint Hilda's song,
> And with the sea-wave and the wind
> Their voices, sweetly shrill, combined,
> And made harmonious close;
> Then, answering from the sandy shore,
> Half-drowned amid the breakers' roar,
> According chorus rose."

The MS. reads here:

> "At each according pause thou spokest aloud
> Thine ardent sympathy sublime and high."

28. *The stag at eve had drunk his fill.* The metre of the poem proper is *iambic*, that is, with the accent on the even syllables, and *octosyllabic*, or eight syllables to the line.

29. *Monan's rill.* St. Monan was a Scotch martyr of the fourth century. We can find no mention of any *rill* named for him.

31. *Glenartney.* A valley to the north-east of Callander, with *Benvoirlich* (which rises to the height of 3180 feet) on the north, and *Uam-Var* (see 53 below) on the south, separating it from the valley of the Teith. It takes its name from the Artney, the stream flowing through it.

32. *His beacon red.* The figure is an appropriate one in describing this region, where fires on the hill-tops were so often used as signals in the olden time. Cf. the *Lay*, iii. 379:

> "And soon a score of fires, I ween,
> From height, and hill, and cliff, were seen,
> Each with warlike tidings fraught;
> Each from each the signal caught," etc.

34. *Deep-mouthed.* Cf. Shakespeare, 1 *Hen. VI.* ii. 4. 12: "Between two dogs, which hath the deeper mouth;" and *T. of S.* ind. 1. 18: "the deep-mouthed brach" (that is, hound).

The MS. reads:

> "The bloodhound's notes of heavy bass
> Resounded hoarsely up the pass."

35. *Resounded . . . rocky.* The poet often avails himself of "apt alliteration's artful aid," as here, and in the next two lines; most frequently in pairs of words.

38. *As Chief*, etc. Note here, as often, the simile put *before* that which it illustrates,—an effective rhetorical, though not the logical, arrangement.

45. *Beamed frontlet.* Antlered forehead.

46. *Adown.* An instance of a purely poetical word, not admissible in prose.

49. *Chase.* Here put for those engaged in the chase; as in 101 and 171, below. One of its regular meanings is the *object* of the chase, or the animal pursued.

53. *Uam-Var.* "Ua-Var, as the name is pronounced, or more properly *Uaigh-mor*, is a mountain to the north-east of the village of Callander, in Menteith, deriving its name, which signifies the great den, or cavern, from a sort of retreat among the rocks on the south side, said, by tradition, to have been the abode of a giant. In latter times, it was the refuge of robbers and banditti, who have been only extirpated within these forty or fifty years. Strictly speaking, this stronghold is not a cave, as the name would imply, but a sort of small enclosure, or recess, surrounded with large rocks and open above head. It may have been originally designed as a toil for deer, who might get in from the outside, but would find it difficult to return. This opinion prevails among the old sportsmen and deer-stalkers in the neighborhood" (Scott).

54. *Yelled.* Note the emphatic force of the inversion, as in 59 below. Cf. 38 above.

Opening. That is, barking on view or scent of the game; a hunting term. Cf. Shakespeare, *M. W.* iv. 2. 209: "If I bark out thus upon no trail, never trust me when I open again."

The description of the echo which follows is very spirited.

66. *Cairn.* Literally, a heap of stones; here put poetically for the rocky point which the falcon takes as a look-out.

69. *Hurricane.* A metaphor for the wild rush of the hunt.

71. *Linn.* Literally, a deep pool; but often = cataract, as in *Bracklinn*, ii. 270 below (cf. vi. 488), and sometimes = precipice.

73. *On the lone wood.* Note the musical variation in the measure here; the 1st, 3d, and 4th syllables being accented instead of the 2d and 4th. It is occasionally introduced into iambic metre with admirable effect. Cf. 85 and 97 below.

76. *The cavern*, etc. See on 53 above.

80. *Perforce.* A poetical word. See on 46 above.

84. *Shrewdly.* Severely, keenly; a sense now obsolete. *Shrewd* originally meant evil, mischievous. Cf. Shakespeare, *A. Y. L.* v. 4. 179, where it is said that those

> "That have endur'd shrewd days and nights with us
> Shall share the good of our returned fortune."

In Chaucer (*Tale of Melibœus*) we find, "The prophete saith: Flee shrewdnesse, and do goodnesse" (referring to *Ps.* xxxiv. 14).

89. *Menteith.* The district in the southwestern part of Perthshire, watered by the Teith.

91. *Mountain and meadow*, etc. See on 35 above. *Moss* is used in

the North-of-England sense of a boggy or peaty district, like the famous Chat Moss between Liverpool and Manchester.

93. *Lochard.* Loch Ard is a beautiful lakelet, about five miles south of Loch Katrine. On its eastern side is the scene of Helen Macgregor's skirmish with the King's troops in *Rob Roy;* and near its head, on the northern side, is a waterfall, which is the original of Flora MacIvor's favorite retreat in *Waverley.* *Aberfoyle* is a village about a mile and a half to the east of the lake.

95. *Loch Achray.* A lake between Loch Katrine and Loch Vennachar, lying just beyond the pass of the Trosachs.

97. *Benvenue.* A mountain, 2386 feet in height, on the southern side of Loch Katrine.

98. *With the hope.* The MS. has "with the *thought,*" and "flying *hoof*" in the next line.

102. *'T were.* It would be. Cf. Shakespeare, *Macb.* ii. 2. 73: "To know my deed, 't were best not know myself."

103. *Cambusmore.* The estate of a family named Buchanan, whom Scott frequently visited in his younger days. It is about two miles from Callander, on the wooded banks of the Keltie, a tributary of the Teith.

105. *Benledi.* A mountain, 2882 feet high, northwest from Callander. The name is said to mean "Mountain of God."

106. *Bochastle's heath.* A moor between the east end of Loch Vennachar and Callander. See also on v. 298 below.

107. *The flooded Teith.* The Teith is formed by streams from Loch Voil and from Loch Katrine (by way of Loch Achray and Loch Vennachar), which unite at Callander. It joins the Forth near Stirling.

111. *Vennachar.* As the map shows, this "Lake of the Fair Valley" is the most eastern of the three lakes around which the scenery of the poem lies. It is about five miles long and a mile and a half wide.

112. *The Brigg of Turk.* This *brig,* or *bridge* (cf. Burns's poem of *The Brigs of Ayr*), is over a stream that comes down from Glenfinlas and flows into the one connecting Lochs Achray and Vennachar. According to Graham, it is "the scene of the death of a wild boar famous in Celtic tradition."

114. *Unbated.* Cf. Shakespeare, *M. of V.* ii. 6. 11:

> "Where is the horse that doth untread again
> His tedious measures with the unbated fire
> That he did pace them first?"

115. *Scourge and steel.* Whip and spur. *Steel* is often used for the sword (as in v. 239 below: "foeman worthy of their steel"), the figure being of the same sort as here — "the material put for the thing made of it." Cf. v. 479 below.

117. *Embossed.* An old hunting term. George Turbervile, in his *Noble Art of Venerie or Hunting* (A. D. 1576), says: "When the hart is foamy at the mouth, we say, that he is emboss'd." Cf. Shakespeare, *T. of S.* ind. 1. 17: "Brach Merriman, the poor cur, is emboss'd;" and *A. and C.* iv. 13. 3:

> "the boar of Thessaly
> Was never so emboss'd."

120. *Saint Hubert's breed.* Scott quotes Turbervile here: "The hounds which we call Saint Hubert's hounds are commonly all blacke, yet neuertheless, the race is so mingled at these days, that we find them of all colours. These are the hounds which the abbots of St. Hubert haue always kept some of their race or kind, in honour or remembrance of the saint, which was a hunter with S. Eustace. Whereupon we may conceiue that (by the grace of God) all good huntsmen shall follow them into paradise."

127. *Quarry.* The animal hunted; another technical term. Shakespeare uses it in the sense of a heap of slaughtered game; as in *Cor.* i. 1. 202:

> "Would the nobility lay aside their ruth,
> And let me use my sword, I'd make a quarry
> With thousands of these quarter'd slaves," etc.

Cf. Longfellow, *Hiawatha:*

> "Seldom stoops the soaring vulture
> O'er his quarry in the desert."

130. *Stock.* Tree-stump. Cf. *Job*, xiv. 8.

133. *Turn to bay.* Like *stand at bay*, etc., a term used when the stag, driven to extremity, turns round and faces his pursuers. Cf. Shakespeare, 1 *Hen. VI.* iv. 2. 52, where it is used figuratively (as in vi. 525 below):

> "Turn on the bloody hounds with heads of steel,
> And make the cowards stand aloof at bay;"

and *T. of S.* v. 2. 56: "'T is thought your deer does hold you at a bay," etc.

137. *For the death-wound*, etc. Scott has the following note here:

"When the stag turned to bay, the ancient hunter had the perilous task of going in upon, and killing or disabling, the desperate animal. At certain times of the year this was held particularly dangerous, a wound received from a stag's horn being then deemed poisonous, and more dangerous than one from the tusks of a boar, as the old rhyme testifies:

> 'If thou be hurt with hart, it brings thee to thy bier,
> But barber's hand will boar's hurt heal, therefore thou need'st not fear.'

At all times, however, the task was dangerous, and to be adventured upon wisely and warily, either by getting behind the stag while he was gazing on the hounds, or by watching an opportunity to gallop roundly in upon him, and kill him with the sword. See many directions to this purpose in the *Booke of Hunting*, chap. 41. Wilson, the historian, has recorded a providential escape which befell him in this hazardous sport, while a youth, and follower of the Earl of Essex:

'Sir Peter Lee, of Lime, in Cheshire, invited my lord one summer to hunt the stagg. And having a great stagg in chase, and many gentlemen in the pursuit, the stagg took soyle. And divers, whereof I was one, alighted, and stood with swords drawne, to have a cut at him, at his coming out of the water. The staggs there being wonderfully fierce and dangerous, made us youths more eager to be at him. But he escaped us all. And it was my misfortune to be hindered of my coming nere him, the way being sliperie, by a falle; which gave occasion to some, who did not know mee, to speak as if I had falne for feare. Which being told mee, I left the stagg, and followed the gentleman who [first] spake it. But I found him of that cold temper, that it seems his words made an escape from him; as by his denial and repentance it appeared. But this made mee more violent in the pursuit of the stagg, to recover my reputation. And I happened to be the only horseman in, when the dogs sett him up at bay; and approaching near him on horsebacke, he broke through the dogs, and run at mee, and tore my horse's side with his hornes, close by my thigh. Then I quitted my horse, and grew more cunning (for the dogs had sette him up againe), stealing behind him with my sword, and cut his hamstrings; and then got upon his back, and cut his throate; which, as I was doing, the company came in, and blamed my rashness for running such a hazard' (*Peck's Desiderata Curiosa*, ii. 464)."

138. *Whinyard.* A short stout sword or knife; the same as the *whinger* of the *Lay of Last Minstrel*, v. 7:

> "And whingers, now in friendship bare
> The social meal to part and share,
> Had found a bloody sheath."

142. *Turned him.* In Elizabethan, and still more in earlier English, personal pronouns were often used reflexively; and this, like many other old constructions, is still used in poetry.

145. *Trosachs.* "The *rough* or *bristled* territory" (Graham); the wild district between Lochs Katrine and Vennachar. The name is now especially applied to the pass between Lochs Katrine and Achray.

147. *Close couched.* That is, *as he lay* close couched, or hidden. Such ellipses are common in poetry.

150. *Amain.* With *main*, or full force. We still say "with might and main."

151. *Chiding.* An example of the old sense of the word as applied to any oft-repeated noise; originally a figurative use of *chide* (intransitive) as expressing "loud or impassioned utterance of anger, displeasure, etc." Shakespeare uses it of the barking of dogs in *M. N. D.* iv. i. 120:

> "never did I hear
> Such gallant chiding;"

of the wind, as in *A. Y. L.* ii. 1. 7: "And churlish chiding of the winter's wind;" and of the sea, as in 1 *Hen. IV.* iii. 1. 45:

> "the sea
> That chides the banks of England;"

and *Hen. VIII.* iii. 2. 197: "the chiding flood."

163. *The banks of Seine.* James visited France in 1536, and sued for the hand of Magdalen, daughter of Francis I. He married her the following spring, but she died a few months later. He then married Mary of Guise, whom he had doubtless seen while in France.

166. *Woe worth the chase.* That is, woe be to it. This *worth* is from the A. S. *weorthan*, to become. Cf. Spenser, *F. Q.* ii. 6. 32:

> "Wo worth the man,
> That first did teach the cursed steele to bight
> In his owne flesh, and make way to the living spright!"

See also *Ezek.* xxx. 2.

180. *And on the hunter*, etc. The MS. reads:

> "And on the hunter hied his pace,
> To meet some comrades of the chase;"

and the 1st ed. retains "pace" and "chase."

184. *The western waves*, etc. This description of the Trosachs was written amid the scenery it delineates, in the summer of 1809. The *Quarterly Review* (May, 1810) says of the poet: "He sees everything with a painter's eye. Whatever he represents has a character of individuality, and is drawn with an accuracy and minuteness of discrimination which we are not accustomed to expect from mere verbal description. It is because Mr. Scott usually delineates those objects with which he is perfectly familiar that his touch is so easy, correct, and animated. The rocks, the ravines, and the torrents which he exhibits are not the imperfect sketches of a hurried traveller, but the finished studies of a resident artist." See also on 278 below.

Ruskin (*Modern Painters*, iii. 278) refers to "the love of *color*" as a leading element in Scott's love of beauty. He might have quoted the present passage among the illustrations he adds.

195. *The native bulwarks*, etc. The MS. has "The mimic castles of the pass."

196. *The tower*, etc. Cf. *Gen.* xi. 1–9.

198. *The rocky*. The 1st ed. has "Their rocky," etc.

204. *Nor were*, etc. The MS. reads: "Nor were these mighty bulwarks bare."

208. *Dewdrop sheen*. Not "dewdrops sheen," or "dewdrops' sheen," as sometimes printed. *Sheen* = shining, bright; as in v. 10 below. Cf. Spenser, *F. Q.* ii. 1. 10. "so faire and sheene;" *Id.* iii. 4. 51: "in top of heaven sheene," etc. See Wb. The MS. has here: "Bright glistening with the dewdrop sheen."

212. *Boon*. Bountiful. Cf. Milton, *P. L.* iv. 242:

> "Flowers worthy of Paradise, which not nice art
> In beds and curious knots, but nature boon
> Pour'd forth profuse on hill, and dale, and plain."

See also *P. L.* ix. 793: "jocund and boon."

217. *Bower*. In the old sense of chamber, lodging-place; as in iv. 413 and vi. 218 below. Cf. Spenser, *F. Q.* iii. 1. 58:

> "Eftesoones long waxen torches weren light
> Unto their bowres to guyden every guest."

For *clift* (= cleft), the reading of the 1st ed., every other edition that we have seen reads "cliff." See *Addendum*, p. 269.

219. *Emblems of punishment and pride*. See on iii. 19 below.

222, 223. Note the imperfect rhyme in *breath* and *beneath*. Cf. 224–25, 256–57, 435–36, 445–46 below. Such instances are comparatively rare in Scott's poetry. Some rhymes that *appear* to be imperfect are to be explained by peculiarities of Scottish pronunciation. See on 363 below.

227. *Shattered*. The MS. has "scathed;" also "rugged arms athwart the sky" in 229, and "twinkling" for *glistening* in 231. The 1st ed has "scattered" for *shattered;* corrected in the *Errata*.

231. *Streamers*. Of ivy or other vines.

238. *Affording*, etc. The MS. reads:

"Affording scarce such breadth of flood
As served to float the wild-duck's brood."

247. *Emerging*, etc. The MS. has "Emerging dry-shod from the wood."

254. *And now, to issue from the glen*, etc. "Until the present road was made through the romantic pass which I have presumptuously attempted to describe in the preceding stanzas, there was no mode of issuing out of the defile called the Trosachs, excepting by a sort of ladder, composed of the branches and roots of trees" (Scott).

263. *Loch Katrine*. In a note to *The Fair Maid of Perth*, Scott derives the name from the *Catterans*, or Highland robbers, that once infested the shores of the lake. Others make it "the Lake of the Battle," in memory of some prehistoric conflict.

267. *Livelier*. Because in motion; like *living gold* above.

270. *Benvenue*. See on 97 above.

271. *Down to*. Most editions misprint "down on."

272. *Confusedly*. A trisyllable; as in ii. 161 below, and in the *Lay*, iii. 337: "And helms and plumes, confusedly tossed."

274. *Wildering*. Bewildering. Cf. Dryden, *Aurungzebe*, i. 1: "wilder'd in the way," etc. See also 434 and v. 22 below.

275. *His ruined sides*, etc. The MS. reads:

"His ruined sides and fragments hoar,
While on the north to middle air."

277. *Ben-an*. This mountain, 1800 feet high, is north of the Trosachs, separating that pass from Glenfinlas.

278. *From the steep*, etc. The MS. reads:

"From the high promontory gazed
The stranger, awe-struck and amazed."

The *Critical Review* (Aug. 1820) remarks of this portion of the poem (184 fol.): "Perhaps the art of landscape-painting in poetry has never been displayed in higher perfection than in these stanzas, to which rigid criticism might possibly object that the picture is somewhat too minute, and that the contemplation of it detains the traveller somewhat too long from the main purpose of his pilgrimage, but which it would be an act of the greatest injustice to break into fragments and present by piecemeal. Not so the magnificent scene which bursts upon the bewildered hunter as he emerges at length from the dell, and commands at one view the beautiful expanse of Loch Katrine."

281. *Churchman*. In its old sense of one holding high office in the church. Cf. Shakespeare, 2 *Hen. VI*. i. 3. 72, where Cardinal Beaufort is called "the imperious churchman," etc.

285. *Cloister*. Monastery; originally, the covered walk around the inner court of the building.

287. *Chide*. Here, figuratively, in the modern sense. See on 151 above.

290. *Should lave*. The 1st ed. has "did lave," which is perhaps to be preferred.

294. *While the deep peal's*. For the measure, see on 73 above.

300. *To friendly feast*, etc. The MS. has "To hospitable feast and hall."

302. *Beshrew*. May evil befall (see on *shrewdly*, 84 above); a mild imprecation, often used playfully and even tenderly. Cf. Shakespeare 2 *Hen. IV*. ii. 3. 45:

> "Beshrew your heart,
> Fair daughter, you do draw my spirits from me
> With new lamenting ancient oversights!"

305. *Some mossy bank*, etc. The MS. reads:

> "And hollow trunk of some old tree
> My chamber for the night must be."

313. *Highland plunderers*. "The clans who inhabited the romantic regions in the neighborhood of Loch Katrine were, even until a late period, much addicted to predatory excursions upon their Lowland neighbors" (Scott).

317. *Fall the worst*. If the worst befall that can happen. Cf. Shakespeare, *M. of V*. i. 2. 96: "an the worst fall that ever fell, I hope I shall make shift to go without him."

319. *But scarce again*, etc. The MS. reads:

> "The bugle shrill again he wound,
> And lo! forth starting at the sound;"

and below:

> "A little skiff shot to the bay.
> The hunter left his airy stand,
> And when the boat had touched the sand,
> Concealed he stood amid the brake,
> To view this Lady of the Lake."

336. *Strain*. The 1st ed. has a comma after *strain*, and a period after *art* in 340. The ed. of 1821 points as in the text.

342. *Naiad*. Water nymph.

343. *And ne'er did Grecian chisel*, etc. The MS. reads:

> "A finer form, a fairer face,
> Had never marble Nymph or Grace,
> That boasts the Grecian chisel's trace;"

and in 359 below, "a stranger tongue.'

353. *Measured mood*. The formal manner required by court etiquette.

360. *Dear*. This is the reading of the 1st ed. and almost every other that we have seen. We are inclined, however, to believe that Scott wrote "clear." The facsimiles of his handwriting show that his *d*'s and *cl*'s might easily be confounded by a compositor.

363. *Snood*. The fillet or ribbon with which the Scotch maidens bound their hair. See on iii. 114 below. It is the rich *materials* of *snood*, *plaid*, and *brooch* that betray her birth.

The rhyme of *plaid* with *maid* and *betrayed* is not imperfect, the Scottish pronunciation of *plaid* being like our *played*.

385. *One only*. For the inversion, cf. Shakespeare, *J. C*. i. 2. 157: "When there is in it but one only man;" Goldsmith, *D. V*. 39: "One only master grasps the whole domain," etc.

393. *Awhile she paused*, etc. The MS. reads:

> "A space she paused, no answer came,—
> 'Alpine, was thine the blast?' the name
> Less resolutely uttered fell,
> The echoes could not catch the swell.
> 'Nor foe nor friend,' the stranger said,
> Advancing from the hazel shade.
> The startled maid, with hasty oar,
> Pushed her light shallop from the shore."

and just below:

> "So o'er the lake the swan would spring,
> Then turn to prune its ruffled wing."

404. *Prune*. Pick out damaged feathers and arrange the plumage with the bill Cf. Shakespeare, *Cymb*. v. 4. 118:

> "his royal bird
> Prunes the immortal wing," etc.

408. *Wont*. Are wont, or accustomed; now used only in the participle. The form here is the past tense of the obsolete *won*, or *wone*, to dwell. The present is found in Milton, *P. L.* vii. 457:

> "As from his lair the wild beast, where he wons
> In forest wild, in thicket, brake, or den."

Cf. Spenser, *Virgil's Gnat*:

> "Of Poets Prince, whether he woon beside
> Faire Xanthus sprincled with Chimæras blood,
> Or in the woods of Astery abide;"

and *Colin Clouts Come Home Againe*:

> "I weened sure he was our God alone,
> And only woond in fields and forests here."

See also iv. 278 and 298 below.

409. *Middle age*. As James died at the age of thirty (in 1542), this is not strictly true, but the portrait in other respects is quite accurate. He was fond of going about disguised, and some of his freaks of this kind are pleasantly related in Scott's *Tales of a Grandfather*. See on vi. 740 below.

425. *Slighting*, etc. "Treating lightly his need of food and shelter."

432. *At length*. The 1st ed. has "at last."

433. *That Highland halls were*, etc. The MS. has "Her father's hall was," etc.

434. *Wildered*. See on 274 above.

438. *A couch*. That is, the *heather* for it. Cf. 666 below.

441. *Mere*. Lake; as in *Windermere*, etc.

443. *Rood*. Cross, or crucifix. *By the rood* was a common oath; so *by the holy rood*, as in Shakespeare, *Rich. III*. iii. 2. 77, iv. 4. 165. Cf. the name of *Holyrood Palace* in Edinburgh. See ii. 221 below.

451. *Romantic*. The MS. has "enchanting."

457. *Yesternight*. We have lost this word, though we retain *yesterday*. Cf. *yester-morn* in v. 104 below. *As far* = as far back as.

460. *Was on*, etc. The MS. reads: "Is often on the future bent."

"If force of evidence could authorize us to believe facts inconsistent with the general laws of nature, enough might be produced in favor of the existence of the second-sight. It is called in Gaelic *Taishitaraugh*, from *Taish*, an unreal or shadowy appearance; and those possessed of the faculty are called *Taishatrin*, which may be aptly translated visionaries. Martin, a steady believer in the second-sight, gives the following account of it: —

'The second-sight is a singular faculty of seeing an otherwise invisible object without any previous means used by the person that uses it for that end: the vision makes such a lively impression upon the seers, that they neither see nor think of any thing else, except the vision, as long as it continues; and then they appear pensive or jovial, according to the object that was represented to them.

'At the sight of a vision, the eyelids of the person are erected, and the eyes continue staring until the object vanish. This is obvious to others who are by when the persons happen to see a vision, and occurred more than once to my own observation, and to others that were with me. . . .

'If a woman is seen standing at a man's left hand, it is a presage that she will be his wife, whether they be married to others, or unmarried at the time of the apparition.

'To see a spark of fire fall upon one's arm or breast is a forerunner of a dead child to be seen in the arms of those persons; of which there are several fresh instances. . . .

'To see a seat empty at the time of one's sitting in it, is a presage of that person's death soon after' (*Martin's Description of the Western Islands*, 1716, 8vo, p. 300, *et seq.*).

"To these particulars innumerable examples might be added, all attested by grave and credible authors. But, in despite of evidence which neither Bacon, Boyle, nor Johnson were able to resist, the *Taish*, with all its visionary properties, seems to be now universally abandoned to the use of poetry. The exquisitely beautiful poem of *Lochiel* will at once occur to the recollection of every reader" (Scott).

462. *Birchen.* Shaded by birches. Cf. Milton's "cedarn alleys" in *Comus*, 990.

464. *Lincoln green.* A cloth made in Lincoln, much worn by hunters.

467. *Heron.* The early eds. have "heron's."

475. *Errant-knight.* Knight-errant.

476. *Sooth.* True. We find *soothest* in Milton, *Comus*, 823. The noun *sooth* (truth) is more common, and still survives in *soothsayer* (teller of *hidden* truth). Cf. v. 64 below.

478. *Emprise.* Enterprise. Cf. Spenser, *F. Q.* ii. 7. 39: "But give me leave to follow my emprise," etc.

485. *His noble hand.* The MS. has "This gentle hand; and in the next line, "the oars he drew."

490. *Frequent.* Often; one of the many instances of the adjective used adverbially in the poem.

492. *The rocky isle.* It is still known as *Ellen's Isle.* "It is rather high, and irregularly pyramidal. It is mostly composed of dark-gray rocks, mottled with pale and gray lichens, peeping out here and there amid trees that mantle them, — chiefly light, graceful birches, intermingled with red-berried mountain ashes and a few dark-green, spiry

pines. The landing is beneath an aged oak; and, as did the Lady and the Knight, the traveller now ascends 'a clambering unsuspected road,' by rude steps, to the small irregular summit of the island. A more poetic, romantic retreat could hardly be imagined: it is unique. It is completely hidden, not only by the trees, but also by an undergrowth of beautiful and abundant ferns and the loveliest of heather" (*Hunnewell's Lands of Scott*).

500. *Winded.* Wound; used for the sake of the measure, as in v. 22 below. We find the participle *winded* in *Much Ado*, i. 1. 243, but it is = blown. The verb in that sense is derived from the noun *wind* (air in motion), and has no connection with *wind*, to turn. Cf. Wb

504. *Here for retreat*, etc. Scott has the following note here:

"The Celtic chieftains, whose lives were continually exposed to peril, had usually, in the most retired spot of their domains, some place of retreat for the hour of necessity, which, as circumstances would admit, was a tower, a cavern, or a rustic hut, in a strong and secluded situation. One of these last gave refuge to the unfortunate Charles Edward, in his perilous wanderings after the battle of Culloden.

'It was situated in the face of a very rough, high, and rocky mountain, called Letternilichk, still a part of Benalder, full of great stones and crevices, and some scattered wood interspersed. The habitation called the Cage, in the face of that mountain, was within a small thick bush of wood. There were first some rows of trees laid down, in order to level the floor for a habitation; and as the place was steep, this raised the lower side to an equal height with the other: and these trees, in the way of joists or planks, were levelled with earth and gravel. There were betwixt the trees, growing naturally on their own roots, some stakes fixed in the earth, which, with the trees, were interwoven with ropes, made of heath and birch twigs, up to the top of the Cage, it being of a round or rather oval shape; and the whole thatched and covered over with fog. The whole fabric hung, as it were, by a large tree, which reclined from the one end, all along the roof, to the other, and which gave it the name of the Cage; and by chance there happened to be two stones at a small distance from one another, in the side next the precipice, resembling the pillars of a chimney, where the fire was placed. The smoke had its vent out here, all along the fall of the rock, which was so much of the same color, that one could discover no difference in the clearest day' (*Home's History of the Rebellion*, Lond. 1802, 4to, p. 381)."

525. *Idæan vine.* Some have taken this to refer to the "red whortleberry," the botanical name of which is *Vaccinium vitis Idæa;* but as that is not a climber, it is more probable that the common vine is here meant. *Idæan* is from *Ida*, a mountain near ancient Troy (there was another in Crete), famous for its vines.

526. *Clematis.* The *Clematis vitalba*, one of the popular English names of which is *virgin-bower*.

528. *And every favored plant could bear.* That is, *which* could endure. This ellipsis of the relative was very common in Elizabethan English. Cf Shakespeare, *M. for M.* ii. 2. 23: "I have a brother is condemned to die;" *Rich. II.* ii. 2. 128: "The hate of those love not the king," etc See also [illegible] iii. [illegible]

532. *On heaven and on thy lady call.* This is said *gayly*, or sportively, as keeping up the idea of a knight-errant. Cf. 475 above.

542. *Careless.* See on 490 above.

546. *Target.* Buckler; the *targe* of iii. 445, etc. See Scott's note on v. 380 below.

548. *Store.* Stored, laid up; an obsolete adjective. Cf. iii. 3 below, and see also on vi. 124.

551. *And there the wild-cat's*, etc. The MS. reads:

> "There hung the wild-cat's brindled hide,
> Above the elk's branched brow and skull,
> And frontlet of the forest bull."

559. *Garnish forth.* Cf. *furnish forth* in 442 above.

566. *Brook.* Bear, endure; now seldom used except with reference to what is endured against one's will or inclination. It seems to be a favorite word with Scott.

573. *Ferragus or Ascabart.* "These two sons of Anak flourished in romantic fable. The first is well known to the admirers of Ariosto by the name of Ferrau. He was an antagonist of Orlando, and was at length slain by him in single combat. . . . Ascapart, or Ascabart, makes a very material figure in the *History of Bevis of Hampton*, by whom he was conquered. His effigies may be seen guarding one side of the gate at Southampton, while the other is occupied by Bevis himself" (Scott).

580. *To whom, though more than kindred knew.* The MS. reads:

> "To whom, though more remote her claim,
> Young Ellen gave a mother's name."

She was the maternal aunt of Ellen, but was loved as a mother by her, or *more than* (such) *kindred* (usually) *knew* (in way of affection).

585. *Though all unasked*, etc. "The Highlanders, who carried hospitality to a punctilious excess, are said to have considered it as churlish to ask a stranger his name or lineage before he had taken refreshment. Feuds were so frequent among them, that a contrary rule would in many cases have produced the discovery of some circumstance which might have excluded the guest from the benefit of the assistance he stood in need of" (Scott).

591. *Snowdoun.* An old name of Stirling Castle. See vi. 789 below.

592. *Lord of a barren heritage.* "By the misfortunes of the earlier Jameses, and the internal feuds of the Scottish chiefs, the kingly power had become little more than a name. Each chief was a petty king in his own district, and gave just so much obedience to the king's authority as suited his convenience" (Taylor).

596. *Wot.* Knows; the present of the obsolete *wit* (the infinitive *to wit* is still used in legal forms), not of *weet*, as generally stated. See Mätzner, *Eng. Gram.* i. 382. Cf. Shakespeare, *Rich. III.* ii. 3. 18: "No, no, good friends, God wot." He also uses *wots* (as in *Hen. V.* iv. 1. 299) and a participle *wotting* (in *W. T.* iii. 2. 77).

602. *Require.* Request, ask; as in Elizabethan English. Cf. Shakespeare, *Hen. VIII.* ii. 4. 144: "In humblest manner I require your highness," etc.

603. *The elder lady's mien.* The MS. has "the mother's easy mien."

606. *Ellen, though more*, etc. The MS. reads:

> "Ellen, though more her looks betrayed
> The simple heart of mountain maid,
> In speech and gesture, form and grace,
> Showed she was come of gentle race;
> 'T was strange, in birth so rude, to find
> Such face, such manners, and such mind.
> Each anxious hint the stranger gave,
> The mother heard with silence grave."

616. *Weird women we*, etc. See on 35 above. *Weird* here = skilled in witchcraft; like the "weird sisters" of *Macbeth*. *Down* = hill (the Gaelic *dun*).

622. *A harp unseen*. Scott has the following note here:

"'"They [the Highlanders] delight much in musicke, but chiefly in harps and clairschoes of their own fashion. The strings of the clairschoes are made of brasse wire, and the strings of the harps of sinews; which strings they strike either with their nayles, growing long, or else with an instrument appointed for that use. They take great pleasure to decke their harps and clairschoes with silver and precious stones; the poore ones that cannot attayne hereunto, decke them with christall. They sing verses prettily compound, contayning (for the most part) prayses of valiant men. There is not almost any other argument, whereof their rhymes intreat. They speak the ancient French language, altered a little."[1]

'The harp and clairschoes are now only heard of in the Highlands in ancient song. At what period these instruments ceased to be used, is not on record; and tradition is silent on this head. But, as Irish harpers occasionally visited the Highlands and Western Isles till lately, the harp might have been extant so late as the middle of the present century. Thus far we know, that from remote times down to the present, harpers were received as welcome guests, particularly in the Highlands of Scotland; and so late as the latter end of the sixteenth century, as appears by the above quotation, the harp was in common use among the natives of the Western Isles. How it happened that the noisy and inharmonious bagpipe banished the soft and expressive harp, we cannot say; but certain it is, that the bagpipe is now the only instrument that obtains universally in the Highland districts' (*Campbell's Journey through North Britain*. London, 1808, 4to, i. 175).

"Mr. Gunn, of Edinburgh, has lately published a curious *Essay upon the Harp and Harp Music of the Highlands of Scotland*. That the instrument was once in common use there, is most certain. Cleland numbers an acquaintance with it among the few accomplishments which his satire allows to the Highlanders:—

> 'In nothing they're accounted sharp,
> Except in bagpipe or in harp.'"

624. *Soldier, rest!* etc. The metre of this song is *trochaic;* that is, the accents fall regularly on the odd syllables.

[1] Vide *Certayne Matters concerning the Realms of Scotland, etc., as they were Anno Domini* 1597. London, 1603.

631. *In slumber dewing.* That is, bedewing. For the metaphor, cf. Shakespeare, *Rich. III.* iv. 1. 84: "the golden dew of sleep;" and *J. C.* ii. 1. 230: "the honey-heavy dew of slumber."

635. *Morn of toil*, etc. The MS. has "Noon of hunger, night of waking;" and in the next line, "rouse" for *reach.*

638. *Pibroch.* "A Highland air, suited to the particular passion which the musician would either excite or assuage; generally applied to those airs that are played on the bagpipe before the Highlanders when they go out to battle" (Jamieson). Here it is put for the bagpipe itself. See also on ii. 363 below.

642. *And the bittern sound his drum.* Goldsmith (*D. V.* 44) calls the bird "the hollow-sounding bittern;" and in his *Animated Nature*, he says that of all the notes of waterfowl "there is none so dismally hollow as the booming of the bittern."

648. *She paused*, etc. The MS. has "She paused — but waked again the lay."

655. The MS. reads: "Slumber sweet our spells shall deal ye;" and in 657:

"Let our slumbrous spells { avail ye.
beguile ye."

657. *Reveillé.* The call to rouse troops or huntsmen in the morning.

669. *Forest sports.* The MS. has "mountain chase."

672. *Not Ellen's spell.* That is, not *even* Ellen's spell.

On the passage, cf. *Rokeby*, i. 2:

"Sleep came at length, but with a train
Of feelings true and fancies vain,
Mingling, in wild disorder cast,
The expected future with the past."

693. *Or is it all a vision now?* Lockhart quotes here Thomson's *Castle of Indolence:*

"Ye guardian spirits, to whom man is dear,
From these foul demons shield the midnight gloom:
Angels of fancy and of love, be near,
And o'er the blank of sleep diffuse a bloom:
Evoke the sacred shades of Greece and Rome,
And let them virtue with a look impart;
But chief, awhile, O! lend us from the tomb
Those long-lost friends for whom in love we smart,
And fill with pious awe and joy-mixt woe the heart.

"Or are you sportive? — bid the morn of youth
Rise to new light, and beam afresh the days
Of innocence, simplicity, and truth;
To cares estranged, and manhood's thorny ways.
What transport, to retrace our boyish plays,
Our easy bliss, when each thing joy supplied;
The woods, the mountains, and the warbling maze
Of the wild brooks!"

The *Critical Review* says of the following stanza (xxxiv): "Such a strange and romantic dream as may be naturally expected to flow from the extraordinary events of the past day. It might, perhaps, be quoted as one of Mr. Scott's most successful efforts in descriptive poetry. Some few lines of it are indeed unrivalled for delicacy and melancholy tenderness."

704. *Grisly.* Grim, horrible; an obsolete word, much used in old poetry. Cf. Spenser, *F. Q.* i. 5. 30: "her darke griesly looke;" Shakespeare, 1 *Hen. VI.* i. 4. 47: "My grisly countenance made others fly," etc. See also iv. 322, etc. below.

723. *Played,* etc. The MS. reads:

> "Played on { the bosom of the lake,
> Loch Katrine's still expanse;
> The birch, the wild rose, and the broom
> Wasted around their rich perfume . . .
> The birch-trees wept in balmy dew;
> The aspen slept on Benvenue;
> Wild were the heart whose passions' power
> Defied the influence of the hour."

724. *Passion's.* The reading of the 1st ed. and that of 1821; some recent eds. have "passions'."

738. *Orisons.* The 1st ed. has "orison" both here and in 740 (the ed. of 1821 only in the latter); but the word is almost invariably plural, both in poetry and prose — always in Shakespeare and Milton.

CANTO SECOND.

7. *A minstrel gray.* "That Highland chieftains, to a late period, retained in their service the bard, as a family officer, admits of very easy proof. The author of the *Letters from the North of Scotland,* an officer of engineers, quartered at Inverness about 1720, who certainly cannot be deemed a favorable witness, gives the following account of the office, and of a bard, whom he heard exercise his talent of recitation: — 'The bard is skilled in the genealogy of all the Highland families, sometimes preceptor to the young laird, celebrates in Irish verse the original of the tribe, the famous warlike actions of the successive heads, and sings his own lyricks as an opiate to the chief, when indisposed for sleep; but poets are not equally esteemed and honored in all countries. I happened to be a witness of the dishonour done to the muse, at the house of one of the chiefs, where two of these bards were set at a good distance, at the lower end of a long table, with a parcel of Highlanders of no extraordinary appearance, over a cup of ale. Poor inspiration! They were not asked to drink a glass of wine at our table, though the whole company consisted only of the *great man,* one of his near relations, and myself. After some little time, the chief ordered one of them to sing me a Highland song. The bard readily obeyed, and with a hoarse voice, and in a tune of few various notes, began, as I was told, one of his own lyricks; and when he had proceeded to the fourth or fifth stanza, I perceived, by the names of several persons, glens, and mountains, which I had known or heard of before, that it was an account of some clan battle. But in his going on, the chief (who piques himself upon his school-learning) at some particular passage, bid him cease, and cryed out, "There's nothing like that in Virgil

or Homer." I bowed, and told him I believed so. This you may believe was very edifying and delightful'" (Scott).

15. *Than men*, etc. "It is evident that the old bard, with his second-sight, has a glimmering notion who the stranger is. He speaks below [311] of 'courtly spy,' and James's speech had betrayed a knowledge of the Douglas" (Taylor).

20. *Battled.* The reading of the 1st ed. and that of 1821; "battle" in most others. Cf. i. 626 above.

22. *Where beauty*, etc. The MS. has "At tourneys where the brave resort." The reference is to the tournaments, "Where," as Milton says (*L'Allegro*, 119),

> "throngs of knights and barons bold,
> In weeds of peace, high triumphs hold,
> With store of ladies, whose bright eyes
> Rain influence, and judge the prize
> Of wit or arms, while both contend
> To win her grace whom all commend."

Cf. 87 below.

26. *Love's.* The reading of the 1st ed. and that of 1821; most eds. have "love."

29. *Plaided.* The plaid was properly the dress of a *Highlander*, though it was worn also in the Lowlands.

51. *The Harper on the islet beach.* "This picture is touched with the hand of the true poet" (Jeffrey).

56. *As from.* As *if* from. Cf. 64 and 83 below. This ellipsis was common in Elizabethan English. Cf. Shakespeare, *Macb.* ii. 2. 28:

> "One cried 'God bless us!' and 'Amen' the other,
> As they had seen me with these hangman's hands."

65. *In the last sound.* For the measure, see on i. 73 above.
69. *His fleet.* That is, of ducks. Cf. i. 239 above.
80. *Would scorn.* Who would scorn. See on i. 528 above.
84. *Turned him.* See on i. 142 above, and cf. 106 below.
86. *After.* Afterwards; as in Shakespeare, *Temp.* ii. 2. 10: "And after bite me," etc. The word is not now used adverbially of *time*, though we may say "he followed after," etc. The 1st ed. reads "that knight."

94. *Parts.* Departs; as often in poetry and earlier English. Cf. Goldsmith, *D. V.* 171: "Beside the bed where parting life was laid;" Gray, *Elegy*, 1: "the knell of parting day," etc. On the other hand, *depart* was used in the sense of *part.* In the Marriage Service "till death us do part" is a corruption of "till death us depart." Wiclif's Bible, in *Matt.* xix. 6, has "therfor a man departe not that thing that God hath ioyned."

103. *Another step*, etc. The MS. has "The loveliest Lowland fair to spy;" and the 1st ed. reads "The step of parting fair to spy."

109. *The Græme.* Scott has the following note here: "The ancient and powerful family of Graham (which, for metrical reasons, is here spelled after the Scottish pronunciation) held extensive possessions in the counties of Dumbarton and Stirling. Few families can boast of more historical renown, having claim to three of the most remarkable

characters in the Scottish annals. Sir John the Græme, the faithful and undaunted partaker of the labors and patriotic warfare of Wallace, fell in the unfortunate field of Falkirk, in 1298. The celebrated Marquis of Montrose, in whom De Retz saw realized his abstract idea of the heroes of antiquity, was the second of these worthies. And, notwithstanding the severity of his temper, and the rigor with which he executed the oppressive mandates of the princes whom he served, I do not hesitate to name as the third, John Græme, of Claverhouse, Viscount of Dundee, whose heroic death, in the arms of victory, may be allowed to cancel the memory of his cruelty to the non-conformists, during the reigns of Charles II. and James II."

112. *Bower.* The word meant a chamber (see on i. 217 above), and was often used of the ladies' apartments in a house. *In hall and bower* = among men and women. The words are often thus associated. Cf. Spenser, *Astrophel*, 28: "Merily masking both in bowre and hall," etc.

115. *Arose.* The 1st ed. misprints "Across;" not noted in the *Errata.*

126. *And the proud march.* See on i. 73 above.

131. *Saint Modan.* A Scotch abbot of the 7th century. Scott says here: "I am not prepared to show that Saint Modan was a performer on the harp. It was, however, no unsaintly accomplishment; for Saint Dunstan certainly did play upon that instrument, which retaining, as was natural, a portion of the sanctity attached to its master's character, announced future events by its spontaneous sound. 'But labouring once in these mechanic arts for a devout matrone that had sett him on work, his violl, that hung y him on the wall, of its own accord, without anie man's helpe, distinctly sounded this anthime: *Gaudent in cœlis animæ sanctorum qui Christi vestigia sunt secuti; et quia pro eius amore sanguinem suum fuderunt, ideo cum Christo gaudent æternum.* Whereat all the companie being much astonished, turned their eyes from beholding him working, to looke on that strange accident. . . . Not long after, manie of the court that hitherunto had born a kind of fayned friendship towards him, began now greatly to envie at his progresse and rising in goodness, using manie crooked, backbiting meanes to diffame his vertues with the black markes of hypocrisie. And the better to authorise their calumnie, they brought in this that happened in the violl, affirming it to have been done by art magick. What more? this wicked rumour encreased dayly, till the king and others of the nobilitie taking hould thereof, Dunstan grew odious in their sight. Therefore he resolued to leaue the court, and goe to Elphegus, surnamed the Bauld, then bishop of Winchester, who was his cozen. Which his enemies understanding, they layd wayte for him in the way, and hauing throwne him off his horse, beate him, and dragged him in the durt in the most miserable manner, meaning to have slaine him, had not a companie of mastiue dogges, that came unlookt uppon them, defended and redeemed him from their crueltie. When with sorrow he was ashamed to see dogges more humane than they. And giuing thankes to Almightie God, he sensibly againe perceaued that the tunes of his violl had giuen him a warning of future accidents' (*Flower of*

the Lives of the most renowned Saincts of England, Scotland, and Ireland, by the R. Father Hierome Porter. Doway, 1632. 4to. tome i. p. 438).

"The same supernatural circumstance is alluded to by the anonymous author of *Grim, the Collier of Croydon:*

> '―――――― [*Dunstan's harp sounds on the wall.*]
> '*Forrest.* Hark, hark, my lord, the holy abbot's harp
> Sounds by itself so hanging on the wall!
> '*Dunstan.* Unhallow'd man, that scorn'st the sacred rede,
> Hark, how the testimony of my truth
> Sounds heavenly music with an angel's hand,
> To testify Dunstan's integrity,
> And prove thy active boast of no effect.'"

141. *Bothwell's bannered hall.* The picturesque ruins of Bothwell Castle stand on the banks of the Clyde, about nine miles above Glasgow. Some parts of the walls are 14 feet thick, and 60 feet in height. They are covered with ivy, wild roses, and wall-flowers.

> "The tufted grass lines Bothwell's ancient hall,
> The fox peeps cautious from the creviced wall,
> Where once proud Murray, Clydesdale's ancient lord,
> A mimic sovereign, held the festal board."

142. *Ere Douglases, to ruin driven.* Scott says: "The downfall of the Douglases of the house of Angus, during the reign of James V., is the event alluded to in the text. The Earl of Angus, it will be remembered, had married the queen dowager, and availed himself of the right which he thus acquired, as well as of his extensive power, to retain the king in a sort of tutelage, which approached very near to captivity. Several open attempts were made to rescue James from this thraldom, with which he was well known to be deeply disgusted; but the valor of the Douglases, and their allies, gave them the victory in every conflict. At length, the king, while residing at Falkland, contrived to escape by night out of his own court and palace, and rode full speed to Stirling Castle, where the governor, who was of the opposite faction, joyfully received him. Being thus at liberty, James speedily summoned around him such peers as he knew to be most inimical to the domination of Angus, and laid his complaint before them, says Pitscottie, 'with great lamentations: showing to them how he was holden in subjection, thir years bygone, by the Earl of Angus, and his kin and friends, who oppressed the whole country, and spoiled it, under the pretence of justice and his authority; and had slain many of his lieges, kinsmen, and friends, because they would have had it mended at their hands, and put him at liberty, as he ought to have been, at the counsel of his whole lords, and not have been subjected and corrected with no particular men, by the rest of his nobles: Therefore, said he, I desire, my lords, that I may be satisfied of the said earl, his kin, and friends; for I avow, that Scotland shall not hold us both, while [*i. e.* till] I be revenged on him and his.

'The lords hearing the king's complaint and lamentation, and also the great rage, fury, and malice, that he bure toward the Earl of Angus, his kin and friends, they concluded all and thought it best, that he should be summoned to underly the law; if he fand not caution, nor yet compear himself, that he should be put to the horn, with all his kin and friends, so many as were contained in the letters. And further, the lords ordained, by advice of his majesty, that his brother and friends should be summoned to find caution to underly the law within a certain day, or else be put to the horn. But the earl appeared not, nor none for him; and so he was put to the horn, with all his kin and friends: so many as were contained in the summons, that compeared not, were banished, and holden traitors to the king.'"

159. *From Tweed to Spey.* From the *Tweed*, the southern boundary of Scotland, to the *Spey*, a river far to the north in Inverness-shire; that is, from one end of the land to the other.

170. *Reave.* Tear away. The participle *reft* is still used, at least in poetry. Cf. Shakespeare, *V. and A.* 766: "Or butcher-sire that reaves his son of life" (that is, bereaves); Spenser, *F. Q.* i. 3. 36: "He to him lept, in minde to reave his life;" *Id.* ii. 8. 15: "I will him reave of arms," etc.

178. *It drinks*, etc. The MS. has "No blither dewdrop cheers the rose."

195, 196. *To see . . . dance.* This couplet is not in the MS.

200. *The Lady of the Bleeding Heart.* The *bleeding heart* was the cognizance of the Douglas family. Robert Bruce, on his death-bed, bequeathed his heart to his friend, the good Lord James, to be borne in war against the Saracens. "He joined Alphonso, King of Leon and Castile, then at war with the Moorish chief Osurga, of Granada, and in a keen contest with the Moslems he flung before him the casket containing the precious relic, crying out, 'Onward as thou wert wont, thou noble heart, Douglas will follow thee.' Douglas was slain, but his body was recovered, and also the precious casket, and in the end Douglas was laid with his ancestors, and the heart of Bruce deposited in the church of Melrose Abbey" (*Burton's Hist. of Scotland*).

201. *Fair.* The 1st ed. (and probably the MS., though not noted by Lockhart) has "Gay."

203. *Yet is this*, etc. The MS. and 1st ed. read:

> "This mossy rock, my friend, to me
> Is worth gay chair and canopy."

205. *Footstep.* The reading of the 1st and other early eds.; "footsteps" in recent ones.

206. *Strathspey.* A Highland dance, which takes its name from the *strath*, or broad valley, of the *Spey* (159 above).

213. *Clan-Alpine's pride.* "The *Siol Alpine*, or race of Alpine, includes several clans who claimed descent from Kenneth McAlpine, an ancient king. These are the Macgregors, the Grants, the Mackies, the Mackinnans, the MacNabs, the MacQuarries, and the Macaulays. Their common emblem was the pine, which is now confined to the Macgregors" (Taylor).

214. *Loch Lomond.* This beautiful lake, "the pride of Scottish lakes," is about 23 miles in length and 5 miles in its greatest breadth. At the southern end are many islands, one of which, *Inch-Cailliach* (the Island of Women, so called from a nunnery that was once upon it), was the burial-place of Clan-Alpine. See iii. 191 below.

216. *A Lennox foray.* That is, a raid in the lands of the Lennox family, bordering on the southern end of Loch Lomond. On the island of Inch-Murrin, the ruins of Lennox Castle, formerly a residence of the Earls of Lennox, are still to be seen. There was another of their strongholds on the shore of the lake near Balloch, where the modern Balloch Castle now stands.

217. *Her glee.* The 1st ed. misprints "his glee;" not noted in the *Errata.*

220. *Black Sir Roderick.* Roderick *Dhu,* or the *Black,* as he was called.

221. *In Holy-Rood a knight he slew.* That is, in Holyrood Palace. "This was by no means an uncommon occurrence in the Court of Scotland; nay, the presence of the sovereign himself scarcely restrained the ferocious and inveterate feuds which were the perpetual source of bloodshed among the Scottish nobility" (Scott).

223. *Courtiers give place,* etc. The MS. reads:

> "Courtiers give place with heartless stride
> Of the retiring homicide."

227. *Who else,* etc. The MS. has the following couplet before this line:

> "Who else dared own the kindred claim
> That bound him to thy mother's name?"

229. *The Douglas,* etc. Scott says here: "The exiled state of this powerful race is not exaggerated in this and subsequent passages. The hatred of James against the race of Douglas was so inveterate, that numerous as their allies were, and disregarded as the regal authority had usually been in similar cases, their nearest friends, even in the most remote part of Scotland, durst not entertain them, unless under the strictest and closest disguise. James Douglas, son of the banished Earl of Angus, afterwards well known by the title of Earl of Morton, lurked, during the exile of his family, in the north of Scotland, under the assumed name of James Innes, otherwise *James the Grieve* (*i.e.* reve or bailiff). 'And as he bore the name,' says Godscroft, 'so did he also execute the office of a grieve or overseer of the lands and rents, the corn and cattle of him with whom he lived.' From the habits of frugality and observation which he acquired in his humble situation, the historian traces that intimate acquaintance with popular character which enabled him to rise so high in the state, and that honorable economy by which he repaired and established the shattered estates of Angus and Morton (*History of the House of Douglas,* Edinburgh, 1743, vol. ii. p. 160)."

235. *Guerdon.* Reward; now rarely used except in poetry. Cf. Spenser, *F. Q.* i. 10. 59: "That glory does to them for guerdon graunt," etc.

236. *Dispensation.* As Roderick and Ellen were cousins, they could not marry without a dispensation from the Pope.

251. *Orphan.* Referring to *child,* not to *she,* as its position indicates.

254. *Shrouds.* Shields, protects. Cf. Spenser, *F. Q.* i. 1. 6: "And this faire couple eke to shroud themselves were fain" (that is, from the

rain). So the noun = shelter, protection; as in Shakespeare, *A. and C.* iii. 13. 71: "put yourself under his shroud," etc. See also on 757 below.

260. *Maronnan's cell.* "The parish of *Kilmaronock*, at the eastern extremity of Loch Lomond, derives its name from a *cell*, or chapel, dedicated to Saint Maronock, or Marnock, or Maronnan, about whose sanctity very little is now remembered" (Scott). *Kill* = cell; as in *Colmekill* (*Macb.* ii. 4. 33), "the cell of Columba," now known as Icolmkill, or Iona.

270. *Bracklinn's thundering wave.* This beautiful cascade is on the Keltie, a mile from Callander. The height of the fall is about fifty feet. "A few years ago a marriage party of Lowland peasants met with a tragic end here, two of them having tumbled into the broken, angry waters, where they had no more chance of life than if they had dropped into the crater of Hecla" (Black).

271. *Save.* Unless; here followed by the subjunctive.

274. *Claymore.* The word means "a large sword" (Gaelic *claidheamh*, sword, and *more*, great).

294. *Shadowy plaid and sable plume.* Appropriate to Roderick *Dhu*. See on 220 above.

303. *Woe the while.* Woe be to the time, alas the time! Cf. Shakespeare, *J. C.* i. 3. 82: "But, woe the while! our fathers' minds are dead," etc. See also on i. 166 above.

306. *Tine-man.* "Archibald, the third Earl of Douglas, was so unfortunate in all his enterprises, that he acquired the epithet of 'tine-man,' because he *tined*, or lost, his followers in every battle which he fought. He was vanquished, as every reader must remember, in the bloody battle of Homildon-hill, near Wooler, where he himself lost an eye, and was made prisoner by Hotspur. He was no less unfortunate when allied with Percy, being wounded and taken at the battle of Shrewsbury. He was so unsuccessful in an attempt to besiege Roxburgh Castle, that it was called the 'Foul Raid,' or disgraceful expedition. His ill fortune left him indeed at the battle of Beaugé, in France; but it was only to return with double emphasis at the subsequent action of Vernoil, the last and most unlucky of his encounters, in which he fell, with the flower of the Scottish chivalry, then serving as auxiliaries in France, and about two thousand common soldiers, A. D. 1424" (Scott).

307. *What time*, etc. That is, at the time when Douglas allied himself with Percy in the rebellion against Henry IV. of England. See Shakespeare, 1 *Hen. IV.*

309. *Did, self-unscabbarded*, etc. Scott says here:

"The ancient warriors, whose hope and confidence rested chiefly in their blades, were accustomed to deduce omens from them, especially from such as were supposed to have been fabricated by enchanted skill, of which we have various instances in the romances and legends of the time. The wonderful sword Skofnung, wielded by the celebrated Hrolf Kraka, was of this description. It was deposited in the tomb of the monarch at his death, and taken from thence by Skeggo, a celebrated pirate, who bestowed it upon his son-in-law, Kormak, with the following curious directions: '"The manner of using it will appear strange to you. A small bag is attached to it, which take heed not to violate. Let not the rays of the sun touch the upper part of the handle, nor unsheathe it, unless thou art ready for battle. But when thou comest to the place of fight, go aside from the rest, grasp and extend the sword, and breathe upon it. Then a small worm will creep out of the handle; lower the handle, that he may more easily return into it." Kormak, after having received the sword, returned home to his mother. He showed the sword, and attempted to draw it, as unnecessarily as ineffectually, for he could not pluck it out of the sheath. His mother, Dalla, exclaimed, "Do not despise the counsel given to thee, my son." Kormak, however, repeating his efforts, pressed down the handle with his feet, and tore off the bag, when Skofnung emitted a hollow groan; but still he could not unsheathe the sword. Kormak then went out with Bessus, whom he had challenged to fight with him, and drew apart at the place of combat. He sat down upon the ground, and ungirding the sword, which he bore above his vestments, did not remember to shield the hilt from the rays of the sun. In vain he endeavored to draw it, till he placed his foot against the hilt; then the worm issued from it. But Kormak did not rightly handle the weapon, in consequence whereof good fortune deserted it. As he unsheathed Skofnung, it emitted a hollow murmur' (*Bartholini de Causis Contemptæ a Danis adhuc Gentilibus Mortis, Libri Tres.* Hafniæ, 1689, 4to, p. 574).

"To the history of this sentient and prescient weapon, I beg leave to add, from memory, the following legend, for which I cannot produce any better authority. A young nobleman, of high hopes and fortune, chanced to lose his way in the town which he inhabited, the capital, if I mistake not, of a German province. He had accidentally involved himself among the narrow and winding streets of a suburb, inhabited by the lowest order of the people, and an approaching thunder-shower determined him to ask a short refuge in the most decent habitation that was near him. He knocked at the door, which was opened by a tall man, of a grisly and ferocious aspect, and sordid dress. The stranger was readily ushered to a chamber, where swords, scourges, and machines, which seemed to be implements of torture, were suspended on the wall. One of these swords dropped from its scabbard, as the nobleman, after a moment's hesitation, crossed the threshold. His host immediately stared at him with such a marked expression, that the young man could not help demanding his name and business, and the meaning of his looking at him so fixedly. 'I am,' answered the man, 'the public executioner of this city; and the incident you have observed is a sure augury that I shall, in discharge of my duty, one day cut off your head with the weapon which has just now spontaneously unsheathed itself.' The nobleman lost no time in leaving his place of refuge; but, engaging in some of the plots of the period, was shortly after decapitated by that very man and instrument.

"Lord Lovat is said, by the author of the *Letters from Scotland* (vol. ii. p. 214), to have affirmed that a number of swords that hung up in the hall of the mansion-house, leaped of themselves out of the scabbard at the instant he was born. The story passed current among his clan, but, like that of the story I have just quoted, proved an unfortunate omen."

311. *If courtly spy hath*, etc. The 1st ed. has "If courtly spy, and harbored," etc. The ed. of 1821 reads "had harbored."

319. *Beltane.* The first of May, when there was a Celtic festival in honor of the sun. *Beltane* = *Beal-tein*, or the fire of Beal, a Gaelic name for the sun. It was celebrated by kindling fires on the hill-tops at night, and other ceremonies, followed by dances and merry-making. Cf. 410 below. See also *The Lord of the Isles*, i. 8: "The shepherd lights his beltane-fire;" and *Glenfinlas:*

> "But o'er his hills, in festal day,
> How blazed Lord Ronald's beltane-tree!"

323. *But hark!* etc. "The moving picture — the effect of the sounds — and the wild character and strong peculiar nationality of the whole procession, are given with inimitable spirit and power of expression" (Jeffrey).

327. *The canna's hoary beard.* The down of the *canna*, or cotton-grass.

335. *Glengyle.* A valley at the northern end of Loch Katrine.

337. *Brianchoil.* A promontory on the northern shore of the lake.

342. *Spears, pikes, and axes.* The 1st ed. and that of 1821 have *Spears*, but all the recent ones misprint "Spear." The "Globe" ed. has "Spear, spikes," etc.

343. *Tartans.* The checkered woollen cloth so much worn in Scotland. Curiously enough, the name is not Gaelic but French. See Jamieson or Wb.

Brave. Fine, beautiful; the same word as the Scottish *braw.* Cf. Shakespeare, *Sonn.* 12. 2: "And see the brave day sunk in hideous night;" *Ham.* ii. 2. 312: "This brave o'erhanging firmament," etc It is often used of dress, as also is *bravery* (= finery); as in *T. of S.* iv. 3. 57: "With scarfs and fans and double change of bravery." See also Spenser, *Mother Hubberds Tale*, 858: "Which oft maintain'd his masters braverie" (that is, dressed as well as his master).

351. *Chanters.* The *pipes* of the bagpipes, to which long ribbons were attached.

357. *The sounds.* Misprinted "the sound" in the ed. of 1821, and all the more recent eds. that we have seen. Cf. 363 below.

363. *Those thrilling sounds*, etc. Scott says here: "The connoisseurs in pipe-music affect to discover in a well-composed pibroch, the imitative sounds of march, conflict, flight, pursuit, and all the 'current of a heady fight.' To this opinion Dr. Beattie has given his suffrage, in the following elegant passage: — 'A *pibroch* is a species of tune, peculiar, I think, to the Highlands and Western Isles of Scotland. It is performed on a bagpipe, and differs totally from all other music. Its rhythm is so irregular, and its notes, especially in the quick movement, so mixed and huddled together, that a stranger finds it impossible to reconcile his ear to it, so as to perceive its modulation. Some of these pibrochs, being intended to represent a battle, begin with a grave motion, resembling a march; then gradually quicken into the onset; run off with noisy confusion, and turbulent rapidity, to imitate the conflict and pursuit; then swell into a few flourishes of triumphant joy

and perhaps close with the wild and slow wailings of a funeral procession' (*Essay on Laughter and Ludicrous Composition*, chap. iii. note)."

367. *Hurrying.* Referring to *their*, or rather to the *them* implied in that word.

392. *The burden bore.* That is, sustained the *burden*, or chorus, of the song. Cf. Shakespeare, *Temp.* i. 2. 381: "And, sweet sprites, the burden bear."

399. *Hail to the Chief*, etc. The metre of the song is *dactylic;* the accents being on the 1st, 4th, 7th, and 10th syllables. It is little used in English. Tennyson's *Charge of the Light Brigade* and Longfellow's *Skeleton in Armor* are familiar examples of it.

405. *Bourgeon.* Bud. Cf. Fairfax, *Tasso*, vii. 76: "When first on trees bourgeon the blossoms soft;" and Tennyson, *In Memoriam*, 115:

> "Now burgeons every maze of quick
> About the flowering squares," etc.

408. *Roderigh Vich Alpine dhu.* "Besides his ordinary name and surname, which were chiefly used in the intercourse with the Lowlands, every Highland chief had an epithet expressive of his patriarchal dignity as head of the clan, and which was common to all his predecessors and successors, as Pharaoh to the kings of Egypt, or Arsaces to those of Parthia. This name was usually a patronymic, expressive of his descent from the founder of the family. Thus the Duke of Argyll is called MacCallum More, or the *son of Colin the Great.* Sometimes, however, it is derived from armorial distinctions, or the memory of some great feat; thus Lord Seaforth, as chief of the Mackenzies, or Clan-Kennet, bears the epithet of Caber-fae, or *Buck's Head*, as representative of Colin Fitzgerald, founder of the family, who saved the Scottish king, when endangered by a stag. But besides this title, which belonged to his office and dignity, the chieftain had usually another peculiar to himself, which distinguished him from the chieftains of the same race. This was sometimes derived from complexion, as *dhu* or *roy;* sometimes from size, as *beg* or *more;* at other times, from some peculiar exploit, or from some peculiarity of habit or appearance. The line of the text therefore signifies,

> Black Roderick, the descendant of Alpine.

"The song itself is intended as an imitation of the *jorrams*, or boat songs, of the Highlanders, which were usually composed in honor of a favorite chief. They are so adapted as to keep time with the sweep of the oars, and it is easy to distinguish between those intended to be sung to the oars of a galley, where the stroke is lengthened and doubled, as it were, and those which were timed to the rowers of an ordinary boat" (Scott).

410. *Beltane.* See on 319 above.

415. *Roots him.* See on i. 142 above.

416. *Breadalbane.* The district north of Loch Lomond and around Loch Tay. The seat of the Earl of Breadalbane is Taymouth Castle, near the northern end of Loch Tay.

For *Menteith*, see on i. 89 above.

419. *Glen Fruin.* A valley to the southwest of Loch Lomond. The ruins of the castle of Benuchara, or *Bannochar* (see on 422 just below), still overhang the entrance to the glen.

Glen Luss is another valley draining into the lake, a few miles from Glen Fruin, and *Ross-dhu* is on the shore of the lake, midway between the two. Here stands a tower, the only remnant of the ancient castle of the family of Luss, which became merged in that of Colquhoun.

BEN LOMOND, FROM LUSS.

422. *The best of Loch Lomond,* etc. Scott has the following note here:

"The Lennox, as the district is called which encircles the lower extremity of Loch Lomond, was peculiarly exposed to the incursions of the mountaineers, who inhabited the inaccessible fastnesses at the upper end of the lake, and the neighboring district of Loch Katrine. These were often marked by circumstances of great ferocity, of which the noted conflict of Glen Fruin is a celebrated instance. This was a clan-battle, in which the Macgregors, headed by Allaster Macgregor, chief of the clan, encountered the sept of Colquhouns, commanded by Sir Humphry Colquhoun of Luss. It is on all hands allowed that the action was desperately fought, and that the Colquhouns were defeated with slaughter, leaving two hundred of their name dead upon the field. But popular tradition has added other horrors to the tale. It is said that Sir Humphry Colquhoun, who was on horseback, escaped to the Castle of Benechra, or Bannochar, and was next day dragged out and murdered by the victorious Macgregors in cold blood. Buchanan of Auchmar, however, speaks of his slaughter as a subsequent event, and as perpetrated by the Macfarlanes. Again, it is reported that the Macgregors murdered a number of youths, whom report of the intended battle had brought to be spectators, and whom the Colquhouns, anxious for their safety, had shut up in a barn to be out of danger. One account of the Macgregors denies this circumstance entirely; another ascribes it to the savage and bloodthirsty disposition of a single individual, the bastard brother of the Laird of Macgregor, who amused himself with this second massacre of the innocents, in express disobedience to the chief, by whom he was left their guardian during the pursuit of the Colquhouns. It is added that Macgregor bitterly lamented this atrocious action, and prophesied the ruin which it must bring upon their ancient clan. . . .

"The consequences of the battle of Glen Fruin were very calamitous to the family of Macgregor, who had already been considered as an unruly clan. The widows of the slain Colquhouns, sixty, it is said, in number, appeared in doleful procession before the king at Stirling, each riding upon a white palfrey, and bearing in her hand the bloody shirt of her husband displayed upon a pike. James VI. was so much moved by the complaints of this 'choir of mourning dames,' that he let loose his vengeance against the Macgregors without either bounds or moderation. The very name of the clan was proscribed, and those by whom it had been borne were given up to sword and fire, and absolutely hunted down by bloodhounds like wild beasts. Argyll and the Campbells, on the one hand, Montrose, with the Grahames and Buchanans, on the other, are said to have been the chief instruments in suppressing this devoted clan. The Laird of Macgregor surrendered to the former, on condition that he would take him out of Scottish ground. But, to use Birrel's expression, he kept 'a Highlandman's promise;' and, although he fulfilled his word to the letter, by carrying him as far as Berwick, he afterwards brought him back to Edinburgh, where he was executed with eighteen of his clan (*Birrel's Diary*, 2d Oct. 1603). The clan Gregor being thus driven to utter despair, seem to have renounced the laws from the benefit of which they were excluded, and their depredations produced new acts of council, confirming the severity of their proscription, which had only the effect of rendering them still more united and desperate. It is a most extraordinary proof of the ardent and invincible spirit of clanship, that, notwithstanding the repeated proscriptions providently ordained by the legislature, 'for the *timeous preventing* the disorders and oppression that may fall out by the said name and clan of Macgregors, and their followers,' they were, in 1715 and 1745, a potent clan, and continue to subsist as a distinct and numerous race."

426. *Leven-glen.* The valley of the *Leven*, which connects Loch Lomond with the Clyde.

431. *The rosebud.* That is, Ellen. "Note how this song connects Allan's forebodings with Roderick's subsequent offer" (Taylor).

444. *And chorus wild*, etc. The MS. has "The chorus to the chieftain's fame."

476. *Weeped.* The form is used for the rhyme. Cf. note on i. 508 above.

477. *Nor while*, etc. The MS. reads:

> "Nor while on Ellen's faltering tongue
> Her filial greetings eager hung,
> Marked not that awe (affection's proof)
> Still held yon gentle youth aloof;

INCHMAHONE ISLAND, LAKE MENTEITH.

"No! not till Douglas named his name,
Although the youth was Malcolm Græme.
Then with flushed cheek and downcast eye,
Their greeting was confused and shy."

495. *Bothwell.* See on 141 above.

497. *Percy's Norman pennon.* Taken in the raid which led to the battle of Otterburn, in Northumberland, in the year 1388, and which forms the theme of the ballads of *Chevy Chase.*

501. *Pomp.* Triumphal procession; the original meaning of *pomp.*

504. *The waned crescent.* The Buccleuch family, defeated in their attempt to restore the king. For the crescent as the Buccleuch badge, see our ed. of *Lay of Last Minstrel*, p. 225.

506. *Blantyre.* A priory, the ruins of which are still to be seen on a height above the Clyde, opposite Bothwell Castle.

521. *The dogs*, etc. The MS. has "The dogs with whimpering notes repaid."

525. *Unhooded.* The falcon was carried on the wrist, with its head covered, or *hooded*, until the prey was seen, when it was *unhooded* for flight. Cf. vi. 665 below.

526. *Trust.* Believe me.

527. *Goddess.* The MS. has "huntress;" that is, Diana.

534. *Stature fair.* The reading of the 1st ed. and that of 1821; "stature tall" in most of the other eds.

541. *The ptarmigan.* A *white* bird.

543. *Menteith.* See on i. 89 above.

548. *Ben Lomond.* This is much the highest (3192 feet) of the mountains on the shores of Loch Lomond. The following lines on the ascent

were scratched upon the window-pane of the old inn at Tarbet a hundred years or more ago:

> "Trust not at first a quick adventurous pace;
> Six miles its top points gradual from its base;
> Up the high rise with panting haste I past,
> And gained the long laborious steep at last;
> More prudent thou — when once you pass the deep,
> With cautious steps and slow ascend the steep."

549. *Not a sob.* That is, without *panting*, or getting out of breath, like the degenerate modern tourist.

574. *Glenfinlas.* A wooded valley between Ben-an and Benledi, the entrance to which is between Lochs Achray and Vennachar. It is the scene of Scott's ballad, *Glenfinlas, or Lord Ronald's Coronach.* A mile from the entrance are the falls of the *Hero's Targe.* See iv. 84 below.

577. *Still a royal ward.* Still under age, with the king for guardian.

583. *Strath-Endrick.* A valley to the southeast of Loch Lomond, drained by Endrick Water.

584. *Peril aught.* Incur any peril. Milton uses the verb intransitively in *Reason of Church Government*, ii. 3: "it may peril to stain itself."

587. *Not in action.* The 1st ed. has "nor in action."

594. *News.* Now generally used as a singular; but in old writers both as singular and as plural. Cf. Shakespeare, *K. John*, iii. 4. 164: "at that news he dies;" and *Id.* v. 7. 65: "these dead news," etc.

601. *As.* As if. See on 56 above.

606. *Glozing.* That *glosses* over the truth, not plain and outspoken. Sometimes it means to flatter, or deceive with smooth words; as in Spenser, *F. Q.* iii. 8. 14:

> "For he could well his glozing speaches frame
> To such vaine uses that him best became;"

Smith, *Sermons* (A. D. 1609): "Every smooth tale is not to be believed; and every glosing tongue is not to be trusted;" Milton, *P. L.* iii. 93: "his glozing lies;" *Id.* ix. 549: "So glozed the Tempter;" *Comus*, 161: "well-placed words of glozing courtesy," etc.

615. *The King's vindictive pride*, etc. Scott says here: "In 1529, James made a convention at Edinburgh, for the purpose of considering the best mode of quelling the Border robbers, who, during the license of his minority, and the troubles which followed, had committed many exorbitances. Accordingly he assembled a flying army of ten thousand men, consisting of his principal nobility and their followers, who were directed to bring their hawks and dogs with them, that the monarch might refresh himself with sport during the intervals of military execution. With this array he swept through Ettrick Forest, where he hanged over the gate of his own castle Piers Cockburn of Henderland, who had prepared, according to tradition, a feast for his reception. He caused Adam Scott of Tushielaw also to be executed, who was distinguished by the title of King of the Border. But the most noted victim of justice during that expedition was John Armstrong of Gilnockie, famous in Scottish song, who, confiding in his own supposed

innocence, met the King, with a retinue of thirty-six persons, all of whom were hanged at Carlenrig, near the source of the Teviot. The effect of this severity was such, that, as the vulgar expressed it, 'the rush-bush kept the cow,' and 'thereafter was great peace and rest a long time, wherethrough the King had great profit; for he had ten thousand sheep going in the Ettrick Forest in keeping by Andrew Bell, who made the King as good count of them as they had gone in the bounds of Fife' (*Pitscottie's History*, p. 153)."

623. *Meggat's mead.* The *Meggat*, or *Megget*, is a mountain stream flowing into the *Yarrow*, a branch of the *Ettrick*, which is itself a branch of the Tweed. The *Teviot* is also a branch of the Tweed.

627. *The dales*, etc. The MS. has "The dales where clans were wont to bide."

634. *By fate of Border chivalry.* Scott says: "James was, in fact, equally attentive to restrain rapine and feudal oppression in every part of his dominions. 'The King past to the isles, and there held justice courts, and punished both thief and traitor according to their demerit. And also he caused great men to show their holdings, wherethrough he found many of the said lands in non-entry; the which he confiscate and brought home to his own use, and afterwards annexed them to the crown, as ye shall hear. Syne brought many of the great men of the isles captive with him, such as Mudyart, M'Connel, M'Loyd of the Lewes, M'Neil, M'Lane, M'Intosh, John Mudyart, M'Kay, M'Kenzie, with many other that I cannot rehearse at this time. Some of them he put in ward and some in court, and some he took pledges for good rule in time coming. So he brought the isles, both north and south, in good rule and peace; wherefore he had great profit, service, and obedience of people a long time hereafter; and as long as he had the heads of the country in subjection, they lived in great peace and rest, and there was great riches and policy by the King's justice' (*Pitscottie*, p. 152)."

638. *Your counsel.* That is, give me your counsel. *Streight* = strait.

659. *The Bleeding Heart.* See on 200 above.

662. *Quarry.* See on i. 127 above.

672. *To wife.* For wife. Cf. Shakespeare, *Temp.* ii. 1. 75: "such a paragon to their queen;" *Rich. II.* iv. 1. 306: "I have a king here to my flatterer," etc. See also *Matt.* iii. 9, *Luke*, iii. 8, etc.

674. *Enow.* The old plural of *enough;* as in Shakespeare, *Hen. V.* iv. 1. 240: "we have French quarrels enow," etc.

678. *The Links of Forth.* The windings of the Forth between Stirling and Alloa.

679. *Stirling's porch.* The gate of Stirling Castle.

683. *Blench.* Start, shrink.

685. *Heat.* Misprinted "heart" in many eds.

690. *From pathless glen.* The MS. has "from hill and glen."

692. *There are who have.* For the ellipsis, cf. Shakespeare, *Temp.* ii 1. 262: "There be that can rule Naples," etc. See also iii. 10 below.

694. *That beetled o'er.* Cf. *Hamlet*, i. 4. 71:

> "the dreadful summit of the cliff
> That beetles o'er his base into the sea."

696. *Their dangerous dream.* The MS. has "their desperate dream."

702. *Battled.* Battlemented; as in vi. 7 below.

703. *It waved.* That it waved; an ellipsis very common in Elizabethan and earlier English. Cf. 789 below.

708. *Astound.* Astounded. This contraction of the participle (here used for the sake of the rhyme) was formerly not uncommon in verbs ending in *d* and *t*. Thus in Shakespeare we find the participles *bloat* (*Ham.* iii. 4. 182), *enshield* (*M. for M.* ii. 4. 80), *taint* (1 *Hen. VI.* v. 3. 183), etc.

710. *Crossing.* Conflicting.

716. *Ere.* The 1st ed. misprints "e'er."

731. *Level.* Aim; formerly a technical term. Cf. 2 *Hen. IV.* iii. 2. 286: "The foeman may with as great aim level at the edge of a penknife," etc.

747. *Nighted.* Benighted. It is to be regarded as a contraction of that word; like *lated* for *belated* in *Macbeth*, iii. 3. 6, etc. *Nighted* (= dark, black) in *Hamlet*, i. 2. 68 ("thy nighted colour") is an adjective formed from the noun *night*.

757. *Checkered shroud.* Tartan plaid. The original meaning of *shroud* (see Wb.) was garment.

763. *Parting.* Departing. See on 94 above.

768. *So deep*, etc. According to Lockhart, the MS. reads:

> "The deep-toned anguish of despair
> Flushed, in fierce jealousy, to air;"

but we suspect that "Flushed" should be "Flashed."

774. *So lately.* At the "Beltane game" (319 above).

781. *Thus as they strove*, etc. The MS. reads:

> "Thus, as they strove, each better hand
> Grasped for the dagger or the brand."

786. *I hold*, etc. Scott has the following note on the last page of the 1st ed.: "The author has to apologize for the inadvertent appropriation of a whole line from the tragedy of *Douglas*: 'I hold the first who strikes my foe.'"

789. *His daughter's hand*, etc. For the ellipsis of *that*, see on 703 above. *Deemed* is often misprinted "doomed."

791. *Sullen and slowly*, etc. The MS. reads:

> "Sullen and slow the rivals bold
> Loosed at his hest their desperate hold,
> But either still on other glared," etc.

795. *Brands.* A pet word with Scott. Note how often it has been used already in the poem.

798. *As faltered.* See on 601 above.

801. *Pity 't were*, etc. Scott says here: "Hardihood was in every respect so essential to the character of a Highlander, that the reproach of effeminacy was the most bitter which could be thrown upon him. Yet it was sometimes hazarded on what we might presume to think slight grounds. It is reported of old Sir Ewen Cameron of Lochiel, when upwards of seventy, that he was surprised by night on a hunting or military expedition. He wrapped him in his plaid, and lay con-

tentedly down upon the snow, with which the ground happened to be covered. Among his attendants, who were preparing to take their rest in the same manner, he observed that one of his grandsons, for his better accommodation, had rolled a large snow-ball, and placed it below his head. The wrath of the ancient chief was awakened by a symptom of what he conceived to be degenerate luxury. 'Out upon thee,' said he, kicking the frozen bolster from the head which it supported, 'art thou so effeminate as to need a pillow?' The officer of engineers, whose curious Letters from the Highlands have been more than once quoted, tells a similar story of Macdonald of Keppoch, and subjoins the following remarks: 'This and many other stories are romantick; but there is one thing, that at first thought might seem very romantick, of which I have been credibly assured, that when the Highlanders are constrained to lie among the hills, in cold dry windy weather, they sometimes soak the plaid in some river or burn (*i. e.* brook), and then holding up a corner of it a little above their heads, they turn themselves round and round, till they are enveloped by the whole mantle. They then lay themselves down on the heath, upon the leeward side of some hill, where the wet and the warmth of their bodies make a steam, like that of a boiling kettle. The wet, they say, keeps them warm by thickening the stuff, and keeping the wind from penetrating. I must confess I should have been apt to question this fact, had I not frequently seen them wet from morning to night, and, even at the beginning of the rain, not so much as stir a few yards to shelter, but continue in it without necessity, till they were, as we say, wet through and through. And that is soon effected by the looseness and spunginess of the plaiding; but the bonnet is frequently taken off, and wrung like a dishclout, and then put on again. They have been accustomed from their infancy to be often wet, and to take the water like spaniels, and this is become a second nature, and can scarcely be called a hardship to them, insomuch that I used to say, they seemed to be of the duck kind, and to love water as well. Though I never saw this preparation for sleep in windy weather, yet, setting out early in a morning from one of the huts, I have seen the marks of their lodging, where the ground has been free from rime or snow, which remained all round the spot where they had lain' (*Letters from Scotland*, Lond. 1754, 8vo, ii. p. 108)."

809. *His henchman.* Scott quotes again the *Letters from Scotland* (ii. 159): "This officer is a sort of secretary, and is to be ready, upon all occasions, to venture his life in defence of his master; and at drinking-bouts he stands behind his seat, at his haunch, from whence his title is derived, and watches the conversation, to see if any one offends his patron. An English officer being in company with a certain chieftain, and several other Highland gentlemen, near Killichumen, had an argument with the *great man;* and both being well warmed with usky [whiskey], at last the dispute grew very hot. A youth who was henchman, not understanding one word of English, imagined his chief was insulted, and thereupon drew his pistol from his side, and snapped it at the officer's head: but the pistol missed fire, otherwise it is more than probable he might have suffered death from the hand of that little vermin. But it is very disagreeable to an Englishman over a bottle

with the Highlanders, to see every one of them have his gilly, that is, his servant, standing behind him all the while, let what will be the subject of conversation."

829. *On the morn.* Modifying *should circle*, not the nearer verb *had sworn.*

831. *The Fiery Cross.* See on iii. 18 below.

846. *Point.* Point out, appoint. Cf. Shakespeare, *Sonn.* 14. 6:

> "Nor can I fortune to brief minutes tell,
> Pointing to each his thunder, rain, and wind."

The word in this and similar passages is generally printed "'point" by modern editors, but it is not a contraction of *appoint.*

860. *Then plunged,* etc. The MS. has "He spoke, and plunged into the tide."

862. *Steered him.* See on i. 142 above.

865, 866. *Darkening . . . gave.* In the 1st ed. these lines are joined to what precedes, as they evidently should be; in all the more recent eds. they are joined to what follows.

CANTO THIRD.

3. *Store.* See on i. 548 above.

5. *That be.* In old English, besides the present tense *am*, etc., there was also this form *be*, from the Anglo-Saxon *beon.* The 2d person singular was *beest.* The 1st and 3d person plural *be* is often found in Shakespeare and the Bible.

10. *Yet live there still,* etc. See on ii. 692 above.

15 *What time.* Cf. ii. 307 above.

17. *The gathering sound.* The *sound*, or signal, for the *gathering.* The phrase illustrates the difference between the participle and the verbal noun (or whatever it may be called) in *-ing.* Cf. "a laboring man" and "a laboring day" (*Julius Cæsar*, i. 1. 4); and see our ed. of *J. C.* p. 126.

18. *The Fiery Cross.* Scott says here: "When a chieftain designed to summon his clan, upon any sudden or important emergency, he slew a goat, and making a cross of any light wood, seared its extremities in the fire, and extinguished them in the blood of the animal. This was called the *Fiery Cross*, also *Crean Tarigh*, or the *Cross of Shame*, because disobedience to what the symbol implied, inferred infamy. It was delivered to a swift and trusty messenger, who ran full speed with it to the next hamlet, where he presented it to the principal person, with a single word, implying the place of rendezvous. He who received the symbol was bound to send it forward, with equal despatch, to the next village; and thus it passed with incredible celerity through all the district which owed allegiance to the chief, and also among his allies and neighbors, if the danger was common to them. At sight of the Fiery Cross, every man, from sixteen years old to sixty, capable of

[illegible] was obliged instantly to repair, in his best arms and accoutrements, to the place of rendezvous. He who failed to appear suffered the extremities of fire and sword, which were emblematically denounced to the disobedient by the bloody and burnt marks upon this warlike signal. During the civil war of 1745–6, the Fiery Cross often made its circuit; and upon one occasion it passed through the whole district of Breadalbane, a tract of thirty-two miles, in three hours. The late Alexander Stewart, Esq., of Invernahyle, described to me his having sent round the Fiery Cross through the district of Appine, during the same commotion. The coast was threatened by a descent from two English frigates, and the flower of the young men were with the army of Prince Charles Edward, then in England; yet the summons was so effectual that even old age and childhood obeyed it; and a force was collected in a few hours, so numerous and so enthusiastic, that all attempt at the intended diversion upon the country of the absent warriors was in prudence abandoned, as desperate."

19. *The Summer dawn's reflected hue*, etc. Mr. Ruskin says (*Modern Painters*, iii. 278): "And thus Nature becomes dear to Scott in a threefold way: dear to him, first, as containing those remains or memories of the past, which he cannot find in cities, and giving hope of Prætorian mound or knight's grave in every green slope and shade of its desolate places; dear, secondly, in its moorland liberty, which has for him just as high a charm as the fenced garden had for the mediæval; . . . and dear to him, finally, in that perfect beauty, denied alike in cities and in men, for which every modern heart had begun at last to thirst, and Scott's, in its freshness and power, of all men's most earnestly.

"And in this love of beauty, observe that the love of *color* is a leading element, his healthy mind being incapable of losing, under any modern false teaching, its joy in brilliancy of hue. . . . In general, if he does not mean to say much about things, the *one* character which he will give is color, using it with the most perfect mastery and faithfulness."

After giving many illustrations of Scott's use of color in his poetry, Ruskin quotes the present passage, which he says is "still more interesting, because it has *no form* in it *at all* except in one word (*chalice*), but wholly composes its imagery either of color, or of that delicate half-believed life which we have seen to be so important an element in modern landscape."

"Two more considerations," he adds, "are, however, suggested by the above passage. The first, that the love of natural history, excited by the continual attention now given to all wild landscape, heightens reciprocally the interest of that landscape, and becomes an important element in Scott's description, leading him to finish, down to the minutest speckling of breast, and slightest shade of attributed emotion, the portraiture of birds and animals; in strange opposition to Homer's slightly named 'sea-crows, who have care of the works of the sea,' and Dante's singing-birds, of undefined species. Compare carefully the 2d and 3d stanzas of *Rokeby*.

"The second point I have to note is Scott's habit of drawing a slight *moral* from every scene, . . . and that this slight moral is almost always melancholy. Here he has stopped short without entirely expressing it:

> 'The mountain-shadows . .
> . . . . lie
> Like future joys to Fancy's eye.'

His completed thought would be, that these future joys, like the mountain-shadows, were never to be attained. It occurs fully uttered in many other places. He seems to have been constantly rebuking his own worldly pride and vanity, but never purposefully:

> 'The foam-globes on her eddies ride,
> Thick as the schemes of human pride
> That down life's current drive amain,
> As frail, as frothy, and as vain.'"

Ruskin adds, among other illustrations, the reference to "foxglove and nightshade" in i. 218, 219 above.

28. *Like future joys*, etc. This passage, quoted by Ruskin above, also illustrates what is comparatively rare in figurative language — taking the immaterial to exemplify the material. The latter is constantly used to symbolize or elucidate the former; but one would have to search long in our modern poetry to find a dozen instances where, as here, the relation is reversed. Cf. 639 below. We have another example in the second passage quoted by Ruskin. Cf. also Tennyson's

> "thousand wreaths of dangling water-smoke,
> That like a broken purpose waste in air;"

and Shelley's

> "Our boat is asleep on Serchio's stream:
> Its sails are folded like thoughts in a dream."

30. *Reared*. The 1st ed. has "oped."

32. After this line the MS. has the couplet,

> "Invisible in fleecy cloud,
> The lark sent down her matins loud,"

which reappears in altered form below.

33. *Gray mist*. The MS. has "light mist."

38. *Good-morrow gave*, etc. Cf. Byron, *Childe Harold*:

> "and the bills
> Of summer-birds sing welcome as ye pass."

39. *Cushat dove*. Ring-dove.

46. *His impatient blade*. Note the "transferred epithet." It is not the *blade* that is impatient.

47. *Beneath a rock*, etc. The MS. reads:

> "Hard by, his vassals' early care
> The mystic ritual prepare."

50. *Antiquity*. The men of old; "the abstract for the concrete."

59. *With her broad shadow*, etc. Cf. Longfellow, *Maidenhood*:

> "Seest thou shadows sailing by,
> As the dove, with startled eye,
> Sees the falcon's shadow fly?"

62. *Rowan*. The mountain-ash.

71. *That monk, of savage form and face.* Scott says here: "The state of religion in the middle ages afforded considerable facilities for those whose mode of life excluded them from regular worship, to secure, nevertheless, the ghostly assistance of confessors, perfectly willing to adapt the nature of their doctrine to the necessities and peculiar circumstances of their flock. Robin Hood, it is well known, had his celebrated domestic chaplain Friar Tuck. And that same curtal friar was probably matched in manners and appearance by the ghostly fathers of the Tynedale robbers, who are thus described in an excommunication fulminated against their patrons by Richard Fox, Bishop of Durham, tempore Henrici VIII.: 'We have further understood, that there are many chaplains in the said territories of Tynedale and Redesdale, who are public and open maintainers of concubinage, irregular, suspended, excommunicated, and interdicted persons, and withal so utterly ignorant of letters, that it has been found by those who objected this to them, that there were some who, having celebrated mass for ten years, were still unable to read the sacramental service. We have also understood there are persons among them who, although not ordained, do take upon them the offices of priesthood, and, in contempt of God, celebrate the divine and sacred rites, and administer the sacraments, not only in sacred and dedicated places, but in those which are prophane and interdicted, and most wretchedly ruinous, they themselves being attired in ragged, torn, and most filthy vestments, altogether unfit to be used in divine, or even in temporal offices. The which said chaplains do administer sacraments and sacramental rites to the aforesaid manifest and infamous thieves, robbers, depredators, receivers of stolen goods, and plunderers, and that without restitution, or intention to restore, as evinced by the act; and do also openly admit them to the rites of ecclesiastical sepulchre, without exacting security for restitution, although they are prohibited from doing so by the sacred canons, as well as by the institutes of the saints and fathers. All which infers the heavy peril of their own souls, and is a pernicious example to the other believers in Christ, as well as no slight, but an aggravated injury, to the numbers despoiled and plundered of their goods, gear, herds, and chattels.'"

74. *Benharrow.* A mountain near the head of Loch Lomond.

77. *Brook.* See on i. 566 above.

81. *The hallowed creed.* The Christian creed, as distinguished from *heathen lore*. The MS. has "While the blest creed," etc.

85. *Bound.* That is, of his haunts.

87. *Glen or strath.* A *glen* is the deep and narrow valley of a small stream, a *strath* the broader one of a river.

89. *He prayed*, etc. The MS. reads:

> "He prayed, with many a cross between,
> And terror took devotion's mien."

91. *Of Brian's birth*, etc. Scott says that the legend which follows is not of his invention, and goes on to show that it is taken with slight variation from "the geographical collections made by the Laird of Macfarlane."

102. *Bucklered.* Served as a *buckler* to, shielded.

114. *Snood.* Cf. i. 363 above. Scott has the following note here: "The *snood*, or riband, with which a Scottish lass braided her hair, had an emblematical signification, and applied to her maiden character. It was exchanged for the *curch*, *toy*, or coif, when she passed, by marriage, into the matron state. But if the damsel was so unfortunate as to lose pretensions to the name of maiden, without gaining a right to that of matron, she was neither permitted to use the snood, nor advanced to the graver dignity of the curch. In old Scottish songs there occur many sly allusions to such misfortune; as in the old words to the popular tune of 'Ower the muir amang the heather:'

> 'Down amang the broom, the broom,
> Down amang the broom, my dearie,
> The lassie lost her silken snood,
> That gard her greet till she was wearie.'"

120. *Or . . . or.* For *either . . . or*, as often in poetry.

131. *Till, frantic*, etc. The MS. reads:

> "Till, driven to frenzy, he believed
> The legend of his birth received."

136. *The cloister.* Here personified as feminine.

138. *Sable-lettered.* "Black-letter;" the technical term for the "old English" form of letter, used in the earliest English manuscripts and books.

142. *Cabala.* Mysteries. For the original meaning of the word, see Wb.

144. *Curious.* Inquisitive, prying into hidden things.

148. *Hid him.* See on i. 142 above.

149. *The desert gave him*, etc. Scott says here: "In adopting the legend concerning the birth of the Founder of the Church of Kilmallie, the author has endeavored to trace the effects which such a belief was likely to produce, in a barbarous age, on the person to whom it related. It seems likely that he must have become a fanatic or an impostor, or that mixture of both which forms a more frequent character than either of them, as existing separately. In truth, mad persons are frequently more anxious to impress upon others a faith in their visions, than they are themselves confirmed in their reality; as, on the other hand, it is difficult for the most cool-headed impostor long to personate an enthusiast, without in some degree believing what he is so eager to have believed. It was a natural attribute of such a character as the supposed hermit, that he should credit the numerous superstitions with which the minds of ordinary Highlanders are almost always imbued. A few of these are slightly alluded to in this stanza. The River Demon, or River-horse, for it is that form which he commonly assumes, is the Kelpy of the Lowlands, an evil and malicious spirit, delighting to forebode and to witness calamity. He frequents most Highland lakes and rivers; and one of his most memorable exploits was performed upon the banks of Loch Vennachar, in the very district which forms the scene of our action: it consisted in the destruction of a funeral procession, with all its attendants. The 'noontide hag,' called in Gaelic

Glas-lich, a tall, emaciated, gigantic female figure, is supposed in particular to haunt the district of Knoidart. A goblin dressed in antique armor, and having one hand covered with blood, called, from that circumstance, *Lham-dearg*, or Red-hand, is a tenant of the forests of Glenmore and Rothiemurcus. Other spirits of the desert, all frightful in shape and malignant in disposition, are believed to frequent different mountains and glens of the Highlands, where any unusual appearance, produced by mist, or the strange lights that are sometimes thrown upon particular objects, never fails to present an apparition to the imagination of the solitary and melancholy mountaineer."

161. *Mankind*. Accented on the first syllable: as it is almost invariably in Shakespeare, except in *Timon of Athens*, where the modern accent prevails. Milton uses either accent, as suits the measure. We find both in *P. L.* viii. 358: "Above mankind, or aught than mankind higher."

166. *Alpine's*. Some eds. misprint "Alpine;" also "horsemen" in 172 below.

168. *The fatal Ben-Shie's boding scream*. The MS. reads:

> "The fatal Ben-Shie's dismal scream,
> And seen her wrinkled form, the sign
> Of woe and death to Alpine's line."

Scott has the following note here: "Most great families in the Highlands were supposed to have a tutelar, or rather a domestic, spirit, attached to them, who took an interest in their prosperity, and intimated, by its wailings, any approaching disaster. That of Grant of Grant was called *May Moullach*, and appeared in the form of a girl, who had her arm covered with hair. Grant of Rothiemurcus had an attendant called *Bodach-an-dun*, or the Ghost of the Hill; and many other examples might be mentioned. The Ben-Shie implies the female fairy whose lamentations were often supposed to precede the death of a chieftain of particular families. When she is visible, it is in the form of an old woman, with a blue mantle and streaming hair. A superstition of the same kind is, I believe, universally received by the inferior ranks of the native Irish.

"The death of the head of a Highland family is also sometimes supposed to be announced by a chain of lights of different colors, called *Dr'eug*, or death of the Druid. The direction which it takes marks the place of the funeral." [See the Essay on Fairy Superstitions in Scott's *Border Minstrelsy*.]

169. *Sounds, too, had come*, etc. Scott says: "A presage of the kind alluded to in the text, is still believed to announce death to the ancient Highland family of M'Lean of Lochbuy. The spirit of an ancestor slain in battle is heard to gallop along a stony bank, and then to ride thrice around the family residence, ringing his fairy bridle, and thus intimating the approaching calamity. How easily the eye as well as the ear may be deceived upon such occasions, is evident from the stories of armies in the air, and other spectral phenomena with which history abounds. Such an apparition is said to have been witnessed upon the side of Southfell mountain, between Penrith and Keswick, upon the 23d

June, 1744, by two persons, William Lancaster of Blakehills, and Daniel Stricket his servant, whose attestation to the fact, with a full account of the apparition, dated the 21st July, 1745, is printed in Clarke's *Survey of the Lakes.* The apparition consisted of several troops of horse moving in regular order, with a steady rapid motion, making a curved sweep around the fell, and seeming to the spectators to disappear over the ridge of the mountain. Many persons witnessed this phenomenon, and observed the last, or last but one, of the supposed troop, occasionally leave his rank, and pass, at a gallop, to the front, when he resumed the same steady pace. The curious appearance, making the necessary allowance for imagination, may be perhaps sufficiently accounted for by optical deception."

171. *Shingly.* Gravelly, pebbly.

173. *Thunderbolt.* The 1st ed. has "thunder too."

188. *Framed.* The reading of the 1st ed.; commonly misprinted "formed," which occurs in 195.

190. *Limbs.* The 1st ed. has "limb."

191. *Inch-Cailliach.* Scott says: "*Inch-Cailliach*, the Isle of Nuns, or of Old Women, is a most beautiful island at the lower extremity of Loch Lomond. The church belonging to the former nunnery was long used as the place of worship for the parish of Buchanan, but scarce any vestiges of it now remain. The burial-ground continues to be used, and contains the family places of sepulture of several neighboring clans. The monuments of the lairds of Macgregor, and of other families claiming a descent from the old Scottish King Alpine, are most remarkable. The Highlanders are as zealous of their rights of sepulture as may be expected from a people whose whole laws and government, if clanship can be called so, turned upon the single principle of family descent. 'May his ashes be scattered on the water,' was one of the deepest and most solemn imprecations which they used against an enemy." [See a detailed description of the funeral ceremonies of a Highland chieftain in the *Fair Maid of Perth.*]

203. *Dwelling low.* That is, burial-place.

207. *Each clansman's execration*, etc. The MS. reads:

"Our warriors, on his worthless bust,
Shall speak disgrace and woe;"

and below:

"Their clattering targets hardly strook;
And first they muttered low."

212. *Strook.* One of the old forms of *struck*. In the early eds. of Shakespeare, we find *struck*, *stroke*, and *strook* (or *strooke*) for the past tense, and all these, together with *stricken*, *strucken*, *stroken*, and *strooken*, for the participle. Cf. Milton, *Hymn on Nativity*, 95:

"When such music sweet
Their hearts and ears did greet
As never was by mortal finger strook;"

where, as here, it is used for the sake of the rhyme.

214. *Then, like the billow*, etc. The repetition of the same rhyme here gives well the *cumulative* effect of the rising billow.

217. *Burst, with loud roar.* See on i. 73 above; and cf. 227 below.

228. *Holiest name.* The MS. has "holy name."

245. *Mingled with childhood's babbling trill*, etc. "The whole of this stanza is very impressive; the mingling of the *children's* curses is the climax of horror. Note the meaning of the triple curse. The cross is of ancestral yew — the defaulter is cut off from communion with his clan; it is seared in the fire — the fire shall destroy his dwelling; it is dipped in blood — his heart's blood is to be shed" (Taylor).

253. *Coir-Uriskin.* See on 622 below.

255. *Beala-nam-bo.* "The pass of the cattle," on the other side of Benvenue from the Goblin's Cave; "a magnificent glade, overhung with birch-trees, by which the cattle, taken in forays, were conveyed within the protection of the Trosachs" (Black).

279. *This sign.* That is, the cross. *To all*, which we should not expect with *bought*, was apparently suggested by the antithetical *to him* in the preceding line. For the allusion to the Scriptural doctrine of redemption, cf. *Acts*, xx. 28, 1 *Cor.* xi. 20, vii. 23, etc.

281. *The murmur*, etc. The MS. has "The slowly muttered deep Amen."

286. *The muster-place*, etc. The MS. reads "Murlagan is the spot decreed."

Lanrick Mead is a meadow at the northwestern end of Loch Vennachar.

300. *The dun deer's hide*, etc. Scott says: "The present *brogue* of the Highlanders is made of half-dried leather, with holes to admit and let out the water; for walking the moors dry-shod is a matter altogether out of question. The ancient buskin was still ruder, being made of undressed deer's hide, with the hair outwards, — a circumstance which procured the Highlanders the well-known epithet of *Red-shanks*. The process is very accurately described by one Elder (himself a Highlander), in the project for a union between England and Scotland, addressed to Henry VIII.: 'We go a-hunting, and after that we have slain red-deer, we flay off the skin by and by, and setting of our barefoot on the inside thereof, for want of cunning shoemakers, by your grace's pardon, we play the cobblers, compassing and measuring so much thereof as shall reach up to our ankles, pricking the upper part thereof with holes, that the water may repass where it enters, and stretching it up with a strong thong of the same above our said ankles. So, and please your noble grace, we make our shoes. Therefore, we using such manner of shoes, the rough hairy side outwards, in your grace's dominions of England, we be called *Rough-footed Scots'* (*Pinkerton's History*, vol. ii. p. 397)."

Cf. *Marmion*, v. 5:

> "The hunted red-deer's undressed hide
> Their hairy buskins well supplied."

304. *Steepy.* For the word (see also iv. 374 below) and the line, cf. Shakespeare, *T. of A.* i. 1. 75:

> "Bowing his head against the steepy mount
> To climb his happiness."

309. *Questing.* Seeking its game. Bacon (*Adv. of Learning,* v. 5) speaks of "the questing of memory."

310. *Scaur.* Cliff, precipice; the same word as *scar.* Cf. Tennyson's *Bugle Song:* "O sweet and far, from cliff and scar;" and in the *Idyls of the King:* "shingly scaur."

314. *Herald of battle,* etc. The MS. reads:

> "Dread messenger of fate and fear,
> Herald of danger, fate, and fear,
> Stretch onward in thy fleet career!
> Thou track'st not now the stricken doe,
> Nor maiden coy through greenwood bough."

322. *Fast as the fatal symbol flies,* etc. "The description of the starting of the Fiery Cross bears more marks of labor than most of Mr. Scott's poetry, and borders, perhaps, on straining and exaggeration; yet it shows great power" (Jeffrey).

332. *Cheer.* In its original sense of countenance, or look. Cf. Shakespeare, *M. N. D.* iii. 2. 96: "pale of cheer;" Spenser, *F. Q.* i. 1. 2: "But of his cheere did seeme too solemne sad;" Dryden, *Hind and Panther,* iii. 437: "Till frowning skies began to change their cheer," etc.

333. *His scythe.* The reading of the 1st and other early eds.; "the scythe" in more recent ones.

342. *Alas, thou lovely lake!* etc. "Observe Scott's habit of looking at nature, neither as dead, nor merely material, nor as altered by his own feelings; but as having an animation and pathos of *its own,* wholly irrespective of human passion — an animation which Scott loves and sympathizes with, as he would with a fellow creature, forgetting himself altogether, and subduing his own humanity before what seems to him the power of the landscape. . . . Instead of making Nature anywise subordinate to himself, he makes himself subordinate to *her* — follows her lead simply — does not venture to bring his own cares and thoughts into her pure and quiet presence — paints her in her simple and universal truth, adding no result of momentary passion or fancy, and appears, therefore, at first shallower than other poets, being in reality wider and healthier" (Ruskin).

344. *Bosky.* Bushy, woody. Cf. Milton, *Comus,* 313: "And every bosky bourn from side to side;" Shakespeare, *Temp.* iv. i. 81: "My bosky acres and my unshrubb'd down," etc.

347. *Seems for the scene,* etc. The MS. has "Seems all too lively and too loud."

349. *Duncraggan's huts.* A homestead between Lochs Achray and Vennachar, near the Brigg of Turk.

355. *Shot him.* See on i. 142 above. Scott is much given to this construction.

357. *The funeral yell,* etc. The MS. has "'T is woman's scream, 't is childhood's wail."

Yell may at first seem too strong a word here, but it is in keeping with the people and the times described. Besides Scott was familiar with old English poetry, in which it was often used where a modern writer would choose another word. Cf. Surrey, *Virgil's Æneid:*

DUNCRAGGAN.

"With wailing great and women's shrill yelling;" and Gascoigne, *De Profundis*:

> "From depth of doole wherein my soule dooth dwell,
>
> . . . .
>
> O gracious God, to thee I crie and yell."

362. *Torch's ray.* The 1st ed. reads "torches ray" and "supply; corrected in the *Errata* to read as in the text. Most eds. print "torches' ray."

369. *Coronach.* Scott has the following note here: "The *Coronach* of the Highlanders, like the *Ululatus* of the Romans, and the *Ululoo* of the Irish, was a wild expression of lamentation, poured forth by the mourners over the body of a departed friend. When the words of it were articulate, they expressed the praises of the deceased, and the loss the clan would sustain by his death. The following is a lamentation of this kind, literally translated from the Gaelic, to some of the ideas of which the text stands indebted. The tune is so popular that it has since become the war-march, or gathering of the clan.

CORONACH ON SIR LAUCHLAN, CHIEF OF MACLEAN.

'Which of all the Senachies
Can trace thy line from the root, up to Paradise,
But Macvuirih, the son of Fergus?
No sooner had thine ancient stately tree
Taken firm root in Albin,
Than one of thy forefathers fell at Harlaw.—
'T was then we lost a chief of deathless name.

''T is no base weed—no planted tree,
Nor a seedling of last Autumn;
Nor a sapling planted at Beltain; [1]
Wide, wide around were spread its lofty branches—
But the topmost bough is lowly laid!
Thou hast forsaken us before Sawaine. [2]

[1] See on ii. 319 above.

[2] Hallowe'en.

'Thy dwelling is the winter house ;—
Loud, sad, and mighty is thy death-song !
Oh ! courteous champion of Montrose !
Oh ! stately warrior of the Celtic Isles !
Thou shalt buckle thy harness on no more !'

"The coronach has for some years past been suspended at funerals by the use of the bagpipe; and that also is, like many other Highland peculiarities, falling into disuse, unless in remote districts."

370. *He is gone*, etc. As Taylor remarks, the metre of this dirge seems to be *amphibrachic;* that is, made up of *feet*, or metrical divisions, of three syllables, the *second* of which is accented. Some of the lines appear to be *anapestic* (made up of trisyllabic feet, with the *last* syllable accented); but the *rhythm* of these is amphibrachic; that is, the rhythmic pause is after the syllable that follows the accent.

"(He) is góne on | the móuntain,
(Like) a súmmer- | dried fóuntain."

Ten lines out of twenty-four are distinctly amphibrachic, as

"To Dúncan | no mórrow."

So that it seems best to treat the rest as amphibrachic, with a superfluous unaccented syllable at the beginning of the line. Taylor adds: "The song is very carefully divided. To each of the three things, *mountain*, *forest*, *fountain*, four lines are given, in the order 3, 1, 2."

384. *In flushing*. In full bloom. Cf. *Hamlet*, iii. 3. 81: "broad blown, as flush as May."

386. *Correi*. A hollow in the side of a hill, where game usually lies.

387. *Cumber*. Trouble, perplexity. Cf. Fairfax, *Tasso*, ii. 73: "Thus fade thy helps, and thus thy cumbers spring;" and Sir John Harrington, *Epigrams*, i. 94: "without all let [hindrance] or cumber."

388. *Red*. Bloody, not afraid of the hand-to-hand fight.

394. *Stumah*. "*Faithful;* the name of a dog" (Scott).

410. *Angus, the heir*, etc. The MS. reads:

"Angus, the first of Duncan's line,
Sprung forth and seized the fatal sign,
And then upon his kinsman's bier
Fell Malise's suspended tear.
In haste the stripling to his side
His father's targe and falchion tied."

439. *Hest*. Behest, bidding; used only in poetry. Cf. Shakespeare, *Temp*. iii. 1. 37: "I have broke your hest to say so;" *Id*. iv. 1. 65: "at thy hest," etc.

452. *Benledi saw the Cross of Fire*, etc. Scott says here: "Inspection of the provincial map of Perthshire, or any large map of Scotland, will trace the progress of the signal through the small district of lakes and mountains, which, in exercise of my poetical privilege, I have subjected to the authority of my imaginary chieftain, and which, at the period of my romance, was really occupied by a clan who claimed a descent from Alpine,—a clan the most unfortunate and most persecuted, but neither the least distinguished, least powerful, nor least brave of the tribes of the Gael.

"The first stage of the Fiery Cross is to Duncraggan, a place near the Brigg of Turk, where a short stream divides Loch Achray from Loch Vennachar. From thence, it passes towards Callander, and then, turning to the left up the pass of Leny, is consigned to Norman at the Chapel of Saint Bride, which stood on a small and romantic knoll in the middle of the valley, called Strath-Ire. Tombea and Arnandave, or Ardmandave, are names of places in the vicinity. The alarm is then supposed to pass along the Lake of Lubnaig, and through the various glens in the district of Balquidder, including the neighboring tracts of Glenfinlas and Strath-Gartney."

THE CHAPEL OF SAINT BRIDE.

435. *Strath-Ire.* This valley connects Lochs Voil and Lubnaig. The *Chapel of Saint Bride* is about half a mile from the southern end of Loch Lubnaig, on the banks of the River Leny, a branch of the Teith (hence "Teith's *young* waters"). The churchyard with a few remains of the chapel are all that now mark the spot.

458. *Until, where,* etc. The MS. reads:

> "And where a steep and wooded knoll
> Graced the dark strath with emerald green."

465. *Though reeled his sympathetic eye.* That is, his eye reeled in sympathy with the movement of the waters — a poetic expression of what every one has felt when looking into a "dizzily dancing" stream.

478. *That morning-tide.* That morning time. *Tide* in this sense is now used only in a few poetic compounds like *eventide, springtide,* etc. See iv. 59 below. For its former use, cf. Spenser, *F. Q.* i. 2. 29: "and rest their weary limbs a tide;" *Id.* iii. 6. 21: "that mine may be your paine another tide," etc. See also Scott's *Lay,* vi. 50: "Me lists not at this tide declare."

483. *Bridal.* Bridal party; used as a collective noun.

485. *Coif-clad.* Wearing the *coif*, or *curch.* See on 114 above; a also for *snooded.*

488. *Unwitting.* Unknowing. Cf. 367 above. For the verb *wit*, see on i. 596 above.

495. *Kerchief.* Curch, which is etymologically the same word, and means a covering for the head. Some eds. print "'kerchief," as if the word were a contraction of *handkerchief.*

508. *Muster-place.* The 1st ed. has "mustering place;" and in 519 "brooks" for *brook.*

510. *And must he*, etc. The MS. reads: "And must he then exchange the hand."

528. *Lubnaig's lake.* Loch Lubnaig is about four miles long and a mile broad, hemmed in by steep and rugged mountains. The view of Benledi from the lake is peculiarly grand and impressive.

530. *The sickening pang*, etc. Cf. *The Lord of the Isles,* vi. 1: "The heartsick faintness of the hope delayed." See *Prov.* xiii. 12.

531. *And memory*, etc. The MS. reads:

> "And memory brought the torturing train
> Of all his morning visions vain;
> But mingled with impatience came
> The manly love of martial fame."

541. *Brae.* The *brow* or side of a hill.

545. *The heath*, etc. The metre of the song is the same as that of the poem, the only variation being in the order of the rhymes.

546. *Bracken.* Fern; "the *Pteris aquilina*" (Taylor).

553. *Fancy now.* The MS. has "image now."

561. *A time will come*, etc. The MS. reads:

> "A time will come for love and faith,
> For should thy bridegroom yield his breath.
> 'T will cheer him in the hour of death,
> The boasted right to thee, Mary."

570. *Balquidder.* A village near the eastern end of *Loch Voil*, the burial-place of Rob Roy and the scene of many of his exploits. The *Braes* extend along the north side of the lake and of the *Balvaig* which flows into it.

Scott says here: "It may be necessary to inform the Southern reader that the heath on the Scottish moorlands is often set fire to, that the sheep may have the advantage of the young herbage produced, in room of the tough old heather plants. This custom (execrated by sportsmen) produces occasionally the most beautiful nocturnal appearances, similar almost to the discharge of a volcano. This simile is not new to poetry. The charge of a warrior, in the fine ballad of *Hardyknute*, is said to be 'like fire to heather set.'"

575. *Nor faster speeds it*, etc. "The eager fidelity with which this fatal signal is hurried on and obeyed, is represented with great spirit and felicity" (Jeffrey).

577. *Coil.* Turmoil. Cf. Shakespeare, *Temp.* i. 2. 207:

> "Who was so firm, so constant, that this coil
> Would not infect his reason?"

C. of E. iii. 1. 48: "What a coil is there, Dromio?" etc.

579. *Loch Doine.* A lakelet just above Loch Voil, and almost forming a part of it. The epithets *sullen* and *still* are peculiarly appropriate to this valley. "Few places in Scotland have such an air of solitude and remoteness from the haunts of men" (Black).

582. *Strath-Gartney.* The north side of the basin of Loch Katrine.

583. *Each man might claim.* That is, *who* could claim. See on i. 528 above.

600. *No law but Roderick Dhu's command.* Scott has the following note here:

"The deep and implicit respect paid by the Highland clansmen to their chief, rendered this both a common and a solemn oath. In other respects, they were like most savage nations, capricious in their ideas concerning the obligatory power of oaths. One solemn mode of swearing was by kissing the *dirk*, imprecating upon themselves death by that, or a similar weapon, if they broke their vow. But for oaths in the usual form, they are said to have had little respect. As for the reverence due to the chief, it may be guessed from the following odd example of a Highland point of honor:

'The clan whereto the above-mentioned tribe belongs, is the only one I have heard of which is without a chief; that is, being divided into families, under several chieftains, without any particular patriarch of the whole name. And this is a great reproach, as may appear from an affair that fell out at my table, in the Highlands, between one of that name and a Cameron. The provocation given by the latter was, "Name your chief." The return of it at once was, "You are a fool." They went out next morning, but having early notice of it, I sent a small party of soldiers after them, which, in all probability, prevented some barbarous mischief that might have ensued; for the chiefless Highlander, who is himself a petty chieftain, was going to the place appointed with a small-sword and pistol, whereas the Cameron (an old man) took with him only his broadsword, according to the agreement.

'When all was over, and I had, at least seemingly, reconciled them, I was told the words, of which I seemed to think but slightly, were, to one of the clan, the greatest of all provocations' (*Letters from Scotland*, vol. ii. p. 221)."

604. *Menteith.* See on i. 89 above.

607. *Rednock.* The ruins of *Rednock Castle* are about two miles to the north of Loch Menteith, on the road to Callander. *Cardross Castle* (in which Robert Bruce died) was on the banks of the Clyde, a few miles below Dumbarton. *Duchray Castle* is a mile south of Lochard. *Loch Con*, or *Chon*, is a lakelet, about three miles northwest from Lochard (into which it drains) and two miles south of Loch Katrine.

611. *Wot ye.* Know ye. See on i. 596 above.

622. *Coir-nan-Uriskin.* Scott has the following note here: "This is a very steep and most romantic hollow in the mountain of Benvenue, overhanging the southeastern extremity of Loch Katrine. It is surrounded with stupendous rocks, and overshadowed with birch-trees, mingled with oaks, the spontaneous production of the mountain, even where its cliffs appear denuded of soil. A dale in so wild a situation, and amid a people whose genius bordered on the romantic, did not

LOCH CON.

remain without appropriate deities. The name literally implies the Corri, or Den, of the Wild or Shaggy Men. Perhaps this, as conjectured by Mr. Alexander Campbell (*Journey from Edinburgh*, 1802, p. 109), may have originally only implied its being the haunt of a ferocious banditti. But tradition has ascribed to the *Urisk*, who gives name to the cavern, a figure between a goat and a man; in short, however much the classical reader may be startled, precisely that of the Grecian Satyr. The *Urisk* seems not to have inherited, with the form, the petulance of the silvan deity of the classics; his occupation, on the contrary, resembled those of Milton's Lubbar Fiend, or of the Scottish Brownie, though he differed from both in name and appearance. 'The *Urisks*,' says Dr. Graham, 'were a sort of lubberly supernaturals, who, like the Brownies, could be gained over by kind attention to perform the drudgery of the farm, and it was believed that many families in the Highlands had one of the order attached to it. They were supposed to be dispersed over the Highlands, each in his own wild recess, but the solemn stated meetings of the order were regularly held in this Cave of Benvenue. This current superstition, no doubt, alludes to some circumstance in the ancient history of this country' (*Scenery on the Southern Confines of Perthshire*, p. 19, 1806). It must be owned that the *Coir*, or Den, does not, in its present state, meet our ideas of a subterraneous grotto or cave, being only a small and narrow cavity, among huge fragments of rocks rudely piled together. But such a scene is liable to convulsions of nature which a Lowlander cannot estimate, and which may have choked up what was originally a cavern. At least the name and tradition warrant the author of a fictitious tale to assert its having been such at the remote period in which this scene is laid."

639. *With such a glimpse*, etc. See on 28 above.

641. *Still.* Stillness; the adjective used substantively, for the sake of the rhyme.

656. *Satyrs.* "The *Urisk*, or Highland satyr" (Scott).

664. *Beal-nam-bo.* See on 255 above; and for the measure of the first half of the line, on i. 73 above.

667. *'Cross.* Scott (1st ed.) prints "cross," as in 750 below.

672. *A single page,* etc. Scott says: "A Highland chief, being as absolute in his patriarchal authority as any prince, had a corresponding number of officers attached to his person. He had his body-guards, called *Luichttach,* picked from his clan for strength, activity, and entire devotion to his person. These, according to their deserts, were sure to share abundantly in the rude profusion of his hospitality. It is recorded, for example, by tradition, that Allan MacLean, chief of that clan, happened upon a time to hear one of these favorite retainers observe to his comrade, that their chief grew old. 'Whence do you infer that?' replied the other. 'When was it,' rejoined the first, 'that a soldier of Allan's was obliged, as I am now, not only to eat the flesh from the bone, but even to tear off the inner skin, or filament?' The hint was quite sufficient, and MacLean next morning, to relieve his followers from such dire necessity, undertook an inroad on the mainland, the ravage of which altogether effaced the memory of his former expeditions for the like purpose.

"Our officer of Engineers, so often quoted, has given us a distinct list of the domestic officers who, independent of *Luichttach,* or *gardes de corps,* belonged to the establishment of a Highland chief. These are, 1. *The Henchman.* 2. The Bard. See preceding notes. 3. *Bladier,* or spokesman. 4. *Gillie-more,* or sword-bearer, alluded to in the text. 5. *Gillie-casflue,* who carried the chief, if on foot, over the fords. 6. *Gillie-comstraine,* who leads the chief's horse. 7. *Gillie-Trushanarinsh,* the baggage-man. 8. The piper. 9. The piper's gillie, or attendant, who carries the bagpipe (*Letters from Scotland,* vol. ii. p. 158). Although this appeared, naturally enough, very ridiculous to an English officer, who considered the master of such a retinue as no more than an English gentleman of £500 a-year, yet in the circumstances of the chief, whose strength and importance consisted in the number and attachment of his followers, it was of the last consequence, in point of policy, to have in his gift subordinate offices, which called immediately round his person those who were most devoted to him, and, being of value in their estimation, were also the means of rewarding them."

693. *To drown,* etc. The MS. reads:

> "To drown his grief in war's wild roar,
> Nor think of love and Ellen more."

713. *Ave Maria!* etc. "The metrical peculiarity of this song is that the rhymes of the even lines of the first quatrain (or set of four lines) are taken up as those of the odd lines in the second, and that they are the same in all three stanzas" (Taylor).

722. *We now must share.* The MS. has "my sire must share;" and in 725 "The murky grotto's noxious air."

733. *Bow us.* See on i. 142, and cf. 749 below.

754. *Lanrick height.* Overlooking Lanrick Mead. See on 286 above.

755. *Where mustered,* etc. The MS. reads:

> "Where broad extending far below,
> Mustered Clan-Alpine's martial show."

On the first of these lines, cf. i. 88 above.

773. *Yell.* See on 357 above.

774. *Bochastle's plain.* See on i. 106 above.

CANTO FOURTH.

2. ***And hope***, etc. The MS. has "And rapture dearest when obscured by fears."

5. *Wilding.* Wild; a rare word, used only in poetry. Cf. Tennyson, *Geraint and Enid:* "And like a crag was gay with wilding flowers." Spenser has the noun (=wild apples) in *F. Q.* iii. 7. 17: "Oft from the forrest wildings he did bring," etc. *Whom* is used on account of the personification.

9. *What time.* Cf. ii. 307 and iii. 15 above.

19. *Braes of Doune.* The undulating region between Callander and Doune, on the north side of the Teith. The *Doune* of 37 below is the old *Castle* of that name, the ruins of which still form a majestic pile on the steep banks of the Teith. It figures in *Waverley* as the place where the hero was confined by the Highlanders.

36. *Boune.* Prepared, ready; a Scottish word. Cf. 157 and vi. 396 below.

42. *Bide.* Endure; not to be printed *'bide*, as if a contraction of *abide.* Cf. Shakespeare, *Lear*, iii. 4. 29: "That bide the pelting of this pitiless storm," etc.

Bout. Turn (of fortune).

47. *Repair.* That is, *to* repair.

55. *'Tis well advised.* Well thought of, well planned. Cf. *advised* = careful, well considered; as in *M. of V.* i. 1. 142: "with more advised watch," etc.

The MS. reads:

> "'Tis well advised — a prudent plan,
> Worthy the father of his clan."

59. *Evening-tide.* See on iii. 478 above.

63. *The Taghairm.* Scott says here: "The Highlanders, like all rude people, had various superstitious modes of inquiring into futurity. One of the most noted was the *Taghairm*, mentioned in the text. A person was wrapped up in the skin of a newly-slain bullock, and deposited beside a waterfall, or at the bottom of a precipice, or in some other strange, wild, and unusual situation, where the scenery around him suggested nothing but objects of horror. In this situation, he revolved in his mind the question proposed; and whatever was impressed upon him by his exalted imagination, passed for the inspiration of the disembodied spirits, who haunt these desolate recesses. In some of the Hebrides they attributed the same oracular power to a large black stone by the sea-shore, which they approached with certain solemnities, and considered the first fancy which came into their own minds, after they did so, to be the undoubted dictate of the tutelar deity of the stone, and, as such, to be, if possible, punctually complied with."

68. *Gallangad.* Near Kilmaronock (p. 201), on a small tributary of the Endrick, and within the district referred to in Scott's note inserted here: "I know not if it be worth observing that this passage is taken almost literally from the mouth of an old Highland kern, or Ketteran, as they were called. He used to narrate the merry doings of the good

old time when he was follower of Rob Roy MacGregor. This leader, on one occasion, thought proper to make a descent upon the lower part of the Loch Lomond district, and summoned all the heritors and farmers to meet at the Kirk of Drymen, to pay him black-mail; *i. e.*, tribute for forbearance and protection. As this invitation was supported by a band of thirty or forty stout fellows, only one gentleman, an ancestor, if I mistake not, of the present Mr. Grahame of Gartmore, ventured to decline compliance. Rob Roy instantly swept his land of all he could drive away, and among the spoil was a bull of the old Scottish wild breed, whose ferocity occasioned great plague to the Ketterans. 'But ere we had reached the Row of Dennan,' said the old man, 'a child might have scratched his ears.' The circumstance is a minute one, but it paints the time when the poor beeve was compelled

> 'To hoof it o'er as many weary miles,
> With goading pikemen hollowing at his heels,
> As e'er the bravest antler of the woods' (*Ethwald*)."

73. *Kerns.* The Gaelic and Irish light-armed soldiers, the heavy-armed being known as *gallowglasses.* The names are often associated: as in *Macbeth*, i. 2. 13: "kerns and gallowglasses;" 2 *Hen. VI.* iv. 9. 26: "gallowglasses and stout kerns;" Drayton, *Heroical Epist.*: "the Kerne and Irish Galliglasse," etc.

74. *Beal'maha.* "The pass of the plain," on the east of Loch Lomond, opposite Inch-Cailliach. In the olden time it was one of the established roads for making raids into the Lowlands.

77. *Dennan's Row.* The modern *Rowardennan*, on Loch Lomond at the foot of Ben Lomond, and a favorite starting-point for the ascent of that mountain.

82. *Boss.* Knob; in keeping with *Targe.*

83. *Verge.* Pronounced *varge*, as the rhyme shows. In v. 219 below it has its ordinary sound; but cf. v. 812.

84. *The Hero's Targe.* "There is a rock so named in the Forest of Glenfinlas, by which a tumultuary cataract takes its course. This wild place is said in former times to have afforded refuge to an outlaw, who was supplied with provisions by a woman, who lowered them down from the brink of the precipice above. His water he procured for himself, by letting down a flagon tied to a string into the black pool beneath the fall" (Scott).

98. *Broke.* Quartered. Cf. the quotation from Jonson below. Scott says here: "Everything belonging to the chase was matter of solemnity among our ancestors; but nothing was more so than the mode of cutting up, or, as it was technically called, *breaking*, the slaughtered stag The forester had his allotted portion; the hounds had a certain allowance; and, to make the division as general as possible, the very birds had their share also. 'There is a little gristle,' says Turbervile, 'which is upon the spoone of the brisket, which we call the raven's bone; and I have seen in some places a raven so wont and accustomed to it, that she would never fail to croak and cry for it all the time you were in breaking up of the deer, and would not depart till she had it.' In the very ancient metrical romance of *Sir Tristrem*, that peerless knight

who is said to have been the very deviser of all rules of chase, did not omit the ceremony:

> 'The rauen he yaue his yiftes
> Sat on the fourched tre.' [1]

"The raven might also challenge his rights by the *Book of St. Albans*, for thus says Dame Juliana Berners:

> 'sitteth anon
> The bely to the side, from the corbyn bone;
> That is corbyns fee, at the death he will be.'

Jonson, in *The Sad Shepherd*, gives a more poetical account of the same ceremony:

> '*Marian.* He that undoes him,
> Doth cleave the brisket bone, upon the spoon
> Of which a little gristle grows — you call it —
> *Robin Hood.* The raven's bone.
> *Marian.* Now o'er head sat a raven
> On a sere bough, a grown, great bird, and hoarse,
> Who, all the while the deer was breaking up,
> So croaked and cried for 't, as all the huntsmen,
> Especially old Scathlock, thought it ominous.'"

115. *Rouse.* Rise, stand erect. Cf. *Macbeth*, v. 5. 12:

> "The time has been, my senses would have cool'd
> To hear a night-shriek, and my fell of hair
> Would at a dismal treatise rouse and stir
> As life were in 't."

119. *Mine.* Many eds. have "my."

128. *Fateful.* The reading of 1st ed. and that of 1821; "fatal" in some recent eds.

132. *Which spills*, etc. The MS. has "Which foremost spills a foeman's life."

"Though this be in the text described as a response of the Taghairm, or Oracle of the Hide, it was of itself an augury frequently attended to. The fate of the battle was often anticipated, in the imagination of the combatants, by observing which party first shed blood. It is said that the Highlanders under Montrose were so deeply imbued with this notion, that on the morning of the battle of Tippermoor, they murdered a defenceless herdsman, whom they found in the fields, merely to secure an advantage of so much consequence to their party" (Scott).

140. *A spy.* That is, Fitz-James. For *has sought*, the 1st ed. has "hath sought."

144. *Red Murdoch*, etc. The MS. has "The clansman vainly deemed his guide," etc.

147. *Those shall bring him down.* For the ellipsis of *who*, see on i. 528 above. The MS. has "stab him down."

153. *Pale.* In the heraldic sense of "a broad perpendicular stripe in an escutcheon." See Wb.

155. *I love to hear*, etc. Cf. v. 238 below.

[1] To the raven that sat on the forked tree he gave his gifts

156. *When move they on?* etc. The MS. reads:

> "'When move they on?' {'This sun / 'To-day} at noon
> 'T is said will see them march from Doune.'
> 'To-morrow then {makes / sees} meeting stern.'"

160. *Earn.* That is, the district about Loch Earn and the river of the same name flowing from the lake.

164. *Shaggy glen.* As already stated, *Trosachs* means *bristling.*

174. *Stance.* Station; a Scottish word.

177. *Trusty targe.* The MS. has "Highland targe."

197. *Shifting like flashes,* etc. That is, like the Northern Lights. Cf the *Lay,* ii. 86:

> "And red and bright the streamers light
> Were dancing in the glowing north.
>
> . . . . .
>
> He knew by the streamers that shot so bright
> That spirits were riding the northern light."

The MS. reads:

> "Thick as the flashes darted forth
> By morrice-dancers of the north;
> And saw at morn their {barges ride, / little fleet,}
> Close moored by the lone islet's side.
> Since this rude race dare not abide
> Upon their native mountain side,
> 'T is fit that Douglas should provide
> For his dear child some safe abode,
> And soon he comes to point the road."

207. *No, Allan,* etc. The MS. reads:

> "No, Allan, no! His words so kind
> Were but pretexts my fears to blind.
> When in such solemn tone and grave
> Douglas a parting blessing gave."

212. *Fixed and high.* Often misprinted "fixed on high."

215. *Stroke.* The MS. has "shock," and in the next line "adamantine" for *invulnerable.*

223. *Trowed.* Trusted, believed. Cf. Spenser, *F. Q.* v. 2. 34: "So much is more then [than] just to trow." See also *Luke,* xvii. 9.

231. *Cambus-kenneth's fane.* Cambus-kenneth Abbey, about a mile from Stirling, on the other side of the Forth. The massive tower is now the only part remaining entire.

235. *Friends'.* Many recent eds. misprint "friend's."

250. *Sooth.* True. See on i. 476 above.

261. *Merry it is,* etc. Scott says: "This little fairy tale is founded upon a very curious Danish ballad which occurs in the *Kæmpe Viser,* a collection of heroic songs first published in 1591, and reprinted in 1695, inscribed by Anders Sofrensen, the collector and editor, to Sophia, Queen of Denmark."

The measure is the common ballad-metre, the basis of which is a line of eight syllables followed by one of six, the even syllables accented, with the alternate lines rhyming, so as to form a four-line stanza. It is varied by extra unaccented syllables, and by rhymes within the longer lines (both of which modifications we have in 263 and 271), and by "double rhymes" (like *singing* and *ringing*).

262. *Mavis and merle.* Thrush and blackbird.

267. *Wold.* Open country, as opposed to *wood.* Cf. Tennyson, *In Memoriam*, 11: "Calm and deep peace on this high wold," etc. See also 724 below.

274. *Glaive.* Broadsword. Cf. Spenser, *F. Q.* iv. 7. 38: "laying both his hands upon his glave," etc. See also v. 253 below.

277. *Pall.* A rich fabric used for making *palls*, or mantles. Cf. *F. Q.* i. 7. 16. "He gave her gold and purple pall to weare."

278. *Wont.* Were accustomed. See on i. 408 above.

282. *'Twas but*, etc. The MS. reads:

> "'Twas but a midnight chance;
> For blindfold was the battle plied,
> And fortune held the lance."

283. *Darkling.* In the dark; a poetical word. Cf. Milton, *P. L.* iii. 39:

> "as the wakeful bird
> Sings darkling;"

Shakespeare, *Lear*, i. 4. 237: "So out went the candle, and we were left darkling," etc. See also 711 below.

285. *Vair.* The fur of the squirrel. See Wb.

286. *Sheen.* See on i. 208 above.

291. *Richard.* Here accented on the final syllable. Such license is not unusual in ballad poetry.

298. *Woned.* Dwelt. See on i. 408 above. Scott has the following note here:

"In a long dissertation upon the Fairy Superstitions, published in the *Minstrelsy of the Scottish Border*, the most valuable part of which was supplied by my learned and indefatigable friend, Dr. John Leyden, most of the circumstances are collected which can throw light upon the popular belief which even yet prevails respecting them in Scotland. Dr. Grahame, author of an entertaining work upon the *Scenery of the Perthshire Highlands*, already frequently quoted, has recorded with great accuracy the peculiar tenets held by the Highlanders on this topic, in the vicinity of Loch Katrine. The learned author is inclined to deduce the whole mythology from the Druidical system, — an opinion to which there are many objections.

'The *Daoine Shi'*, or Men of Peace, of the Highlanders, though not absolutely malevolent, are believed to be a peevish, repining race of beings, who, possessing themselves but a scanty portion of happiness, are supposed to envy mankind their more complete and substantial enjoyments. They are supposed to enjoy, in their subterraneous recesses, a sort of shadowy happiness, — a tinsel grandeur; which, however, they would willingly exchange for the more solid joys of mortality.

'They are believed to inhabit certain round grassy eminences, where they celebrate their nocturnal festivities by the light of the moon. About a mile beyond the source of the Forth, above Loch Con, there is a place called *Coirshi'an*, or the Cove of the Men of Peace, which is still supposed to be a favorite place of their residence. In the neighborhood are to be seen many round conical eminences, particularly one near the head of the lake, by the skirts of which many are still afraid to pass after sunset. It is believed that if, on Hallow-eve, any person, alone, goes round one of these hills nine times, towards the left hand (*sinistrorsum*) a door shall open, by which he will be admitted into their subterraneous abodes. Many, it is said, of mortal race have been entertained in their secret recesses. There they have been received into the most splendid apartments, and regaled with the most sumptuous banquets and delicious wines. Their females surpass the daughters of men in beauty. The *seemingly* happy inhabitants pass their time in festivity, and in dancing to notes of the softest music. But unhappy is the mortal who joins in their joys or ventures to partake of their dainties. By this indulgence he forfeits for ever the society of men, and is bound down irrevocably to the condition of *Shi'ich*, or Man of Peace.' "

301. *Why sounds*, etc. "It has been already observed that fairies, if not positively malevolent, are capricious, and easily offended. They are, like other proprietors of forests, peculiarly jealous of their rights of *vert* and *venison*. . . . This jealousy was also an attribute of the northern *Duergar*, or dwarfs; to many of whose distinctions the fairies seem to have succeeded, if, indeed, they are not the same class of beings. In the huge metrical record of German chivalry entitled the *Helden-Buch*, Sir Hildebrand, and the other heroes of whom it treats, are engaged in one of their most desperate adventures, from a rash violation of the rose-garden of an Elfin or Dwarf King.

"There are yet traces of a belief in this worst and most malicious order of fairies among the Border wilds. Dr. Leyden has introduced such a dwarf into his ballad entitled *The Cout of Keeldar*, and has not forgot his characteristic detestation of the chase.

'The third blast that young Keeldar blew,
Still stood the limber fern,
And a wee man, of swarthy hue,
Upstarted by a cairn.

'His russet weeds were brown as heath
That clothes the upland fell,
And the hair of his head was frizzly red
As the purple heather-bell.

'An urchin, clad in prickles red,
Clung cow'ring to his arm;
The hounds they howl'd, and backward fled,
As struck by fairy charm.

'"Why rises high the staghound's cry,
Where staghound ne'er should be?
Why wakes that horn the silent morn,
Without the leave of me?" —

'"Brown Dwarf, that o'er the muirland strays,
Thy name to Keeldar tell!" —
"The Brown Man of the Muirs, who stays
Beneath the heather-bell.

'"'Tis sweet beneath the heather-bell
To live in autumn brown;
And sweet to hear the lav'rock's swell,
Far, far from tower and town.

'"But woe betide the shrilling horn,
The chase's surly cheer!
And ever that hunter is forlorn
Whom first at morn I hear."'

"The poetical picture here given of the Duergar corresponds exactly with the following Northumberland legend, with which I was lately favored by my learned and kind friend, Mr. Surtees of Mainsforth, who has bestowed indefatigable labor upon the antiquities of the English Border counties. The subject is in itself so curious, that the length of the note will, I hope, be pardoned:

'I have only one record to offer of the appearance of our Northumbrian Duergar. My narratrix is Elizabeth Cockburn, an old wife of Offerton, in this county, whose credit, in a case of this kind, will not, I hope, be much impeached when I add that she is by her dull neighbors supposed to be occasionally insane, but by herself to be at those times endowed with a faculty of seeing visions and spectral appearances which shun the common ken.

'In the year before the great rebellion, two young men from Newcastle were sporting on the high moors above Eldson, and after pursuing their game several hours, sat down to dine in a green glen near one of the mountain streams. After their repast, the younger lad ran to the brook for water, and after stooping to drink, was surprised, on lifting his head again, by the appearance of a brown dwarf, who stood on a crag covered with brackens, across the burn. This extraordinary personage did not appear to be above half the stature of a common man, but was uncommonly stout and broad-built, having the appearance of vast strength. His dress was entirely brown, the color of the brackens, and his head covered with frizzled red hair. His countenance was expressive of the most savage ferocity, and his eyes glared like a bull. It seems he addressed the young man first, threatening him with his vengeance for having trespassed on his demesnes, and asking him if he knew in whose presence he stood? The youth replied that he now supposed him to be the lord of the moors; that he offended through ignorance; and offered to bring him the game he had killed. The dwarf was a little mollified by this submission, but remarked that nothing could be more offensive to him than such an offer, as he considered the wild animals as his subjects, and never failed to avenge their destruction. He condescended further to inform him that he was, like himself, mortal, though of years far exceeding the lot of common humanity, and (what I should not have had an idea of) that he hoped for salvation. He never, he added, fed on anything that had life, but lived in the summer on whortleberries, and in winter on nuts and apples, of which he had great store in the woods. Finally, he invited his new acquaintance to accompany him home and partake his hospitality, an offer which the youth was on the point of accepting, and was just going to spring across the brook (which if he had done, says Elizabeth, the dwarf would certainly have torn him in pieces), when his foot was arrested by the voice of his companion, who thought he had tarried long, and on looking round again, "the wee brown man was fled." The story adds that he was imprudent enough to slight the admonition, and to sport over the moors on his way homewards, but soon after his return he fell into a lingering disorder, and died within the year'" (Scott).

302. *Our moonlight circle's.* The MS. has "Our fairy ringlet's."

306. *The fairies' fatal green.* "As the *Daoine Shi'*, or Men of Peace, wore green habits, they were supposed to take offence when any mortals ventured to assume their favorite color. Indeed, from some reason, which has been, perhaps originally a general superstition, *green* is held in Scotland to be unlucky to particular tribes and counties. The Caithness men, who hold this belief, allege as a reason that their bands wore that color when they were cut off at the battle of Flodden; and for the same reason they avoid crossing the Ord on a Monday, being the day of the week on which their ill-omened array set forth. Green is also disliked by those of the name of Ogilvy; but more especially it is held fatal to the whole clan of Grahame. It is remembered of an aged gentleman of that name that when his horse fell in a fox-chase, he accounted for it at once by observing that the whipcord attached to his lash was of this unlucky color" (Scott).

308. *Wert christened man.* Scott says: "The Elves were supposed greatly to envy the privileges acquired by Christian initiation, and they gave to those mortals who had fallen into their power a certain precedence, founded upon this advantageous distinction. Tamlane, in the old ballad, describes his own rank in the fairy procession:

> 'For I ride on a milk-white steed,
> And aye nearest the town;
> Because I was a christen'd knight,
> They give me that renown.'"

312. *The curse of the sleepless eye.* Cf. *Macbeth*, i. 3. 19:

> "Sleep shall neither night nor day
> Hang upon his pent-house lid," etc.

313. *Part.* Depart. See on ii. 94 above.

322. *Grisly.* See on i. 704 above.

330. *Kindly.* Kindred, natural. See Wb., and cf. Shakespeare, *Much Ado*, iv. 1. 75:

> "that fatherly and kindly power
> That you have in her," etc.

345. *All is glistening show.* "No fact respecting Fairy-land seems to be better ascertained than the fantastic and illusory nature of their apparent pleasure and splendor. It has been already noticed in the former quotations from Dr. Grahame's entertaining volume, and may be confirmed by the following Highland tradition:—'A woman, whose new-born child had been conveyed by them into their secret abodes, was also carried thither herself, to remain, however, only until she should suckle her infant. She one day, during this period, observed the *Shi'ichs* busily employed in mixing various ingredients in a boiling

caldron, and as soon as the composition was prepared, she remarked that they all carefully anointed their eyes with it, laying the remainder aside for future use. In a moment when they were all absent, she also attempted to anoint her eyes with the precious drug, but had time to apply it to one eye only, when the *Daoine Shi'* returned. But with that eye she was henceforth enabled to see everything as it really passed in their secret abodes; she saw every object, not as she hitherto had done, in deceptive splendor and elegance, but in its genuine colors and form. The gaudy ornaments of the apartment were reduced to the walls of a gloomy cavern. Soon after, having discharged her office, she was dismissed to her own home. Still, however, she retained the faculty of seeing, with her medicated eye, everything that was done, anywhere in her presence, by the deceptive art of the order. One day, amidst a throng of people, she chanced to observe the *Shi'ich*, or man of peace, in whose possession she had left her child, though to every other eye invisible. Prompted by maternal affection, she inadvertently accosted him, and began to inquire after the welfare of her child. The man of peace, astonished at being thus recognized by one of mortal race, demanded how she had been enabled to discover him. Awed by the terrible frown of his countenance, she acknowledged what she had done. He spat in her eye, and extinguished it for ever.'

"It is very remarkable that this story, translated by Dr. Grahame from popular Gaelic tradition, is to be found in the *Otia Imperialia* of Gervase of Tilbury.[1] A work of great interest might be compiled upon the original of popular fiction, and the transmission of similar tales from age to age, and from country to country. The mythology of one period would then appear to pass into the romance of the next century, and that into the nursery tale of the subsequent ages. Such an investigation, while it went greatly to diminish our ideas of the richness of human invention, would also show that these fictions, however wild and childish, possess such charms for the populace as enable them to penetrate into countries unconnected by manners and language, and having no apparent intercourse to afford the means of transmission. It would carry me far beyond my bounds to produce instances of this community of fable among nations who never borrowed from each other any thing intrinsically worth learning. Indeed the wide diffusion of popular fictions may be compared to the facility with which straws and feathers are dispersed abroad by the wind, while valuable metals cannot be transported without trouble and labor. There lives, I believe, only one gentleman whose unlimited acquaintance with this subject might enable him to do it justice, — I mean my friend Mr. Francis Douce, of the British Museum, whose usual kindness will, I hope, pardon my mentioning his name while on a subject so closely connected with his extensive and curious researches" (Scott).

355. *Snatched away*, etc. "The subjects of Fairy-land were recruited from the regions of humanity by a sort of *crimping* system, which extended to adults as well as to infants. Many of those who were in this

[1] "This story is still current in the moors of Staffordshire, and adapted by the peasantry to their own meridian. I have repeatedly heard it told, exactly as here, by rustics who could not read. My last authority was a *nailer* near Cheadle" (R. Jamieson).

world supposed to have discharged the debt of nature, had only become denizens of the 'Londe of Faery'" (Scott).

357. *But wist I*, etc. But if I knew, etc. *Wist* is the past tense of *wit* (Mätzner). See on i. 596 above.

371. *Dunfermline*. A town in Fifeshire, 17 miles northwest of Edinburgh. It was long the residence of the Scottish kings, and the old abbey, which succeeded Iona as the place of royal sepulture, has been called "the Westminster of Scotland." Robert Bruce was the last sovereign buried here.

374. *Steepy*. Cf. iii. 304 above.

376. *Lincoln green*. See on i. 464 above.

386. *Morning-tide*. Cf. iii. 478 above.

387. *Bourne*. Bound, limit. Cf. the quotation from Milton in note on iii. 344 above.

392. *Scathe*. Harm, mischief. Spenser uses the word often; as in *F. Q.* i. 12. 34: "To worke new woe and improvided scath," etc. Cf. Shakespeare, *K. John*, ii. 1. 75: "To do offence and scathe in Christendom:" *Rich. III.* i. 3. 317: "To pray for them that have done scathe to us," etc.

393. *Kern*. See on 73 above.

395. *Conjure*. In prose we should have to write "conjure *him*."

403. *Yet life I hold*, etc. Cf. *Julius Cæsar*, i. 2. 84:

> "If it be aught toward the general good,
> Set honor in one eye and death i' the other,
> And I will look on both indifferently;
> For let the gods so speed me as I love
> The name of honor more than I fear death."

411. *Near Bochastle*. The MS. has "By Cambusmore." See on i. 103 and 106 above.

413. *Bower*. Lodging, dwelling. See on i. 217 above.

415. *Art*. Affectation.

417. *Before*. That is, at his visit to the Isle. Cf. ii. 96 fol. above.

418. *Was idly soothed*, etc. The MS. has "Was idly fond thy praise to hear."

421. *Atone*. Atone for. Shakespeare uses the verb transitively several times, but in the sense of *reconcile;* as in *Rich. II.* i. 1. 202: "Since we cannot atone you," etc. Cf. v. 735 below.

433. *If yet he is*. If he is still living.

437. *Train*. Lure; as in *Macbeth*, iv. 3. 118:

> "Devilish Macbeth
> By many of these trains hath sought to win me
> Into his power."

Cf. the use of the verb (=allure, entice); as in *C. of E.* iii. 2. 45: "O, train me not, sweet mermaid, with thy note;" Scott's *Lay*, iii. 146: "He thought to train him to the wood," etc. James was much given to gallantry, and many of his travels in disguise were on adventures of this kind. See on i. 409 above and vi. 740 below.

446. *As death*, etc. As if death, etc. See on ii. 56 above, and cf. 459 below.

464. *This ring*. The MS. has "This ring of gold the monarch gave."

471. *Lordship.* Landed estates.
473. *Reck of.* Care for; poetical.
474. *Ellen, thy hand.* The MS. has "Permit this hand;" and below:

> "'Seek thou the King, and on thy knee
> Put forth thy suit, whate'er it be,
> As ransom of his pledge to me;
> My name and this shall make thy way.'
> He put the little signet on," etc.

492. *He stammered*, etc. The MS. reads:

> "He stammered forth confused reply:
> 'Saxon,
'Sir Knight, } I shouted but to scare
> Yon raven from his dainty fare.'"

500. *Fared.* Went; the original sense of the word. Cf. *farewell* (which was at first a friendly wish for "the parting guest"), *wayfarer, thoroughfare*, etc.

506. *In tattered weeds*, etc. The MS. has "Wrapped in a tattered mantle gray." *Weeds* is used in the old sense of garments. Cf. Shakespeare, *M. N. D.* ii. 1. 256: "Weed wide enough to wrap a fairy in;" *Id.* ii. 2. 71: "Weeds of Athens he doth wear;" Milton, *L'Allegro*, 120: "In weeds of peace," etc. See also v. 465 below.

523. *In better time.* That is, in better times or days; not in the musical sense.

524. *Chime.* Accord, sing; a poetical use of the word. Cf. vi. 592 below.

531. *Allan.* "The *Allan* and *Devan* are two beautiful streams — the latter celebrated in the poetry of Burns — which descend from the hills of Perthshire into the great carse, or plain, of Stirling" (Lockhart).

548. *'T is Blanche*, etc. The MS. has:

> "'A Saxon born, a crazy maid —
> T is Blanche of Devan,' Murdoch said."

552. *Bridegroom.* Here accented on the second syllable. In 682 below it has the ordinary accent.

555. *'Scapes.* The word may be so printed here, but not in Elizabethan poetry. We find it in *prose* of that day; as in Bacon, *Adv. of L.* ii. 14. 9: "such as had scaped shipwreck." See Wb., and cf. *state* and *estate*, etc.

559. *Pitched a bar.* That is, in athletic contests. Cf. v. 648 below.

562. *See the gay pennons*, etc. The MS. reads:

> "With thee these pennons will I share,
> Then seek my true love through the air;
> But I 'll not lend that savage groom,
> To break his fall, one downy plume!
> Deep, deep, mid yon disjointed stones,
> The wolf shall batten on his bones."

567. *Batten.* Fatten; as in *Hamlet*, iii. 4. 67: "batten on this moor." Milton uses it transitively in *Lycidas*, 29: "Battening our flocks with the fresh dews of night."

575. *The Lincoln green.* "The Lowland garb" (520). Cf. also 376 above.

578. *For O my sweet William*, etc. The MS. reads:

> "Sweet William was a woodsman true,
> He stole poor Blanche's heart away;
> His coat was of the forest hue,
> And sweet he sung the Lowland Lay."

590. *The toils are pitched.* The nets are set. Cf. Shakespeare, *L. L. L.*, iv. 3. 2: "they have pitched a toil," etc. "The meaning is obvious. The hunters are Clan-Alpine's men; the stag of ten is Fitz James; the wounded doe is herself" (Taylor).

594. *A stag of ten.* "Having ten branches on his antlers" (Scott). Nares says that *antlers* is an error here, the word meaning "the short brow horns, not the branched horns;" but see Wb. Cf. Jonson, *Sad Shepherd*, i. 2:

> "And a hart of ten,
> Madam, I trow to be;"

and Massinger, *Emperor of the East*, iv. 2:

> "He 'll make you royal sport; he is a deer
> Of ten, at least."

595. *Sturdily.* As Taylor notes, the "triple rhymes" in this song are "of a very loose kind."

609. *Blanche's song.* Jeffrey says: "No machinery can be conceived more clumsy for effecting the deliverance of a distressed hero than the introduction of a mad woman, who, without knowing or caring about the wanderer, warns him *by a song* to take care of the ambush that was set for him. The maniacs of poetry have indeed had a prescriptive right to be musical, since the days of Ophelia downwards; but it is rather a rash extension of this privilege to make them sing good sense, and to make sensible people be guided by them."

To this Taylor well replies: "This criticism seems unjust. The cruelty of Roderick's raids in the Lowlands has already been hinted at, and the sight of the Lowland dress might well stir associations in the poor girl's mind which would lead her to look to the knight for help and protection, and also to warn him of his danger. It is plain, from Murdoch's surprise, that her being out of her captors' sight is looked on as dangerous, from which we may infer that she is not entirely crazed. Her song is not the only hint that Fitz-James follows. His suspicions had already twice been excited, so that the episode seems natural enough. As giving a distinct personal ground for the combat in canto v., it serves the poet's purpose still further. Without it, we should sympathize too much with the robber chief, who thinks that 'plundering Lowland field and fold is naught but retribution true;' but the sight of this sad fruit of his raids wins us back to the cause of law and order."

614. *Forth at full speed*, etc. The MS. reads:

> "Forth at full speed the Clansman went,
> But in his race his bow he bent,
> Halted — and back an arrow sent."

617. *Thrilled.* Quivered.

627. *Thine ambushed kin*, etc. The MS. transposes this line and the next, and goes on thus:

> "Resistless as the lightning's flame,
> The thrust betwixt his shoulder came."

Just below it reads:

> "Then o'er him hung, with falcon eye,
> And grimly smiled to see him die."

642. *Daggled*. Wet, soaked. Cf the *Lay*, i. 316: "Was daggled by the dashing spray."

649. *Helpless*. The MS. has "guiltless."

657. *Shred*. Cut off; a sense now obsolete. Cf. Withal's *Dictionary* (ed. 1608): "The superfluous and wast sprigs of vines, being cut and shreaded off, are called *sarmenta*."

659. *My brain*, etc. The MS. has "But now, my champion, it shall wave."

672. *Wreak*. Avenge. Cf. Shakespeare, *R. and J.* iii. 5. 102:

> "To wreak the love I bore my cousin
> Upon his body that hath slaughter'd him;"

Spenser, *F. Q.* ii. 3. 13: "to wreak so foule despight," etc.

679. *God, in my need*, etc. The MS. reads:

> "God, in my need, to me be true,
> As I wreak this on Roderick Dhu."

686. *Favor*. The *token* of the next line; referring to the knightly custom of wearing such a gift of lady-love or mistress. Cf. *Rich. II*. v. 3. 18:

> "And from the common'st creature pluck a glove,
> And wear it as a favor," etc.

See also the *Lay*, iv. 334:

> "With favor in his crest, or glove,
> Memorial of his ladye-love."

691. *At bay*. See on i. 133 above; and for the *dangerous foe*, cf. the note on i. 137.

698. *Couched him*. Lay down. See on i. 142 above.

700. *Rash adventures*. See on 437 above.

701. *Must prove*. The 1st ed. has "will prove."

705. *Bands at Doune*. Cf. 150 above.

711. *Darkling*. See on 283 above.

722. *Not the summer solstice*. Not even the heat of the summer.

724. *Wold*. See on 267 above.

731. *Beside its embers*, etc. The MS. reads:

> "By the decaying flame was laid
> A warrior in his Highland plaid."

For the rhyme here, see on i. 363 above. Cf. 764 below.

741. *I dare*, etc. The MS. reads:

> "I dare! to him and all the swarm
> He brings to aid his murderous arm."

746. *Slip*. A hunter's term for letting loose the greyhounds from the *slips*, or nooses, by which they were held until sent after the game

Turbervile (*Art of Venerie*) says: "We let slip a greyhound, and we cast off a hound." Cf. Shakespeare, *Cor.* i. 6. 39:

> "Holding Corioli in the name of Rome,
> Even like a fawning greyhound in the leash,
> To let him slip at will;"

and for the noun, *Hen. V.* iii. 1. 31:

> "I see you stand like greyhounds in the slips,
> Straining upon the start."

747. ***Who ever recked*, etc.** **Scott says: "St. John** actually used this illustration when engaged in confuting the plea of law proposed for the unfortunate Earl of Strafford: 'It was true, we gave laws to hares and deer, because they are beasts of chase; but it was never accounted either cruelty or foul play to knock foxes or wolves on the head as they can be found, because they are beasts of prey. In a word, the law and humanity were alike: the one being more fallacious, and the other more barbarous, than in any age had been vented in such an authority' (*Clarendon's History of the Rebellion*)."

762. *The hardened flesh of mountain deer.* "The Scottish Highlanders, in former times, had a concise mode of cooking their venison, or rather of dispensing with cooking it, which appears greatly to have surprised the French, whom chance made acquainted with it. The Vidame of Chartres, when a hostage in England, during the reign of Edward VI., was permitted to travel into Scotland, and penetrated as far as to the remote Highlands (*au fin fond des Sauvages*). After a great hunting-party, at which a most wonderful quantity of game was destroyed, he saw these *Scottish savages* devour a part of their venison raw, without any farther preparation than compressing it between two batons of wood, so as to force out the blood, and render it extremely hard. This they reckoned a great delicacy; and when the Vidame partook of it, his compliance with their taste rendered him extremely popular. This curious trait of manners was communicated by Mons. de Montmorency, a great friend of the Vidame, to Brantôme, by whom it is recorded in *Vies des Hommes Illustres*, lxxxix. 14. . . . After all, it may be doubted whether *la chaire nostree*, for so the French called the venison thus summarily prepared, was anything more than a mere rude kind of deer ham" (Scott).

772. *A mighty augury.* That of the Taghairm.

777. *Not for clan.* The 1st ed. has "nor for clan."

785. ***Stock and stone.*** **Cf. i. 130 above.**

787. *Coilantogle's ford.* On the Teith just below its exit from Loch Vennachar.

791. *The bittern's cry.* See on i. 642 above.

797. *And slept*, etc. The MS. has "streak" and "lake" for *beam* and *stream*.

CANTO FIFTH.

1. *Fair as the earliest beam*, etc. "This introductory stanza is well worked in with the story. The morning beam 'lights the fearful path on mountain side' which the two heroes of the poem are to traverse, and the comparison which it suggests enlists our sympathy for Roderick, who is to be the victim of defeat" (Taylor).

5. *And lights*, etc. The MS. has "And lights the fearful way along its side."

10. *Sheen.* See on i. 208.

14. *The dappled sky.* Cf. Milton, *L'Allegro*, 44: "Till the dappled dawn doth rise;" and Shakespeare, *Much Ado*, v. 3. 25:

> "and look, the gentle day,
> Before the wheels of Phœbus, round about
> Dapples the drowsy east with spots of gray."

15. *By.* The word is used for the rhyme, but perhaps gives the idea of hurry — *muttered off* the prayers.

16. *Steal.* The word here is expressive of *haste.*

18. *Gael.* "The Scottish Highlander calls himself *Gael*, or Gaul, and terms the Lowlanders *Sassenach*, or Saxons" (Scott).

22. *Wildering.* Bewildering. See on i. 274 above. For *winded*, see on i. 500.

32. *Bursting through.* That is, as it burst through — "a piece of loose writing" (Taylor).

36. *At length*, etc. The MS. reads:

> "At length they paced the mountain's side,
> And saw beneath the waters wide."

44. *The rugged mountain's scanty cloak*, etc. The MS. reads:

> "The rugged mountain's stunted screen
> Was dwarfish {shrubs / copse} with cliffs between."

46. *Shingles.* Gravel or pebbles. See on iii. 171 above.

Taylor says: "Note how the details of this description are used in stanza ix. — *shingles, bracken, broom.*"

51. *Dank.* Damp, moist. Cf. Shakespeare, *R. and J.* ii. 3. 6: "and night's dank dew;" Milton, *Sonnet to Mr. Lawrence*: "Now that the fields are dank, and ways are mire," etc.

64. *Sooth to tell.* To tell the truth. See on i. 476 above. *Sooth to say, to say sooth, in sooth, in good sooth*, etc., are common in old writers Cf. the *Lay*, introd. 57: "the sooth to speak."

65. *To claim its aid.* The MS. has "to draw my blade."

78. *Enough.* Suffice it that.

81. *A knight's free footsteps*, etc. The MS. reads:

> "{My errant footsteps / A knight's bold wanderings} far and wide."

86. *I urge thee not.* The MS. has "I ask it not," and in 95 "hall" for *Doune.*

106. *Outlawed.* The 1st ed. has "exiled."

128. *In the Regent's court*, etc. Cf. ii. 221 above.

124. *Albany.* The *Regent* of 108 above. He was the son of a younger brother of James III., who had been driven into exile by his brother's attempts on his life. He took refuge in France, where his son was made Lord High Admiral. On the death of James IV. he was called home by the Scottish nobles to assume the regency.

126. *Mewed.* Shut up. The word seems originally to have meant to moult, or shed the feathers; and as a noun, "the place, whether it be abroad or in the house, in which the hawk is put during the time she casts, or doth change her feathers" (R. Holmes's *Academy of Armory*, etc.). Spenser has both noun and verb; as in *F. Q.* i. 5. 20: "forth comming from her darksome mew;" and *Id.* ii. 3. 34: "In which vaine Braggadocchio was mewd." Milton uses the verb in the grand description of Liberty in *Of Unlicensed Printing:* "Methinks I see her as an eagle mewing her mighty youth, and kindling her undazzled eyes at the full midday beam." In England the noun is still used in the plural to denote a stable for horses. Pennant says that the royal stables in London were called *mews* from the fact that the buildings were formerly used for keeping the king's falcons.

Scott says here: "There is scarcely a more disorderly period of Scottish history than that which succeeded the battle of Flodden, and occupied the minority of James V. Feuds of ancient standing broke out like old wounds, and every quarrel among the independent nobility, which occurred daily, and almost hourly, gave rise to fresh bloodshed. 'There arose,' said Pitscottie, 'great trouble and deadly feuds in many parts of Scotland, both in the north and west parts. The Master of Forbes, in the north, slew the Laird of Meldrum, under tryst' (that is, *at an agreed and secure meeting*). 'Likewise, the Laird of Drummelzier slew the Lord Fleming at the hawking; and, likewise, there was slaughter among many other great lords.' Nor was the matter much mended under the government of the Earl of Angus; for though he caused the King to ride through all Scotland, 'under the pretence and color of justice, to punish thief and traitor, none were found greater than were in their own company. And none at that time durst strive with a Douglas, nor yet a Douglas's man; for if they would, they got the worst. Therefore none durst plainzie of no extortion, theft, reiff, nor slaughter done to them by the Douglases or their men; in that cause they were not heard so long as the Douglas had the court in guiding."

150. *Shingles.* Cf. 46 above.

152. *As to your sires.* The *target and claymore* were the weapons of the Ancient Britons. Taylor quotes Tacitus, *Agricola:* "ingentibus gladiis et brevibus cetris."

161. *Rears.* Raises. The word was formerly less restricted in its application than at present. Cf. Shakespeare's "rear my hand" (*Temp.* ii. 1. 295, *J. C.* iii. 1. 30), "rear the higher our opinion" (*A. and C.* ii. 1. 35), etc.; Milton's "he rear'd me," that is, lifted me up (*P. L.* viii. 316), "rear'd her lank head" (*Comus*, 836), etc. Spenser uses it in the sense of take away (like the cant *lift*=steal); as in *F. Q.* iii. 10. 12:

> "She to his closet went, where all his wealth
> Lay hid; thereof she countlesse summes did reare;"

and *Id.* iii. 10. 53:

> "like as a Beare,
> That creeping close among the hives to reare
> An hony-combe," etc.

Wb. does not give this sense, which we believe is found only in Spenser

165. *Shall with strong hand*, etc. Scott has the following note here: "The ancient Highlanders verified in their practice the lines of Gray (*Fragment on the Alliance of Education and Government*):

> 'An iron race the mountain cliffs maintain,
> Foes to the gentler genius of the plain;
> For where unwearied sinews must be found,
> With side-long plough to quell the flinty ground,
> To turn the torrent's swift descending flood,
> To tame the savage rushing from the wood,
> What wonder if, to patient valor train'd,
> They guard with spirit what by strength they gain'd;
> And while their rocky ramparts round they see
> The rough abode of want and liberty
> (As lawless force from confidence will grow),
> Insult the plenty of the vales below?'

"So far, indeed, was a *Creagh*, or foray, from being held disgraceful, that a young chief was always expected to show his talents for command so soon as he assumed it, by leading his clan on a successful enterprise of this nature, either against a neighboring sept, for which constant feuds usually furnished an apology, or against the *Sassenach*, Saxons, or Lowlanders, for which no apology was necessary. The Gael, great traditional historians, never forgot that the Lowlands had, at some remote period, been the property of their Celtic forefathers, which furnished an ample vindication of all the ravages that they could make on the unfortunate districts which lay within their reach. Sir James Grant of Grant is in possession of a letter of apology from Cameron of Lochiel, whose men had committed some depredation upon a farm called Moines, occupied by one of the Grants. Lochiel assures Grant that, however the mistake had happened, his instructions were precise, that the party should foray the province of Moray (a Lowland district), where, as he coolly observes, 'all men take their prey.'"

177. *Good faith.* In good faith, *bona fide*; as often in old writers.

192. *Bower.* See on i. 217 above.

195. *This rebel Chieftain*, etc. The MS. reads:

> "This dark Sir Roderick / This savage Chieftain } and his band;"

and below:

> "From copse to copse the signal flew.
> Instant, through copse and crags, arose;"

and in 205 "shoots" for *sends*.

208. *And every tuft*, etc. The MS. reads:

> "And each lone tuft of broom gives life
> To plaided warrior armed for strife.
> That whistle manned the lonely glen
> With full five hundred armed men;"

and below (214):

> All silent, too, they stood, and still,
> Watching their leader's beck and will,

> While forward step and weapon show
> They long to rush upon the foe,
> Like the loose crag whose tottering mass
> Hung threatening o'er the hollow pass."

219. *Verge.* See on iv. 83 above.

230. *Manned himself.* Cf. Addison's "manned his soul," quoted by Wb.

238. *The stern joy,* etc. Cf. iv. 155 above.

239. *Foeman.* The reading of the 1st ed. and that of 1821; "foe men" in many recent eds.

246. *Their mother Earth,* etc. Alluding to the old myths of the earth-born Giants and of Cadmus.

252. *Glinted.* Flashed; a Scottish word. Jamieson defines *glint* "to glance, gleam, or pass suddenly like a flash of lightning."

253. *Glaive.* See on iv. 274 above. The *jack* was "a horseman's defensive upper garment, quilted and covered with strong leather" (Nares). It was sometimes also strengthened with iron rings, plates, or bosses. Cf. Lyly, *Euphues:* "jackes quilted, and covered over with leather, fustian, or canvas, over thick plates of yron that are sowed to the same." Scott, in the *Eve of St. John*, speaks of "his plate-jack." For *spear* the 1st ed. has "lance."

267. *One valiant hand.* The MS. has "one brave man's hand."

268. *Lay.* Were staked.

270. *I only meant,* etc. Scott says: "This incident, like some other passages in the poem, illustrative of the character of the ancient Gael, is not imaginary, but borrowed from fact. The Highlanders, with the inconsistency of most nations in the same state, were alternately capable of great exertions of generosity and of cruel revenge and perfidy. The following story I can only quote from tradition, but with such an assurance from those by whom it was communicated as permits me little doubt of its authenticity. Early in the last century, John Gunn, a noted Cateran, or Highland robber, infested Inverness-shire, and levied *black-mail* up to the walls of the provincial capital. A garrison was then maintained in the castle of that town, and their pay (country banks being unknown) was usually transmitted in specie under the guard of a small escort. It chanced that the officer who commanded this little party was unexpectedly obliged to halt, about thirty miles from Inverness, at a miserable inn. About nightfall, a stranger in the Highland dress, and of very prepossessing appearance, entered the same house. Separate accommodation being impossible, the Englishman offered the newly-arrived guest a part of his supper, which was accepted with reluctance. By the conversation he found his new acquaintance knew well all the passes of the country, which induced him eagerly to request his company on the ensuing morning. He neither disguised his business and charge, nor his apprehensions of that celebrated freebooter, John Gunn. The Highlander hesitated a moment, and then frankly consented to be his guide. Forth they set in the morning; and in travelling through a solitary and dreary glen, the discourse again turned on John Gunn. 'Would you like to see him?' said the guide; and without waiting an answer to this alarming ques-

tion, he whistled, and the English officer, with his small party, were surrounded by a body of Highlanders, whose numbers put resistance out of question, and who were all well armed. 'Stranger,' resumed the guide, 'I am that very John Gunn by whom you feared to be intercepted, and not without cause; for I came to the inn last night with the express purpose of learning your route, that I and my followers might ease you of your charge by the road. But I am incapable of betraying the trust you reposed in me, and having convinced you that you were in my power, I can only dismiss you unplundered and uninjured.' He then gave the officer directions for his journey, and disappeared with his party as suddenly as they had presented themselves."

277. *Flood.* Flow; used for the sake of the rhyme, like *drew* just below. *Wont* = wonted.

286. *And still*, etc. The MS. reads:

"And still, from copse and heather bush,
Fancy saw spear and broadsword rush."

298. *Three mighty lakes.* Katrine, Achray, and Vennachar. Scott says: "The torrent which discharges itself from Loch Vennachar, the lowest and eastmost of the three lakes which form the scenery adjoining to the Trosachs, sweeps through a flat and extensive moor, called Bochastle. Upon a small eminence called the *Dun* of Bochastle, and indeed on the plain itself, are some intrenchments which have been thought Roman. There is adjacent to Callander a sweet villa, the residence of Captain Fairfoul, entitled the Roman Camp."

301. *Mouldering.* The MS. has "martial."

309. *This murderous Chief*, etc. Cf. 106 above.

315. *All vantageless*, etc. Scott says: "The duellists of former times did not always stand upon those punctilios respecting equality of arms, which are now judged essential to fair combat. It is true that in formal combats in the lists the parties were, by the judges of the field, put as nearly as possible in the same circumstances. But in private duel it was often otherwise. In that desperate combat which was fought between Quelus, a minion of Henry III. of France, and Antraguet, with two seconds on each side, from which only two persons escaped alive, Quelus complained that his antagonist had over him the advantage of a poniard which he used in parrying, while his left hand, which he was forced to employ for the same purpose, was cruelly mangled. When he charged Antraguet with this odds, 'Thou hast done wrong,' answered he, 'to forget thy dagger at home. We are here to fight, and not to settle punctilios of arms.' In a similar duel, however, a young brother of the house of Aubayne, in Angoulesme, behaved more generously on the like occasion, and at once threw away his dagger when his enemy challenged it as an undue advantage. But at this time hardly anything can be conceived more horridly brutal and savage than the mode in which private quarrels were conducted in France. Those who were most jealous of the point of honor, and acquired the title of *Ruffinés*, did not scruple to take every advantage of strength, numbers, surprise, and arms, to accomplish their revenge."

329. *By prophet bred*, etc. See iii. 91 fol. above; and for the expression cf. iv. 124.

347. *Dark lightning*, etc. The MS. has "In lightning flashed the Chief's dark eye," which might serve as a comment on *Dark lightning.*

349. *Kern.* See on iv. 73 above.

351. *He yields not*, etc. The MS. has "He stoops not, he, to James nor Fate."

356. *Carpet knight.* Cf. Shakespeare, *T. N.* iii. 4. 257: "He is knight, dubbed with unhatched rapier and on carpet consideration."

364. *Ruth.* Pity; obsolete, though we still have *ruthless.* Cf. Spenser, *F. Q.* i. 1. 50:

> "to stirre up gentle ruth,
> Both for her noble blood, and for her tender youth;"

Milton, *Lycidas*, 163: "Look homeward, Angel, now, and melt with ruth," etc.

380. *His targe.* Scott says: "A round target of light wood, covered with strong leather and studded with brass or iron, was a necessary part of a Highlander's equipment. In charging regular troops they received the thrust of the bayonet in this buckler, twisted it aside, and used the broadsword against the encumbered soldier. In the civil war of 1745 most of the front rank of the clans were thus armed; and Captain Grose (*Military Antiquities*, vol. i. p. 164) informs us that in 1747 the privates of the 42d regiment, then in Flanders, were for the most part permitted to carry targets. A person thus armed had a considerable advantage in private fray. Among verses between Swift and Sheridan, lately published by Dr. Barrett, there is an account of such an encounter, in which the circumstances, and consequently the relative superiority of the combatants, are precisely the reverse of those in the text.

. . . .

383. *Trained abroad.* That is, in France. See on i. 163 above. Scott says here: "The use of defensive armor, and particularly of the buckler, or target, was general in Queen Elizabeth's time, although that of the single rapier seems to have been occasionally practised much earlier (see Douce's *Illustrations of Shakespeare*, vol. ii. p. 61). Rowland Yorke, however, who betrayed the fort of Zutphen to the Spaniards, for which good service he was afterwards poisoned by them, is said to have been the first who brought the rapier-fight into general use. Fuller, speaking of the swash-bucklers, or bullies, of Queen Elizabeth's time, says, 'West Smithfield was formerly called Ruffians' Hall, where such men usually met, casually or otherwise, to try *masteries* with sword and buckler. More were frightened than hurt, more hurt than killed therewith, it being accounted unmanly to strike beneath the knee. But since that desperate traitor Rowland Yorke first introduced thrusting with rapiers, sword and buckler are disused.' In *The Two Angry Women of Abingdon*, a comedy, printed in 1599, we have a pathetic complaint: 'Sword and buckler fight begins to grow out of use. I am sorry for it; I shall never see good manhood again. If it be once gone, this poking fight of rapier and dagger will come up; then a tall man

and a good sword and buckler man will be spitted like a cat or rabbit.' But the rapier had upon the Continent long superseded, in private duel, the use of sword and shield. The masters of the noble science of defence were chiefly Italians. They made great mystery of their art and mode of instruction, never suffered any person to be present but the scholar who was to be taught, and even examined closets, beds, and other places of possible concealment. Their lessons often gave the most treacherous advantages; for the challenged, having the right to choose his weapons, frequently selected some strange, unusual, and inconvenient kind of arms, the use of which he practised under these instructors, and thus killed at his ease his antagonist, to whom it was presented for the first time on the field of battle. See Brantôme's *Discourse on Duels*, and the work on the same subject, '*si gentement écrit*,' by the venerable Dr. Paris de Puteo. The Highlanders continued to use broadsword and target until disarmed after the affair of 1745–6."

385. *Ward.* Posture of defence; a technical term in fencing. Cf. Falstaff's "Thou knowest my old ward" (1 *Hen. IV.* ii. 4. 215), etc.

387. *While less expert*, etc. The MS. reads:

> "Not Roderick thus, though stronger far,
> More tall, and more inured to war."

401, 402. *And backward*, etc. This couplet is not in the MS.; and the same is true of 405, 406.

406. *Let recreant yield*, etc. The MS. has "Yield they alone who fear to die." Scott says: "I have not ventured to render this duel so savagely desperate as that of the celebrated Sir Ewan of Lochiel, chief of the clan Cameron, called, from his sable complexion, Ewan Dhu. He was the last man in Scotland who maintained the royal cause during the great Civil War, and his constant incursions rendered him a very unpleasant neighbor to the republican garrison at Inverlochy, now Fort William. The governor of the fort detached a party of three hundred men to lay waste Lochiel's possessions and cut down his trees; but in a sudden and desperate attack made upon them by the chieftain with very inferior numbers, they were almost all cut to pieces. The skirmish is detailed in a curious memoir of Sir Ewan's life, printed in the Appendix of Pennant's *Scottish Tour* (vol. i. p. 375):

'In this engagement Lochiel himself had several wonderful escapes. In the retreat of the English, one of the strongest and bravest of the officers retired behind a bush, when he observed Lochiel pursuing, and seeing him unaccompanied with any, he leapt out and thought him his prey. They met one another with equal fury. The combat was long and doubtful: the English gentleman had by far the advantage in strength and size; but Lochiel, exceeding him in nimbleness and agility, in the end tript the sword out of his hand; they closed and wrestled, till both fell to the ground in each other's arms. The English officer got above Lochiel, and pressed him hard, but stretching forth his neck, by attempting to disengage himself, Lochiel, who by this time had his hands at liberty, with his left hand seized him by the collar, and jumping at his extended throat, he bit it with his teeth quite through, and kept such a hold of his grasp, that he brought away his mouthful; this, he said, *was the sweetest bit he ever had in his lifetime.*'"

435. *Unwounded*, etc. The MS. reads:

> "Panting and breathless on the sands,
> But all unwounded, now he stands;"

and just below:

> "Redeemed, unhoped, from deadly strife;
> Next on his foe his look he { cast, threw,
> Whose every breath appeared his last."

447. *Unbonneted.* Past tense, not participle.

449. *Then faint afar.* The MS. has "Faint and afar."

452. *Lincoln green.* See on i. 464 above.

462. *We destined*, etc. Cf. iv. 411 above.

465. *Weed.* Dress. See on iv. 506 above.

466. *Boune.* Ready. See on iv. 36 above.

479. *Steel.* Spur. Cf. i. 115 above.

485. *Carhonie's hill.* About a mile from the lower end of Loch Vennachar.

486. *Pricked.* Spurred. It came to mean ride; as in *F. Q.* i. 1. 1: "A gentle Knight was pricking on the plaine," etc. Cf. 754 below.

490. *Torry and Lendrick.* These places, like *Deanstown*, *Doune* (see on iv. 19 above), *Blair-Drummond*, *Ochtertyre*, and *Kier*, are all on the banks of the Teith, between Callander and Stirling. Lockhart says: "It may be worth noting that the poet marks the progress of the King by naming in succession places familiar and dear to his own early recollections — *Blair-Drummond*, the seat of the Homes of Kaimes; *Kier*, that of the principal family of the name of Stirling; *Ochtertyre*, that of John Ramsay, the well-known antiquary, and correspondent of Burns; and *Craigforth*, that of the Callenders of Craigforth, almost under the walls of Stirling Castle; — all hospitable roofs, under which he had spent many of his younger days."

494. *Sees the hoofs strike fire.* The MS. has "Saw their hoofs of fire."

496. *They mark*, etc. The *to* of the infinitive is omitted in *glance*, as if *mark* had been *see*.

498. *Sweltering.* The 1st ed. has "swelling."

506. *Flinty.* The MS. has "steepy;" and in 514 "gains" for *scales.*

525. *Saint Serle.* "The King himself is in such distress for a rhyme as to be obliged to apply to one of the obscurest saints in the calendar" (Jeffrey). The MS. has "by my word," and "Lord" for *Earl* in the next line.

534. *Cambus-kenneth's abbey gray.* See on iv. 231 above.

547. *By.* Gone by, past.

551. *O sad and fatal mound!* "An eminence on the northeast of the Castle, where state criminals were executed. Stirling was often polluted with noble blood. It is thus apostrophized by J. Johnston:

> 'Discordia tristis
> Heu quoties procerum sanguine tinxit humum!
> Hoc uno infelix, et felix cetera; nusquam
> Laetior aut caeli frons geniusve soli.'

"The fate of William, eighth Earl of Douglas, whom James II. stabbed in Stirling Castle with his own hand, and while under his royal safe-conduct, is familiar to all who read Scottish history. Murdack Duke of Albany, Duncan Earl of Lennox, his father-in-law, and his two sons, Walter and Alexander Stuart, were executed at Stirling, in 1425. They were beheaded upon an eminence without the Castle walls, but making part of the same hill, from whence they could behold their strong Castle of Doune and their extensive possessions. This 'heading hill,' as it was sometimes termed, bears commonly the less terrible name of Hurly-hacket, from its having been the scene of a courtly amusement alluded to by Sir David Lindsay, who says of the pastimes in which the young King was engaged:

'Some harled him to the Hurly-hacket;'

which consisted in sliding — in some sort of chair, it may be supposed — from top to bottom of a smooth bank. The boys of Edinburgh, about twenty years ago, used to play at the hurly-hacket on the Calton Hill, using for their seat a horse's skull" (Scott).

558. *The Franciscan steeple.* The *Greyfriars Church*, built by James IV. in 1594 on the hill not far from the Castle, is still standing, and has been recently restored. Here James VI. was crowned on the 29th of July, 1567, and John Knox preached the coronation sermon.

562. *Morrice-dancers.* The *morrice* or *morris* dance was probably of Spanish (or *Moorish*, as the name implies) origin, but after its introduction into England it became blended with the Mayday games. A full historical account of it is given in Douce's *Illustrations of Shakespeare.* The characters in it in early times were the following: "Robin Hood, Little John, Friar Tuck, Maid Marian (Robin's mistress and the queen or lady of the May), the fool, the piper, and several morris-dancers habited, as it appears, in various modes. Afterwards a hobby-horse and a dragon were added" (Douce). For a description of the game, see Scott's *Abbot*, ch. xiv., and the author's note. See also on 614 below.

564. *The burghers hold their sports to-day.* Scott has the following note here:

"Every burgh of Scotland of the least note, but more especially the considerable towns, had their solemn *play*, or festival, when feats of archery were exhibited, and prizes distributed to those who excelled in wrestling, hurling the bar, and the other gymnastic exercises of the period. Stirling, a usual place of royal residence, was not likely to be deficient in pomp upon such occasions, especially since James V. was very partial to them. His ready participation in these popular amusements was one cause of his acquiring the title of the King of the Commons, or *Rex Plebeiorum*, as Lesley has latinized it. The usual prize to the best shooter was a silver arrow. Such a one is preserved at Selkirk and at Peebles. At Dumfries a silver gun was substituted, and the contention transferred to firearms. The ceremony, as there performed, is the subject of an excellent Scottish poem, by Mr. John Mayne, entitled the *Siller Gun*, 1808, which surpasses the efforts of Fergusson, and comes near those of Burns.

"Of James's attachment to archery, Pitscottie, the faithful though rude recorder of the manners of that period, has given us evidence:

'In this year there came an ambassador out of England, named Lord William Howard, with a bishop with him, with many other gentlemen, to the number of threescore horse, which were all able men and waled [picked] men for all kind of games and pastimes, shooting, louping, running, wrestling, and casting of the stone, but they were well sayed [essayed or tried] ere they past out of Scotland, and that by their own provocation; but ever they tint: till at last, the Queen of Scotland, the King's mother, favoured the English-men, because she was the King of England's sister; and therefore she took an enterprise of archery upon the English-men's hands, contrary her son the King, and any six in Scotland that he would wale, either gentlemen or yeomen, that the English-men should shoot against them either at pricks, revers, or buts, as the Scots pleased.

'The King, hearing this of his mother, was content, and gart her pawn a hundred crowns and a tun of wine upon the English-men's hands; and he incontinent laid down as much for the Scottish-men. The field and ground was chosen in St. Andrews, and three landed men and three yeomen chosen to shoot against the English-men,—to wit, David Wemyss of that ilk, David Arnot of that ilk, and Mr. John Wedderburn, vicar of Dundee; the yeomen, John Thomson, in Leith, Steven Taburner, with a piper, called Alexander Bailie; they shot very near, and warred [worsted] the English-men of the enterprise, and wan the hundred crowns and the tun of wine, which made the King very merry that his men wan the victory.'"

571. *Play my prize.* The same expression occurs in Shakespeare, *T. A.* i. 1. 399: "You have play'd your prize." Cf. also *M. of V.* iii. 2. 142: "Like one of two contending in a prize," etc

575. *The Castle gates.* The main entrance to the Castle, not the *postern gate* of 532 above.

580. *Fair Scotland's King*, etc. The MS. reads:

> "King James and all his nobles went . . .
> Ever the King was bending low
> To his white jennet's saddle-bow,
> Doffing his cap to burgher dame,
> Who smiling blushed for pride and shame."

601. *There nobles*, etc. The MS. reads:

> "Nobles who mourned their power restrained,
> And the poor burgher's joys disdained;
> Dark chief, who, hostage for his clan,
> Was from his home a banished man,
> Who thought upon his own gray tower,
> The waving woods, his feudal bower,
> And deemed himself a shameful part
> Of pageant that he cursed in heart."

611. *With bell at heel.* Douce says that "the number of bells round each leg of the morris-dancers amounted from twenty to forty;" but Scott, in a note to *The Fair Maid of Perth*, speaks of 252 small bells in sets of twelve at regular musical intervals.

612. *Their mazes wheel.* The MS. adds:

> "With awkward stride there city groom
> Would part of fabled knight assume."

THE GATE OF STIRLING CASTLE.

614. *Robin Hood.* Scott says here: "The exhibition of this renowned outlaw and his band was a favorite frolic at such festivals as we are describing. This sporting, in which kings did not disdain to be actors, was prohibited in Scotland upon the Reformation, by a statute of the 6th Parliament of Queen Mary, c. 61, A. D. 1555, which ordered, under heavy penalties, that 'na manner of person be chosen Robert Hude, nor Little John, Abbot of Unreason, Queen of May, nor otherwise.' But in 1561, the 'rascal multitude,' says John Knox, 'were stirred up to make a Robin Hude, whilk enormity was of mony years left and damned by statute and act of Parliament; yet would they not be forbidden.' Accordingly they raised a very serious tumult, and at length made prisoners the magistrates who endeavored to suppress it, and would not release them till they extorted a formal promise that no one should be punished for his share of the disturbance. It would seem, from the complaints of the General Assembly of the Kirk, that these profane festivities were continued down to 1592 (*Book of the Universal Kirk*, p. 414). Bold Robin was, to say the least, equally successful in

maintaining his ground against the reformed clergy of England; for the simple and evangelical Latimer complains of coming to a country church where the people refused to hear him because it was Robin Hood's day, and his mitre and rochet were fain to give way to the village pastime. Much curious information on this subject may be found in the Preliminary Dissertation to the late Mr. Ritson's edition of the songs respecting this memorable outlaw. The game of Robin Hood was usually acted in May; and he was associated with the morrice-dancers, on whom so much illustration has been bestowed by the commentators on Shakespeare. A very lively picture of these festivities, containing a great deal of curious information on the subject of the private life and amusements of our ancestors, was thrown, by the late ingenious Mr. Strutt, into his romance entitled *Queen-hoo Hall*, published after his death, in 1808."

615. *Friar Tuck.* "Robin Hood's fat friar," as Shakespeare calls him (*T. G. of V.* iv. 1. 36), who figures in the Robin Hood ballads and in *Ivanhoe*. *Scarlet* and *Little John* are mentioned in one of Master Silence's snatches of song in 2 *Hen. IV.* v. 3. 107: "And Robin, Scarlet, and John." *Scathelocke* is a brother of Scarlet in Ben Jonson's *Sad Shepherd*, which is a "Tale of Robin Hood," and *Mutch* is a bailiff in the same play.

626. *Stake.* Prize.

627. *Fondly he watched*, etc. The MS. reads:

"Fondly he watched, with watery eye,
For answering glance of sympathy,
But no emotion made reply!
Indifferent as to unknown } wight,
Cold as to unknown yeoman }
The King gave forth the arrow bright."

630. *To archer wight.* That is, to any ordinary archer; or *wight* may be the old adjective = strong. Scott has the following note here:

"The Douglas of the poem is an imaginary person, a supposed uncle of the Earl of Angus. But the King's behavior during an unexpected interview with the Laird of Kilspindie, one of the banished Douglases, under circumstances similar to those in the text, is imitated from a real story told by Hume of Godscroft. I would have availed myself more fully of the simple and affecting circumstances of the old history, had they not been already woven into a pathetic ballad by my friend Mr. Finlay.[1]

'His [the King's] implacability [towards the family of Douglas] did also appear in his carriage towards Archibald of Kilspindie, whom he, when he was a child, loved singularly well for his ability of body, and was wont to call him his Gray-Steill.[2] Archibald, being banished into England, could not well comport with the humor of that nation, which he thought to be too proud, and that they had too high a conceit of themselves, joined with a contempt and despising of all others. Wherefore, being wearied of that life, and remembering the King's favor of old towards him, he determined to try the King's mercifulness and clem-

[1] See *Scottish Historical and Romantic Ballads*, Glasgow, 1808, vol. ii. p. 117.
[2] A champion of popular romance; see *Ellis's Romances*, vol. iii.

ency. So he comes into Scotland, and taking occasion of the King's hunting in the park at Stirling, he casts himself to be in his way, as he was coming home to the Castle. So soon as the King saw him afar off, ere he came near, he guessed it was he, and said to one of his courtiers, "Yonder is my Gray-Steill, Archibald of Kilspindie, if he be alive." The other answered that it could not be he, and that he durst not come into the King's presence. The King approaching, he fell upon his knees and craved pardon, and promised from thenceforward to abstain from meddling in public affairs, and to lead a quiet and private life. The King went by without giving him any answer, and trotted a good round pace up the hill. Kilspindie followed, and though he wore on him a secret, or shirt of mail, for his particular enemies, was as soon at the Castle gate as the King. There he sat him down upon a stone without, and entreated some of the King's servants for a cup of drink, being weary and thirsty; but they, fearing the King's displeasure, durst give him none. When the King was set at his dinner, he asked what he had done, what he had said, and whither he had gone? It was told him that he had desired a cup of drink, and had gotten none. The King reproved them very sharply for their discourtesy, and told them that if he had not taken an oath that no Douglas should ever serve him, he would have received him into his service, for he had seen him sometime a man of great ability. Then he sent him word to go to Leith, and expect his further pleasure. Then some kinsman of David Falconer, the cannonier, that was slain at Tantallon, began to quarrel with Archibald about the matter, wherewith the King showed himself not well pleased when he heard of it. Then he commanded him to go to France for a certain space, till he heard further from him. And so he did, and died shortly after. This gave occasion to the King of England (Henry VIII.) to blame his nephew, alleging the old saying, That a king's face should give grace. For this Archibald (whatsoever were Angus's or Sir George's fault) had not been principal actor of anything, nor no counsellor nor stirrer up, but only a follower of his friends, and that noways cruelly disposed' (*Hume of Godscroft*, ii. 107)."

637. *Larbert* is a town about ten miles to the south of Stirling, and *Alloa* another seven miles to the east on the north side of the Forth.

641. *To Douglas gave a golden ring.* Scott says: "The usual prize of a wrestling was a ram and a ring, but the animal would have embarrassed my story. Thus, in the *Cokes Tale of Gamelyn*, ascribed to Chaucer:

'There happed to be there beside
Tryed a wrestling;
And therefore there was y-setten
A ram and als a ring."

Again, the *Litil Geste of Robin Hood:*

'By a bridge was a wrestling,
And there taryed was he,
And there was all the best yemen
Of all the west countrey.
A full fayre game there was set up,
A white bull up y-pight,
A great courser with saddle and brydle,
With gold burnished full bryght;

> A payre of gloves, a red golde ringe,
> A pipe of wine, good fay;
> What man bereth him best, I wis,
> The prise shall bear away.' "

648. *To hurl the massive bar*. Cf. iv. 559 above.

658. *Scottish strength*. The MS. has "mortal strength."

660. *The Ladies' Rock*. A point in the "valley" between the Castle and the Greyfriars Church. It was formerly the chief place for viewing the games, which were held in this "valley," or depression in the hill on which the Castle stands. It must not be confounded with the *Ladies' Lookout*, a favorite point of view on the Castle walls.

662. *Well filled*. The MS. has "weighed down;" and in 664, "Scattered the gold among the crowd."

674. *Ere Douglas*, etc. The MS. has "Ere James of Douglas' stalwart hand;" and in 677, "worn" for *wrecked*.

681. *Murmurs*. Some eds. have "murmur."

685. *The banished man*. The MS. has "his stately form."

724. *Needs but a buffet*. Only a single blow is needed.

728. *Then clamored*, etc. The MS. and 1st ed. have "Clamored his comrades of the train;" and in 730 the MS. has "warrior's" for *Baron's*.

735. *Atone*. See on iv. 421 above.

744. *But shall a Monarch's presence*, etc. The MS. reads:

> "But in my court injurious blow,
> And bearded thus, and thus out-dared?
> What, ho!" etc.

747. *Ward*. Guarding, confinement under guard. Cf. *Gen*. xl. 3.

752. *Misarray*. Disorder, confusion. Neither Wb. nor Worc. gives the word.

754. *Pricked*. Spurred, rode. See on 486 above.

755. *Repelled*, etc. The MS. has "Their threats repelled by insult loud."

768. *Hyndford*. A village on the Clyde, a few miles above Lanark.

790. *Widow's mate expires*. An instance of *prolepsis*, or "anticipation" in the use of a word. He must expire before she can be a *widow*. Cf. *Macbeth*, iii. 4. 76:

> "Blood hath been shed ere now, i' the olden time,
> Ere human statute purg'd the gentle weal;"

that is, purged it and *made* it *gentle*.

794. *Ward*. Ward off, avert.

796. *The crowd's wild fury*, etc. The MS. reads:

> "The crowd's wild fury ebbed amain
> In tears, as tempests sink in rain."

The 1st ed. reads as in the text, but that of 1821 has "sunk amain."

The figure here is a favorite one with Shakespeare. Cf. *R. of L.* 1788:

> "This windy tempest, till it blow up rain,
> Held back his sorrow's tide, to make it more;
> At last it rains, and busy winds give o'er;"

3 *Hen. VI.* i. 4. 146:

> "For raging wind blows up incessant showers,
> And, when the rage allays, the rain begins;"

Id. ii. 5. 85:

> "see, see, what showers arise,
> Blown with the windy tempest of my heart;"

T. and C. iv. 4. 55: "Where are my tears? rain, to lay this wind, or my heart will be blown up by the root;" and *Macbeth*, i. 7. 25: "That tears shall drown the wind."

808. *The rough soldier.* Sir John of Hyndford (768 above).

811. *He led.* The 1st ed. has "they led," and "their" for *his* in 813.

812. *Verge.* Note the rhyme with *charge*, and see on iv. 83 above.

819. *This common fool.* Cf. Shakespeare's "fool multitude" (*M. of V.* ii. 9. 26). Just below Lockhart quotes *Coriolanus*, i. 1. 180:

> "Who deserves greatness
> Deserves your hate; and your affections are
> A sick man's appetite, who desires most that
> Which would increase his evil. He that depends
> Upon your favors swims with fins of lead
> And hews down oaks with rushes. Hang ye! Trust ye?
> With every minute you do change a mind,
> And call him noble that was now your hate,
> Him vile that was your garland."

821. *Douglas.* The reading of the 1st ed., as in 825 below; not "Douglas'," as in some recent eds.

830. *Vain as the leaf*, etc. The MS. has "Vain as the sick man's idle dream."

838. *Cognizance.* "The sable pale of Mar." See on iv. 153 above.

853. *With scanty train*, etc. The MS. has "On distant chase you will not ride."

856. *Lost it.* Forgot it.

858. *For spoiling of.* For fear of ruining. Cf. Shakespeare, *Sonn.* 52. 4:

> "The which he will not every hour survey,
> For blunting the fine point of seldom pleasure;

T. G. of V. i. 2. 136: "Yet here they shall not lie for catching cold;" Beaumont and Fletcher, *Captain*, iii. 5: "We 'll have a bib for spoiling of thy doublet," etc.

887. *Earl William.* The Douglas who was stabbed by James II. See on 551 above.

CANTO SIXTH.

"Lord Jeffrey has objected to the guard-room scene and its accompanying song as the greatest blemish in the whole poem. The scene contrasts forcibly with the grace which characterizes the rest; but in a poem which rests its interest upon incident, such a criticism seems overstrained. It gives us a vigorous picture of a class of men who played a very important part in the history of the time, especially across the Border; men who, many of them outlaws, and fighting, not for country or for king, but for him who paid them best, were humored with every license when they were not on strict military duty. The requirements of the narrative might have been satisfied without these details, it is true; but the use which Sir Walter has made of them — to show the power of beauty and innocence, and the chords of tenderness and goodness which lie ready to vibrate in the wildest natures — may surely reconcile us to such a piece of realism.

"The scene of Roderick's death harmonizes well with his character. The minstrel's account of the battle the poet himself felt to be somewhat long, and yet it is difficult to see how it could be curtailed without spoiling it. It is full of life and vigor, and our only cause of surprise is that the lay should only come to a *sudden* stand when it is really completed" (Taylor).

6. *Scaring*, etc. The 1st ed. reads: "And scaring prowling robbers to their den."

7. *Battled.* Battlemented; as in ii. 702 above.

9. *The kind nurse of men.* Cf. 2 *Hen. IV.* iii. 1. 5:

> "O sleep, O gentle sleep,
> Nature's soft nurse," etc.

23. *Through narrow loop*, etc. The MS. has "Through blackened arch," etc.; and below:

> "The lights in strange alliance shone
> Beneath the arch of blackened stone."

25. *Struggling with.* Some recent eds. misprint "struggling through."

47. *Adventurers they*, etc. Scott says: "The Scottish armies consisted chiefly of the nobility and barons, with their vassals, who held lands under them for military service by themselves and their tenants. The patriarchal influence exercised by the heads of clans in the Highlands and Borders was of a different nature, and sometimes at variance with feudal principles. It flowed from the *Patria Potestas*, exercised by the chieftain as representing the original father of the whole name, and was often obeyed in contradiction to the feudal superior. James V. seems first to have introduced, in addition to the militia furnished from these sources, the service of a small number of mercenaries, who formed a body-guard, called the Foot-Band. The satirical poet, Sir David Lindsay (or the person who wrote the prologue to his play of the *Three Estaites*), has introduced Finlay of the Foot-Band, who after much swaggering upon the stage is at length put to flight by the Fool, who terrifies him by means of a sheep's skull upon a pole. I have rather chosen to give them the harsh features of the mercenary soldiers of the period, than of this Scottish Thraso. These partook of the character of the Adventurous Companions of Froissart, or the Condottieri of Italy."

53. *The Fleming*, etc. The soil of Flanders is very fertile and productive, in marked contrast to the greater part of Scotland.

60. *Halberd.* A combination of spear and battle-axe. See Wb.

63. *Holytide.* Holiday. For *tide* = time, see on iii. 478 above.

73. *Neighboring to.* That is, lying in adjacent rooms.

75. *Burden.* Alluding to the *burden*, or chorus, of a song. Cf. ii. 392 above. The MS. has "jest" for *joke*; and in the next line "And rude oaths vented by the rest."

78. *Trent.* The English river of that name. Cf. 231 below.

84. *That day.* Modifying *cut short*, not *grieved*.

87. *A merry catch I troll.* Cf. Shakespeare, *Temp.* iii. 2. 126: "will you troll the catch," etc.

88. *Buxom.* Lively, brisk; as in *Hen. V.* iii. 6. 27: "of buxom valour," etc. Its original sense was yielding, obedient; as in *F. Q.* i. 11. 37: "the buxome aire" (see also Milton, *P. L.* ii. 842); and *Id.* iii. 2. 23: "Of them that to him buxome are and prone." For the derivation, see Wb.

90. *Poule.* Paul; an old spelling, found in Chaucer and other writers. The measure of the song is *anapestic* (that is, with the accent on every third syllable), with modifications.

92. *Black-jack.* A kind of pitcher made of leather. Taylor quotes *Old Mortality*, ch. viii: "The large black-jack filled with very small beer."

93. *Sack.* A name applied to Spanish and Canary wines in general; but sometimes the particular kind was specified. Cf. 2 *Hen. IV.* iv. 3. 104: "good sherris-sack" (that is, sherry wine); and Herrick, *Poems*:

> "thy isles shall lack
> Grapes, before Herrick leaves Canarie sack."

95. *Upsees.* "Bacchanalian interjection, borrowed from the Dutch" (Scott). Nares criticises Scott for using the word as a noun. It is generally found in the phrases "upsee Dutch" and "upsee Freeze" (the same thing, *Frise* being = Dutch) which appear to mean "in the Dutch fashion." Cf. Ben Jonson, *Alchemist*, iv. 6:

> "I do not like the dullness of your eye,
> It hath a heavy cast, 't is upsee Dutch;"

that is, looks like intoxication. See also Beaumont and Fletcher, *Beggar's Bush*, iv. 4: "The bowl . . . which must be upsey English, strong, lusty, London beer."

98. *Kerchief.* See on iii. 495 above.

100. *Gillian.* A common old English name (according to Coles and others, a corruption of *Juliana*), often contracted into *Gill* or *Jill*, and used as a familiar term for a woman, as *Jack* was for a man. The two are often associated; as in the proverbs "Every Jack must have his Jill," and "A good Jack makes a good Jill."

103. *Placket.* Explained by some as = stomacher; by others as = petticoat, or the slit or opening in those garments. Cf. Wb. It is often used figuratively for woman, as here. *Placket and pot* = women and wine.

104. *Lurch.* Rob. Cf. Shakespeare, *Cor.* ii. 2. 105: "He lurch'd all swords of the garland;" that is, robbed them all of the prize.

112. *The drum.* The 1st ed. has "your drum."

116. *Plaid.* For the rhyme, see on i. 363 above.

124. *Store of blood.* Plenty of blood. Cf. Milton, *L'Allegro*, 121: "With store of ladies," etc. See also on the adjective, i. 548 above.

127. *Reward thy toil.* The MS. goes on thus:

> "Get thee an ape, and then at once
> Thou mayst renounce the warder's lance,
> And trudge through borough and through land,
> The leader of a juggler band."

Scott has the following note here: "The *jongleurs*, or jugglers, as we learn from the elaborate work of the late Mr. Strutt, on the sports and pastimes of the people of England, used to call in the aid of various assistants, to render these performances as captivating as possible. The glee-maiden was a necessary attendant. Her duty was tumbling and dancing; and therefore the Anglo-Saxon version of Saint Mark's Gospel states Herodias to have vaulted or tumbled before King Herod. In Scotland these poor creatures seem, even at a late period, to have been bondswomen to their masters, as appears from a case reported by Fountainhall: 'Reid the mountebank pursues Scot of Harden and his lady for stealing away from him a little girl, called the tumbling-lassie, that danced upon his stage; and he claimed damages, and produced a contract, whereby he bought her from her mother for £30 Scots. But we have no slaves in Scotland, and mothers cannot sell their bairns; and physicians attested the employment of tumbling would kill her; and her joints were now grown stiff, and she declined to return; though she was at least a 'prentice, and so could not run away from her master; yet some cited Moses's law, that if a servant shelter himself with thee against his master's cruelty, thou shalt surely not deliver him up. The Lords, *renitente cancellario*, assoilzied Harden on the 27th of January (1687)' (Fountainhall's *Decisions*, vol. i. p. 439)."

136. *Purvey*. Provide. Cf. Spenser, *F. Q.* v. 12. 10: "He all things did purvay which for them needfull weare."

147. *Bertram*, etc. The MS. has "Bertram {his / such} violence withstood."

152. *The tartan screen*. That is, the tartan which she had drawn over her head as a veil.

155. *The savage soldiery*, etc. The MS. has "While the rude soldiery, amazed;" and in 164 below, "Should Ellen Douglas suffer wrong."

167. *I shame me*. I shame myself, I am ashamed. The verb was formerly used intransitively in this sense. Cf. Shakespeare, *R. of L.* 1143: "As shaming any eye should thee behold;" *A. Y. L.* iv. 3. 136: "I do not shame to tell you what I was," etc.

170. *Needwood*. A royal forest in Staffordshire.

171. *Poor Rose*, etc. The MS. reads:

> "'My Rose,'—he wiped his iron eye and brow,—
> 'Poor Rose,—if Rose be living now.'"

178. *Part*. Act; used for the rhyme. The expression is not unlike "do the part of an honest man" (*Much Ado*, ii. 1. 172), or "*act* the part," as we should now put it.

183. *Tullibardine*. The name of an old seat of the Murray family, about twenty miles from Stirling.

199. *Errant damosel*. Cf. Spenser, *F. Q.* ii. 1. 19: "Th' adventure of the Errant damozell."

209. *Given by the Monarch*, etc. The MS. has "The Monarch gave to James Fitz-James."

218. *Bower*. Chamber. See on i. 217 above.

222. *Permit I marshal you the way*. Permit *that* I conduct you thither

233. *The vacant purse*, etc. The MS. reads:

> "The silken purse shall serve for me,
> And in my barret-cap shall flee" —

a forced rhyme which the poet did well to get rid of.

234. *Barret-cap.* Cloth cap. Cf. the *Lay*, iii. 216:

> "Old England's sign, St. George's cross,
> His barret-cap did grace."

He puts the purse in his cap as a *favor*. See on iv. 686 above.

242. *Master's.* He means the Douglas, but John of Brent takes it to refer to Roderick. See 305 below.

261. *Wot.* Know, understand. See on i. 596 above.

276. *Rugged vaults.* The MS. has "low broad vaults;" and in 279 "stretching" for *crushing*.

291. *Oaken floor.* The MS. and 1st ed. have "flinty floor;" and below:

> "'thou mayst remain;'
> And then, retiring, bolt and chain,
> And rusty bar, he drew again.
> Roused at the sound," etc.

292, 293. *Such . . . hold.* This couplet is not in the 1st ed., and presumably not in the MS., though the fact is not noted by Lockhart.

295. *Leech.* Physician. Cf. *F. Q.* iii. 3. 18: "Yf any leaches skill," etc.; and in the preceding stanza, "More neede of leach-crafte hath your Damozell," etc.

306. *Prore.* Prow (Latin *prora*); used only in poetry.

309. *Astrand.* On strand (cf. *ashore*), stranded.

316. *At sea.* The MS. has "on main," and "plain" for *lea* in the rhyme. The 1st ed. and that of 1821 have "on sea."

334. *Has never harp*, etc. The MS. reads:

> "Shall never harp of minstrel tell
> Of combat fought so fierce and well."

348. *Strike it!* Scott says: "There are several instances, at least in tradition, of persons so much attached to particular tunes, as to require to hear them on their death-bed. Such an anecdote is mentioned by the late Mr. Riddel of Glenriddel, in his collection of Border tunes, respecting an air called the 'Dandling of the Bairns,' for which a certain Gallovidian laird is said to have evinced this strong mark of partiality. It is popularly told of a famous freebooter, that he composed the tune known by the name of Macpherson's Rant while under sentence of death, and played it at the gallows-tree. Some spirited words have been adapted to it by Burns. A similar story is recounted of a Welsh bard, who composed and played on his death-bed the air called *Dafyddy Garregg Wen.* But the most curious example is given by Brantôme of a maid of honor at the court of France, entitled *Mademoiselle de Limeuil:* 'Durant sa maladie, dont elle trespassa, jamais elle ne cessa, ainsi causa tousjours; car elle estoit fort grande parleuse, brocardeuse, et très-bien et fort à propos, et très-belle avec cela. Quand l'heure de sa fin fut venue, elle fit venir a soy son valet (ainsi que les filles de la cour en ont chacune un), qui s'appelloit Julien, et sçavoit très-bien joüer du violon. "Julien," luy dit elle, "prenez vostre violon, et sonnez moy tousjours

jusques a ce que vous me voyez morte (car je m'y en vais) la Défaite des Suisses, et le mieux que vous pourrez, et quand vous serez sur le mot, 'Tout est perdu,' sonnez le par quatre ou cinq fois, le plus piteusement que vous pourrez," ce qui fit l'autre, et elle-mesme luy aidoit de la voix, et quand ce vint "tout est perdu," elle le réïtera par deux fois; et se tournant de l'autre costé du chevet, elle dit à ses compagnes: "Tout est perdu à ce coup, et à bon escient;" et ainsi décéda. Voila une morte joyeuse et plaisante. Je tiens ce conte de deux de ses compagnes, dignes de foi, qui virent joüer ce mystère' (*Œuvres de Brantôme*, iii. 507). The tune to which this fair lady chose to make her final exit was composed on the defeat of the Swiss at Marignano. The burden is quoted by Panurge in Rabelais, and consists of these words, imitating the jargon of the Swiss, which is a mixture of French and German:

'Tout est verlore,
La Tintelore,
Tout est verlore bi Got.'"

362. *With what*, etc. This line is not in the MS.

369. *Battle of Beal' an Duine.* Scott has the following note here:

"A skirmish actually took place at a pass thus called in the Trosachs, and closed with the remarkable incident mentioned in the text. It was greatly posterior in date to the reign of James V.

'In this roughly-wooded island [1] the country people secreted their wives and children and their most valuable effects from the rapacity of Cromwell's soldiers during their inroad into this country, in the time of the republic. These invaders, not venturing to ascend by the ladders along the side of the lake, took a more circuitous road through the heart of the Trosachs, the most frequented path at that time, which penetrates the wilderness about half way between Binean and the lake by a tract called Yea-chilleach, or the Old Wife's Bog.

'In one of the defiles of this by-road the men of the country at that time hung upon the rear of the invading enemy, and shot one of Cromwell's men, whose grave marks the scene of action, and gives name to that pass.[2] In revenge of this insult, the soldiers resolved to plunder the island, to violate the women, and put the children to death. With this brutal intention, one of the party, more expert than the rest, swam towards the island, to fetch the boat to his comrades, which had carried the women to their asylum, and lay moored in one of the creeks. His companions stood on the shore of the mainland, in full view of all that was to pass, waiting anxiously for his return with the boat. But just as the swimmer had got to the nearest point of the island, and was laying hold of a black rock to get on shore, a heroine, who stood on the very point where he meant to land, hastily snatching a dagger from below her apron, with one stroke severed his head from the body. His party seeing this disaster, and relinquishing all future hope of revenge or conquest, made the best of their way out of their perilous situation. This amazon's great grandson lives at Bridge of Turk, who, besides others, attests the anecdote' (*Sketch of the Scenery*

[1] "That at the eastern extremity of Loch Katrine, so often mentioned in the text."
[2] "Beallach an duine."

near Callander, Stirling, 1806, p. 20). I have only to add to this account that the heroine's name was Helen Stuart."

376. *No ripple on the lake.* "The liveliness of this description of the battle is due to the greater variety of the metre, which resembles that of *Marmion*. The three-accent lines introduced at intervals give it lightness, and the repetition of the same rhyme enables the poet to throw together without break all that forms part of one picture" (Taylor).

377. *Erne.* Eagle. See Wb.

392. *I see*, etc. Cf. iv. 152 above.

396. *Boune.* See on iv. 36 above. Most eds. misprint "bound."

404. *Barded.* The reading of the 1st ed. and that of 1821; "corrected" in all the recent ones into "barbed." Scott doubtless wrote *barded* (= armored, or wearing defensive armor; but applied only to horses), a word found in many old writers. Cf. Holinshed (quoted by Nares): "with barded horses, all covered with iron," etc. See also Wb. Scott has the word again in the *Lay*, i. 311:

> "Above the foaming tide, I ween,
> Scarce half the charger's neck was seen;
> For he was barded from counter to tail,
> And the rider was armed complete in mail."

405. *Battalia.* Battalion, army. The word is not a plural of *battalion*, as some have seemed to think. See Wb.

414. *Vaward.* In the vanward, or vanguard; misprinted "vanward" in some editions. Shakespeare has the noun several times; as in *Hen. V.* iv. 3. 130: "The leading of the vaward;" *Cor.* i. 6. 53: "Their bands i' the vaward;" and figuratively in *M. N. D.* iv. 1. 110: "the vaward of the day," etc.

419. *Pride.* Some eds. misprint "power."

429. *As.* As if. See on ii. 56 above.

434. *Their flight they ply.* The reading of the 1st ed. and that of 1821. Most of the eds. have "plight" for *flight*, and Taylor has the following note on *Their plight they ply:* "The meaning of this is not very clear. Possibly 'they keep up a constant fire,' but they seem in too complete a rout for that." Cf. iii. 318 above.

438. *The rear.* The 1st ed. has "their rear."

443. *Twilight wood.* Cf. 403 above. "The appearance of the spears and pikes was such that in the twilight they might have been mistaken at a distance for a wood" (Taylor).

449-450. *And closely shouldering*, etc. This couplet is not in the MS.

452. *Tinchel.* "A circle of sportsmen, who, by surrounding a great space, and gradually narrowing, brought immense quantities of deer together, which usually made desperate efforts to break through the *Tinchel*" (Scott).

459. *The tide.* The 1st ed. has "their tide."

473. *Now, gallants!* etc. Cf. Macaulay, *Battle of Ivry:*

> "Now by the lips of those ye love,
> Fair gentlemen of France,
> Charge for the golden lilies,—
> Upon them with the lance!"

483. *And refluent*, etc. The MS. reads:

> "And refluent down the darksome pass
> The battle's tide was poured;
> There toiled the spearman's struggling spear,
> There raged the mountain sword."

488. *Linn.* Here the word is = cataract. See on i. 71 and ii. 270 above.

497. *Minstrel, away!* The MS. has "Away! away!"

509. *Surge.* Note the imperfect rhyme. See on i. 223 above.

511. *That sullen.* The reading of the 1st ed. and that of 1821; "the sullen" in many eds.

514. *That parts not*, etc. Lockhart quotes Byron, *Giaour:*

> "the loveliness in death
> That parts not quite with parting breath."

515. *Seeming*, etc. The MS. reads:

> "And seemed, to minstrel ear, to toll
> The parting dirge of many a soul."

For *part* = depart, see on ii. 94 above.

523. *While by the lake*, etc. The MS. reads:

> "While by the darkened lake below
> File out the spearmen of the foe."

525. *At weary bay.* See on i. 133 above.

527. *Tattered sail.* The 1st ed. has "shattered sail;" not noted in the *Errata*.

532. *Saxons.* Some eds. misprint "Saxon."

538. *Wont.* See on i. 408 above.

539. *Store.* See on i. 548 above. *Bonnet-pieces* were gold coins on which the King's head was represented with a bonnet instead of a crown.

540. *To him will swim.* For the ellipsis, see on i. 528 above.

556. *Her billows*, etc. The 1st ed. has "Her billow reared his snowy crest," and "its" for *they* in the next line.

564. *It tinged*, etc. The MS. has "It tinged the boats and lake with flame."

Lines 561–568 are interpolated in the MS. on a slip of paper.

565. *Duncraggan's widowed dame.* Cf. iii. 428 fol. above.

567. *A naked dirk.* The 1st ed. has "Her husband's dirk."

592. *Chime.* Music. Cf. iv. 524 above.

595. *Varied his look*, etc. The MS. has "Glowed in his look, as swelled the song;" and in 600, "his {glazing / fiery} eye."

602. *Thus, motionless*, etc. Cf. the Introduction to *Rob Roy:* "Rob Roy, while on his death-bed, learned that a person, with whom he was at enmity, proposed to visit him. 'Raise me from my bed,' said the invalid; 'throw my plaid around me, and bring me my claymore, dirk, and pistols: it shall never be said that a foeman saw Rob Roy MacGregor defenceless and unarmed.' His foeman, conjectured to be one of the MacLarens, entered and paid his compliments, inquiring after the health of his formidable neighbor. Rob Roy maintained a cold,

haughty civility during their short conference; and so soon as he had left the house, 'Now,' he said, 'all is over — let the piper play *Ha til mi tulidh'* [we return no more], and he is said to have expired before the dirge was finished."

605. *Grim and still.* Originally "stern and still." In a note to the printer, sent with the final stanzas, Scott writes: "I send the grand *finale*, and so exit the Lady of the Lake from the head she has tormented for six months. In canto vi. stanza 21, — *stern* and still, read *grim* and still; sternly occurs four lines higher. For a similar reason, stanza 24, — *dun* deer read *fleet* deer."

608. *And art thou,* etc. The MS. has "'And art thou gone,' the Minstrel said."

609. *Foeman's.* Misprinted "foemen's" in some eds.

610. *Breadalbane.* See on ii. 416 above.

614. *The shelter,* etc. The MS. has "The mightiest of a mighty line."

631. *Even she.* That is, Ellen.

638. *Storied.* Referring to the scenes depicted on the painted glass. Cf. Milton, *Il Penseroso,* 159: "And storied windows, richly dight." The change of tense in *fall* is of course for the rhyme; but we might expect "lighten" for *lightened.*

643. *The banquet,* etc. The MS. reads:

> "The banquet gay, the chamber's pride,
> Scarce drew one curious glance aside;"

and in 653, "earnest on his game."

665. *Of perch and hood.* That is, of enforced idleness. See on ii. 525 above. In some eds. this song is printed without any division into stanzas.

670. *Forest.* The 1st ed. and that of 1821 have "forests," but we suspect that Scott wrote *forest.*

672. *Is meet for me.* The MS. has "was meant for me." For the ellipsis, cf. 540 above.

674. *From yon dull steeple's,"* etc. The MS. has "From darkened steeple's," etc. See on v. 558 above.

677. *The lark,* etc. The MS. has "The lively lark my matins rung," and "sung" in the rhyme. The omission of *to* with *ring* and *sing* is here a poetic license; but in Elizabethan English it is common in many cases where it would not now be admissible. Cf. *Othello,* ii. 3. 190: "you were wont be civil;" *F. Q.* i. 1. 50: "He thought have slaine her," etc.

680. *A hall,* etc. The MS. has "a hall should harbor me."

683. *Fleet deer.* See on 605 above.

707. *At morning prime.* Early in the morning. *Prime* is properly the first canonical hour of prayer, or 6 A.M. For its looser use here cf. *F. Q.* ii. 9. 25: "at evening and at prime."

712. *Stayed.* Supported; not to be printed "staid," as in some editions.

716. *Within,* etc. The MS. reads:

> "Within 't was brilliant all, and bright
> The vision glowed on Ellen's sight."

726. *Presence.* Presence-chamber. Cf. *Rich. II.* i. 3. 289:

> "Suppose the singing birds musicians,
> The grass whereon thou tread'st the presence strew'd"

(that is, strewn with rushes); *Hen. VIII.* iii. 1. 17:

> "the two great cardinals
> Wait in the presence," etc.

727. *For him,* etc. The MS. reads: "For him who owned this royal state."

737. *Sheen.* Bright. See on i. 208 above.

740. *And Snowdoun's Knight is Scotland's King.* Scott says: "This discovery will probably remind the reader of the beautiful Arabian tale of *Il Bondocani.* Yet the incident is not borrowed from that elegant story, but from Scottish tradition. James V., of whom we are treating, was a monarch whose good and benevolent intentions often rendered his romantic freaks venial, if not respectable, since, from his anxious attention to the interests of the lower and most oppressed class of his subjects, he was, as we have seen, popularly termed the *King of the Commons.* For the purpose of seeing that justice was regularly administered, and frequently from the less justifiable motive of gallantry, he used to traverse the vicinage of his several palaces in various disguises. The two excellent comic songs entitled *The Gaberlunzie Man* and *We'll gae nae mair a roving* are said to have been founded upon the success of his amorous adventures when travelling in the disguise of a beggar. The latter is perhaps the best comic ballad in any language.

"Another adventure, which had nearly cost James his life, is said to have taken place at the village of Cramond, near Edinburgh, where he had rendered his addresses acceptable to a pretty girl of the lower rank. Four or five persons, whether relations or lovers of his mistress is uncertain, beset the disguised monarch as he returned from his rendezvous. Naturally gallant, and an admirable master of his weapon, the King took post on the high and narrow bridge over the Almond river, and defended himself bravely with his sword. A peasant who was thrashing in a neighboring barn came out upon the noise, and, whether moved by compassion or by natural gallantry, took the weaker side, and laid about with his flail so effectually as to disperse the assailants, well thrashed, even according to the letter. He then conducted the King into his barn, where his guest requested a basin and a towel, to remove the stains of the broil. This being procured with difficulty, James employed himself in learning what was the summit of his deliverer's earthly wishes, and found that they were bounded by the desire of possessing, in property, the farm of Braehead, upon which he labored as a bondsman. The lands chanced to belong to the Crown; and James directed him to come to the palace of Holyrood and inquire for the Guidman (that is, farmer) of Ballenguich, a name by which he was known in his excursions, and which answered to the *Il Bondocani* of Haroun Alraschid. He presented himself accordingly, and found, with due astonishment, that he had saved his monarch's life, and that he was to be gratified with a crown charter of the lands of Braehead, under the service of presenting a ewer, basin, and towel for the King to wash his hands when he shall happen to pass the bridge of Cramond. This person was ancestor of the Howisons of Braehead, in Mid-Lothian, a respectable family, who continue to hold the lands (now passed into the female line) under the same tenure.[1]

"Another of James's frolics is thus narrated by Mr. Campbell from the *Statistical Account:* 'Being once benighted when out a-hunting, and separated from his attendants, he happened to enter a cottage in the midst of a moor, at the foot of the Ochil hills, near Alloa, where, unknown, he was kindly received. In order to regale their unexpected guest, the *gudeman* desired the *gudewife* to fetch the hen that roosted nearest the cock, which is always the plumpest, for the stranger's supper. The King, highly pleased with his night's lodging and hospitable entertainment, told mine host, at parting, that he should be glad to return his civility, and requested that the first time he came to Stirling he would call at the Castle, and inquire for the *Gudeman of Ballenguich*. Donaldson, the landlord, did not fail to call on the *Gudeman of Ballenguich*, when his astonishment at finding that the King had been his guest afforded no small amusement to the merry monarch and his courtiers; and to carry on the pleasantry, he was thenceforth designated by James with the title of King of the Moors, which name and designation have descended from father to son ever since, and they have continued in possession of the identical spot, the property of Mr. Erskine of Mar, till very lately, when this gentleman with reluctance turned out the descendant and representative of the King of the Moors, on account of his Majesty's invincible indolence, and great dislike to reform or innovation of any kind, although, from the spirited example of his neighbor tenants on the same estate, he is convinced similar exertion would promote his advantage.'

"The author requests permission yet farther to verify the subject of his poem, by an extract from the genealogical work of Buchanan of Auchmar, upon Scottish surnames (*Essay upon the Family of Buchanan*, p. 74):

'This John Buchanan of Auchmar and Arnpryor was afterwards termed King of Kippen [a small district of Perthshire] upon the following account: King James V., a very sociable, debonair prince, residing at Stirling, in Buchanan of Arnpryor's time, carriers were very frequently passing along the common road, being near Arnpryor's house, with necessaries for the use of the King's family; and he, having some extraordinary occasion, ordered one of these carriers to leave his load at his house, and he would pay him for it; which the carrier refused to do, telling him he was the King's carrier, and his load for his Majesty's use; to which Arnpryor seemed to have small regard, compelling the carrier, in the end, to leave his load; telling him, if King James was King of Scotland, he was King of Kippen, so that it was reasonable he should share with his neighbor king in some of these loads, so fre-

[1] "The reader will find this story told at greater length, and with the addition in particular of the King being recognized, like the Fitz-James of the *Lady of the Lake*, by being the only person covered, in the First Series of *Tales of a Grandfather*, vol. iii p. 37. The heir of Braehead discharged his duty at the banquet given to King George IV. in the Parliament House at Edinburgh, in 1822" (Lockhart).

quently carried that road. The carrier representing this usage, and telling the story as Arnpryor spoke it, to some of the King's servants, it came at length to his Majesty's ears, who shortly thereafter, with a few attendants, came to visit his neighbor king, who was in the meantime at dinner. King James, having sent a servant to demand access, was denied the same by a tall fellow with a battle-axe, who stood porter at the gate, telling there could be no access till dinner was over. This answer not satisfying the King, he sent to demand access a second time; upon which he was desired by the porter to desist, otherwise he would find cause to repent his rudeness. His Majesty finding this method would not do, desired the porter to tell his master that the Goodman of Ballangeigh desired to speak with the King of Kippen. The porter telling Arnpryor so much, he, in all humble manner, came and received the King, and having entertained him with much sumptuousness and jollity, became so agreeable to King James, that he allowed him to take so much of any provision he found carrying that road as he had occasion for; and seeing he made the first visit, desired Arnpryor in a few days to return him a second to Stirling, which he performed, and continued in very much favor with the King, always thereafter being termed King of Kippen while he lived.'

"The readers of Ariosto must give credit for the amiable features with which James is represented, since he is generally considered as the prototype of Zerbino, the most interesting hero of the *Orlando Furioso*."

743. *Glided from her stay.* The MS. has "shrinking, quits her stay." Ruskin asks us to "note the northern love of rocks" in this passage, and adds: "Dante could not have thought of his 'cut rocks' as giving rest even to snow. He must put it on the pine branches, if it is to be at peace." Taylor quotes Holmes, *Autocrat of Breakfast Table:* "She melted away from her seat like an image of snow."

780. *Pry.* Look pryingly or curiously. In prose *on* would not be used with *pry*.

784. *To speed.* To a fortunate issue; unless *speed* be the verb, and = pass.

786. *In life's more low but happier way.* The MS. has "In lowly life's more happy way."

789. *The name of Snowdoun.* Scott says: "William of Worcester, who wrote about the middle of the fifteenth century, calls Stirling Castle Snowdoun. Sir David Lindsay bestows the same epithet upon it in his *Complaint of the Papingo:*

> 'Adieu, fair Snawdoun, with thy towers high,
> Thy chaple-royal, park, and table round;
> May, June, and July, would I dwell in thee,
> Were I a man, to hear the birdis sound,
> Whilk doth agane thy royal rock rebound.'

"Mr. Chalmers, in his late excellent edition of Sir David Lindsay's works, has refuted the chimerical derivation of Snawdoun from *snedding*, or cutting. It was probably derived from the romantic legend which connected Stirling with King Arthur, to which the mention of the Round Table gives countenance. The ring within which justs were formerly practised in the Castle park, is still called the Round Table. Snawdoun is the official title of one of the Scottish heralds, whose epithets seem in all countries to have been fantastically adopted from ancient history or romance.

"It appears from the preceding note that the real name by which James was actually distinguished in his private excursions was the *Goodman of Ballenguich;* derived from a steep pass leading up to the Castle of Stirling, so called. But the epithet would not have suited poetry, and would besides at once, and prematurely, have announced the plot to many of my countrymen, among whom the traditional stories above mentioned are still current."

798. *My spell-bound steps.* The MS. has

"Thy sovereign back } to Benvenue."
Thy sovereign's steps }

800. *Glaive.* Sword. See on iv. 274 above.

803. *Pledge of my faith,* etc. The MS. has "Pledge of Fitz-James's faith, the ring."

808. *A lightening.* Some eds. have "A lightning."

809. *And more,* etc. The MS. reads:

"And in her breast strove maiden shame;
More deep she deemed the Monarch's ire
Kindled 'gainst him, who, for her sire,
Against his Sovereign broadsword drew;
And, with a pleading, warm and true,
She craved the grace of Roderick Dhu."

813. *Grace.* Pardon.

825. *Stained.* Reddened.

829. *The Græme.* Jeffrey says: "Malcom Græme has too insignificant a part assigned him, considering the favor in which he is held both by Ellen and the author; and in bringing out the shaded and imperfect character of Roderick Dhu as a contrast to the purer virtue of his rival, Mr. Scott seems to have fallen into the common error of making him more interesting than him whose virtues he was intended to set off, and converted the villain of the piece in some measure into its hero. A modern poet, however, may perhaps be pardoned for an error of which Milton himself is thought not to have kept clear, and for which there seems so natural a cause in the difference between poetical and amiable characters."

837. *Warder.* Guard, jailer.

841. Lockhart quotes here the following extract from a letter of Byron's to Scott, dated July 6, 1812:

"And now, waiving myself, let me talk to you of the Prince Regent. He ordered me to be presented to him at a ball; and after some sayings, peculiarly pleasing from royal lips, as to my own attempts, he talked to me of you and your immortalities: he preferred you to every bard past and present, and asked which of your works pleased me most. It was a difficult question. I answered, I thought the *Lay.* He said his own opinion was nearly similar. In speaking of the others, I told him that I thought you more particularly the poet of *princes,* as *they* never appeared more fascinating than in *Marmion* and *The Lady* of the Lake. He was pleased to coincide, and to dwell on the description of your James's as no less royal than poetical. He spoke alternately of Homer and yourself, and seemed well acquainted with both."

842. *Harp of the North, farewell!* Cf. the introduction to the poem.

846. *Wizard elm.* See on i. 2 above.

850. *Housing.* Returning to the hive.

858. *The grief devoured.* For the figure, cf. *Ps.* xlii. 3, lxxx. 5, and *Isa.* xxx. 20.

859. *O'erlive.* Several eds. misprint "o'erlived."

ADDENDUM.

PROF. W. MINTO, in his Clarendon Press edition of the poem (Oxford, 1891), remarks: "Attention was drawn to the state of the text by Mr. W. J. Rolfe in an edition published at Boston in 1883. Mr. Rolfe pointed out that various misprints, such as 'heart' for 'heat,' 'barbed' for 'barded,' had crept into the Author's Edition, and he weeded these out carefully by collating the text with the editions of 1810 and 1821." After stating that he has been allowed to collate the text with the author's manuscript, he adds: "I have found that Mr. Rolfe was almost invariably right in his corrections, and I have been able to add one or two." In i. 217 he reads "cleft," as in the manuscript; "clift," which led to the blundering substitution of "cliff," being, curiously enough, a misprint in the first edition, unless Scott himself changed the word for the sake of the archaism. In ii. 534 Prof. Minto reads "stature tall," though the manuscript, like the early editions, has "stature fair." He thinks that "tall" was "possibly substituted by Scott himself," and "could hardly have been a misprint;" but stranger misprints have occurred on account of some indistinctness or other imperfection in printed "copy," where the compositor substituted a word which he supposed to be the right one, and which the proof-reader did not question, since it made good sense. In ii. 357 Prof. Minto reads "sound," though the manuscript and the first edition have "sounds," believing that "sound" was "possibly a change made by Scott himself for euphony." These are the only variations from my text noted by Prof. Minto, and I do not see sufficient reason for adopting any one of them. "Cleft" is the only one about which he appears to be quite sure himself, and that seems to me somewhat doubtful. I may add that on i. 360, where we both read "dear," he says: "Mr. Rolfe conjectures that this is a misprint for 'clear,' and the same had occurred to myself independently; but the MS. reading is undoubtedly 'dear.'"

Nov. 15, 1895.

INDEX OF WORDS AND PHRASES EXPLAINED.

PRONOUNCING GLOSSARY.

NOTE.—The present English pronunciation is given, which differs in some cases from that of the old Highland language; as, for instance, in *ch* (or *gh*), a guttural sound not found in English, for which *k* is commonly substituted.

Aberfoyle, ab-er-foil′.
Achray, ăk-rā′.
Alloa, al′-lo-a.
Ascabart, as′-ca-bart.
Balquidder, bal-quid′-er.
Balvaig, bal-vaig′.
Bannochar, ban′-no-kar.
Beal'maha, beal-ma-ha′.
Beala-nam-bo, beal-a-nam-bo′.
Beltane, bĕl′-tāne.
Benharrow, bĕn-har′-rō.
Benledi, bĕn-lĕd′-dĭ.
Ben Lomond, ben-lō′-mond.
Ben Shie, ben-shē′.
Benvenue, ben-ve-nū′.
Benvoirlich, ben-voil′-ĭk.
Blantyre, blăn-tire′.
Bochastle, bō-chăs′-le.
Bracklin, brăk′-lin.
Braes of Doune, brāz of doon.
Breadalbane, brĕd-ăl′-bane.
Brianchoil, brī-an-coil′.
Caledon, căl′-e-don.
Cambus-kenneth, cam-bus-ken′-eth.
Cambusmore, cam-bus-more′.
Carbonie, car-bō′-nĭ.
Coilantogle, coil-ăn-tō′-gle.
Coir-nan-Uriskin, cōr-năn-ū′-ris-kin.
coronach, cŏr′-o-nak.
correi (corri, corrie), cŏr′-ĭ.
Craigforth, crāg-forth′.
Dennan, den′-an.
Devan, dĕv′-an.
Dhu, doo.
Doine, doin.
Duchray, dū-krā′.
Duncraggan, dŭn-crăg′-an.
Dunfermline, dŭm-fer′-lin (local pronunciation).
Earn, ĕrn.
Ferragus, fer′-a-gus (fer- as in ferry).
Fillan, fĭl′-an.
Gallangad, gal′-an-gad.
gallowglasses, gal′-o-glas-es.
Glenartney, glen-art′-nĭ.
Glenfinlas, glen-fĭn′-las.
Glen Fruin, glen frū′-in.
Glengyle, glen-gīle′.
Glen Luss, glen-loos′.
Graeme, grāme.
Holyrood, hō′-ly-rood (or hol′-y-rood).
Hyndford, hīnd′-ford.
Inch-Cailliach, inch-kăl′-yăk.
Katrine, kăt′-reen (or kā′-treen).
Kier, keer.
Kilmarnock, kil-mar′-nok.
Lanrick, lan′-rik.
Larbert, lar′-bert.
Lendrick, lĕn′-drik.
Levenglen, lĕv′-en-glen.
Lochard, lok-ard′.
Lomond, lō′-mond.
Lubnaig, lub-nāg′.
Maronnan, ma-ron′-an.
Meggat, mĕg′-at.
Menteith, mĕn-teeth′.
Modan, mō′-dan.
Monan, mō′-nan.
Ochtertyre, ŏk-ter-tire′.
pibroch, pē′-brok.
plaid, plād (or plăd). See p. 188
Ross-dhu, rŏs-doo′.
Scathelocke, scăth′-e-lŏk.
scaur, scår.
Serle, sĕrl.
Snowdoun, snō′-don.
Strathspey, străth-spā′.
Streight (like straight).
Stumah, stū′-mah.
Taghairm, tăg′-erm.
Teith, teeth.
Teviot, tĕv′-i-ot.
Tinchel, tin′-chel.
Torry, tor′-rĭ.
Trosachs, trŏs′-ăks.
Tullibardine, tul-i-bar′-deen.
Uam-Var, u-a-var′. See p. 182
Vennachar, ven′-a-kar.

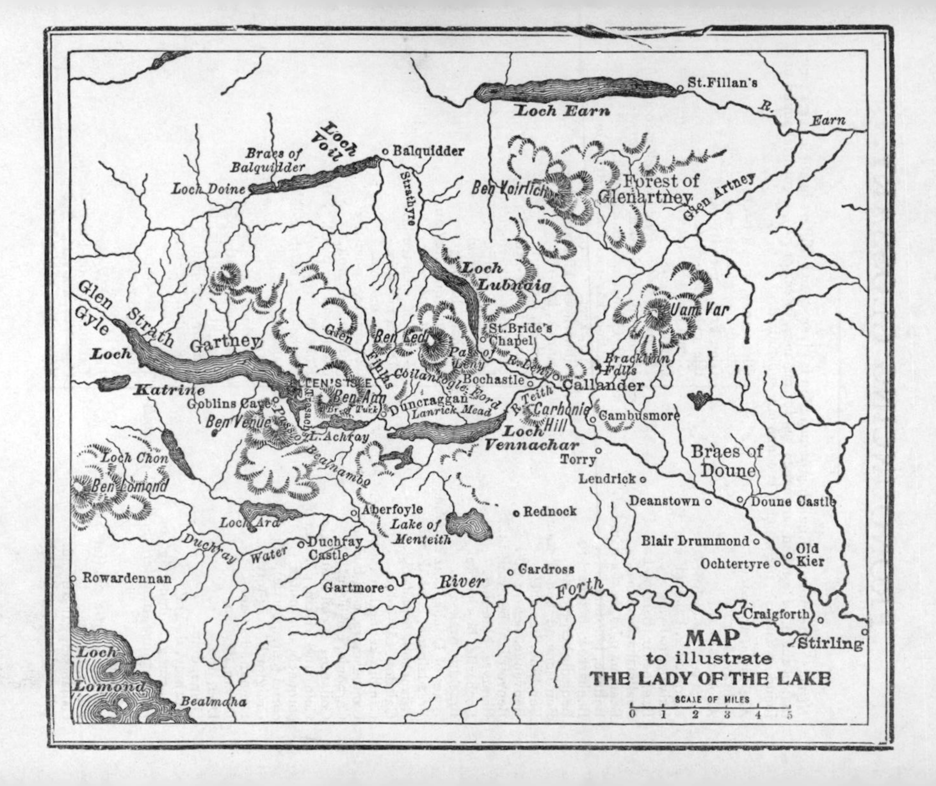
St.Fillan's
Loch Earn
R. Earn
Loch Voil
Balquidder
Braes of Balquidder
Loch Doine
Strathyre
Forest of Glenartney
Glen Artney
Loch Lubnaig
Glen Gyle
Strath Gartney
Loch Katrine
St.Bride's Chapel
Ben Ledi
Pass of Leny
R. Leny
Uam Var
Bracklinn Falls
Callander
Glen Finlas
Coilantogle Ford
Bochastle
Duncraggan
Lanrick Mead
Ben Aan
R. Teith
Carhonie Hill
Cambusmore
Goblins Cave
Ben Venue
L. Achray
Loch Vennachar
Bealnambo
Torry
Braes of Doune
Loch Chon
Ben Lomond
Lendrick
Deanstown
Doune Castle
Aberfoyle
Rednock
Loch Ard
Lake of Menteith
Blair Drummond
Old Kier
Duchray Water
Duchray Castle
Ochtertyre
Rowardennan
Gardross
Gartmore
River Forth
Craigforth
Stirling
Loch Lomond
Bealmaha
MAP
to illustrate
THE LADY OF THE LAKE
SCALE OF MILES
0 1 2 3 4 5

D.C. PUBLIC LIBRARY
3 1172 01406 7094